THE
PRICE OF
INNOCENCE

by
Maurice G. Nash

ISBN
978-0-949001-44-3

C.C.PUBLISHING, MARTINS LANE,
HARGRAVE, CHESTER, CH3 7RX
TEL: 01829 741651. EMAIL: editor@cc-publishing.co.uk
WEBSITE: http://www.cc-publishing.co.uk

This belated work is dedicated to
THE 187 INNOCENT ITALIAN MEN
WHO WERE MASSACRED
BY GERMAN ARMED FORCES
IN THE COMUNE DI CAVRIGLIA
BETWEEN THE 4th & 11th JULY, 1944
and
THE SOLDIERS OF BRITISH 13 CORPS
WHO CONTRIBUTED
TO THE LIBERATION OF ITALY
FROM SEPTEMBER 1943 TO MAY 1945
FOR WHICH MANY GAVE THEIR LIVES.

The Price of Innocence

The Author

MAURICE GORHAM NASH was born at Reading, Berkshire on the 29th May, 1923. His education was received in Reading at Katesgrove and George Palmer Schools, at the end of which he embarked on an apprenticeship in the electrical department of a local engineering firm.

Joining the Army in 1941, he saw active service in the United Kingdom, the Middle East, North Africa, Italy and Austria, being demobilised from the Royal Corps of Mechanical and Electrical Engineers with the rank of Warrant Officer in 1946.

After a brief period as a craftsman at the firm with whom he had been apprenticed, he commenced, in 1947, a four years' course of combined academic studies and practical training which was eventually to lead to his becoming eligible for membership of the major engineering institutions. This course encompassed full-time attendance at technical institutes in London and South Yorkshire, together with a graduate apprenticeship in electricity generation with the Southern Division of the then British Electricity Authority.

1951 saw Maurice Nash move to the north-west of England, progressing over some eight years through a series of appointments in the electricity generation, atomic energy, heavy chemicals and pharmaceutical industries, in order to widen his experience and advance in the engineering profession.

During 1951/52, along with a colleague, he presented to the Institution of Electrical Engineers a paper entitled 'A Review of Modern Power Station Practice' which gained the London Students' Section Prize. 1954 and 1956 saw him granted corporate membership of the Institution of Electrical Engineers and the Institute of Fuel (now the Energy Institute) respectively.

Between 1958 and 1968 he taught Mathematics and Electrical Power Engineering to Higher National Certificate students at Liverpool College of Technology (now John Moores University) on a part-time basis, and from 1961 to 1966 was a governor of John Hamilton High School in Liverpool.

Taking up an appointment with Distillers (Biochemicals) Ltd., in 1959, which company was acquired by Eli Lilly & Co. of Indianapolis in 1963, he worked at the Speke, Liverpool, factory for the remainder of his professional career, taking early retirement in 1982. During this period he held a number of engineering posts, with his final ten years being taken in managing all project engineering at the site.

Although taking part in many forms of sport during his youth and years of military service, he has since middle life taken up walking for recreation, and continues to do so. He is a prolific letter writer and reader; the latter mostly of biographies and military history. Failing to be a musician has not prevented him from developing a great fondness for music, and in particular the works of Puccini, Lehár, Verdi, Donizetti and Gilbert & Sullivan.

Since first being in Italy during World War II, Maurice Nash has made many return visits, and has an overwhelming affection for the people, the countryside and the cuisine.

On 3rd July, 2009, he was awarded Honorary Citizenship of the Comune di Cavriglia.

This is his first and only book, but a story he felt that he had to tell.

The Italian Campaign
Route of British 13 Corps Troops Workshops northwards through Italy: September 1943 to May 1945

1. Reggio di Calabria
2. Palmi
3. Mileto
4. Nicastro
5. Cosenza
6. Scanzano
7. Castel del Monte
8. San Severo
9. Gambatesa
10. Vinchiatura
11. Archi (Gunshop only)
12. Gissi
13. Atessa
14. Vinchiaturo
15. Pietravairano
16. Presenzano
17. MR 9616 (between San Pietro Infine and San Vittore di Lazio)
18. Piedimonte San Germano
19. Valmontone
20. Faleria
21. Orvieto
22. South shore of Lake Trasimeno
23. Near Mugliano
24. Santa Barbara
25. Near Sieci
26. San Piero a Sieve
27. Lugo
28. Chiesa Nuova
29. Mestre
30. Cervignano del Friuli

Foreword

LEANDRO POLVERINI

Professor of Ancient History, University of Rome

July 1944. When 21-year-old Sgt. Maurice Nash of the British Eighth Army first entered Castelnuovo dei Sabbioni, a Tuscan village in the Arno valley south of Florence, he was deeply shocked by the discovery of the brutal massacres which had been carried out by the German forces in that and nearby villages between the 4th and 11th July. A total of 187 male civilians, victims of the most dreadful German reprisals against partisan activity, had paid 'the price of innocence'.

With the British 13th Corps, in whose Troops Workshops he served during the course of the whole Italian campaign, Sgt. Nash soon moved northwards, towards the Gothic Line, but could not forget what he had experienced at Castelnuovo. Indeed, neither had he forgotten it fifteen years later when he first returned to Castelnuovo (1959) nor when he entered it for the third time after fifty-two years (1996). In the autumn of 1996 he had good reasons for deciding to collect his wartime memories. In the previous two years he had carefully revisited the main places of the Italian campaign. Moreover, at the British Public Record Office (now known as the National Archives) he had discovered the War Diary of his own army unit and had gained access to the Eighth Army Special Investigation Branch Reports which dealt with the many atrocities perpetrated by the Germans at and near Castelnuovo. In 1997, invited to attend the official ceremony for the 53rd anniversary of the massacres of July 1944, he amazed everyone present in private and public talks with his deep and precise knowledge of the events as well as with his youthful engagement. The writer of this foreword was one of those who strongly urged Maurice Nash to publish his memoirs as soon as possible.

Here is that book – at last! The first impression might be that we actually have two books: one of general interest about the war in Italy, from the fall of Fascism to April 1945; another of local interest about the massacres of July 1944 in unknown villages deep in Tuscany. On second thoughts, this impression proves to be mistaken. The two parts, or better, the two aspects of the book are so closely connected that they shed significant light on each other, and the whole is a lively and balanced contribution to the history of these crucial and, in Italy, still controversial years. But let the reader judge. As for the writer of this foreword, whose father was one of the innocent men murdered and burned by the Germans at Castelnuovo, he has read this bookwith the utmost interest and with understandable emotion. He sincerely hopes that an Italian edition will follow soon on the English one.

July 2004. The former Sgt. Maurice Nash attended the ceremony for the 60th anniversary of the massacres of July 1944. One of the first British soldiers to enter Castelnuovo after they had been perpetrated, he will now offer the most valuable contribution to the still living memory of the tragic events of sixty years ago.

Contents

Black & White Photographs

Colour Photographs

List of Maps

Acknowledgements

I received a considerable amount of help and guidance from many diverse quarters during the preparation of this book. First and foremost, my sincere thanks go to Signor Emilio Polverini, historian for Castelnuovo dei Sabbioni and the Comune di Cavriglia, who provided me with a vast quantity of invaluable information and material covering the historical and economic evolution of the Comune, together with specific details regarding the massacres carried out by German forces in numerous villages of the Comune in July 1944, and dealt with in Chapters 14 and 15 of the book. The massacres have poignant memories for Signor Polverini since his father, Giuseppe Polverini, was one of the seventy-four Italian civilians put to death at Castelnuovo dei Sabbioni. In addition to the material and information with which he furnished me, Signor Polverini, in 1997, conducted me on a detailed tour of all the locations at which the July 1944 massacres were perpetrated, this embracing the burial places of and monuments to many of the victims.

My warmest thanks go also to Signor Enzo Brogi, the Mayor of Cavriglia, his wife Silvana, and the townsfolk of Castelnuovo dei Sabbioni for all the kindness, consideration and hospitality they extended to myself and my son John during our stay there in July 1997. When attending the ceremonies for the 60th anniversary of the massacres in July 2004, my companion, Mrs Angela Sharples, and myself, were shown the same kindnesses and consideration extended to my son and I during our earlier visit.

A debt of gratitude is owed to Professor Leandro Polverini, younger brother of Emilio, for our several wide-ranging conversations, and particularly those covering present day attitudes and opinions in Italy with regard to the massacres of Italian civilians by the Germans, principally during 1944, and the activities of the Partisans. I thank him too for acting as interpreter between myself and many non-English speaking Italians, and especially for contributing the Foreword to this book.

My grateful thanks go to the staffs of the Public Record Office, the Imperial War Museum Library, the Ministry of Defence Records Department, the Italian Embassy at London, the Italian Cultural Institute, the Comune di Cavriglia and the B.B.C. Document Archives at Caversham Park near Reading, for their patience, courtesy and generous assistance.

I acknowledge the use of copies of four maps from the book entitled Cassino: Portrait of a Battle by Fred Majdalany, published originally by Longmans, Green and Co., in Chapters 9 and 10 of my book which deal with the four battles of Cassino. I also acknowledge reproducing and using copies of thirteen maps from the H.M.S.O. publications History of the Second World War – United Kingdom Military Series when describing in Chapters 7, 11 and 18 the journey of British 13 Corps from Africa through Sicily to Italy and thence northwards through southern, central and northern Italy. Acknowledged too in Chapter 18 of my book is a copy of Map 4 from The Gothic Line by Douglas Orgill, first published by William Heinemann Ltd, showing the early September 1944 attack by the American 5th Army, which included British 13 Corps, on the Gothic Line.

Twenty-six of the photographs shown in Chapters 13, 14, 15 and 17 of this book were provided by and reproduced with the kind permission of the Comune di Cavriglia and Signor Emilio Polverini. Twelve of these photographs of locations in Castelnuovo dei Sabbioni were taken by the local photographer Leo Camici, the remainder either being taken by or reproduced from photographs owned by Signor Emilio Polverini.

The photographs of the four Germans which appear on page 205 of my book are taken from the Supplementary Report on Atrocities Committed by German troops in the Commune of Cavriglia between 4th and 11th July, 1944, prepared by 78 Section of Special Investigation Branch of the British forces in Italy in July 1945.

Permission to use the photographs of Field Marshal Kesselring and General von Mackensen, on page 214 of the book is given by Camera Press Ltd., while that of General Mälzer, which is also on page 214, is granted by Publifoto, Rome, and appears by kind permission of Centro Studi e Archivio della Comunicazione, University of Palma.

The balance of eighteen other photographs which appear in Chapters 5, 9, 10 and 14 were taken by John Nash, son of the author. Chapter 8 of the book, entitled Quae cum ita sint, could not have been written without the ever abiding memories of the close comradeship with many of my fellow soldiers in British 13 Corps Troops Workshops. Of fond memory also is Lt.-Col. C. M. Hunter, who was Officer Commanding the above unit from early October 1943 to mid July 1944, when he then

Acknowledgements

moved to British 13 Corps Headquarters. Subsequent to the war we corresponded, with Col. Hunter acting as a Supporter when, in 1954, I made successful application to become a Chartered Electrical Engineer. I was fortunate enough to be able to visit him at his home in Edinburgh in mid March 1995, a short time before he passed away. I am, of course, more than grateful to my friend of many years, Mr A. E. Snape, and my younger son John, for accompanying me during my several travels throughout Italy to visit or revisit places of relevance to this book. These included locations as widely apart as the Campo Imperatore Hotel on the Gran Sasso from where Mussolini was rescued by the Germans, the Monastery at Monte Cassino and many nearby localities which featured in the four battles of Cassino, the Futa and Il Giogo Passes in the Gothic Line, the British War Cemeteries at Cassino, Arezzo, Orvieto, the Santerno Valley, Bari and the Sangro River, together with many of the locations occupied by British 13 Corps Troops Workshops during the Italian Campaign.

My most sincere thanks go also to my dear friend Mrs Angela Sharples, who has been a constant source of encouragement to me with regard to the completion of this book in addition to rendering invaluable assistance in the compilation of the index. Together, in mid 1999, we visited the Ardeatine Caves near Rome where, in March 1944, the Germans massacred three hundred and thirty-five Italians.

Acknowledgements by me would not be complete without extending my sincere thanks to Mr T. H. Southgate for his many expert translations of letters and documents from Italian into English, and for translating my own letters into Italian. Likewise, I thank Signor Roberto Mobile of the Italian Consulate in Manchester for his help and guidance. The most sincerest of thanks go also to Miss Emma Pyke for acting as my interpreter during my stay in the Comune di Cavriglia in July 1997, and to both Mrs Sylvia Holding and Mrs Joy Hulse for so effectively converting my manuscripts into typed copy suitable for printing.

My gratitude and admiration are extended to Mr. Michael Sherratt for his excellent and detailed proof-reading of the typed copy of my book; thereby correcting the many errors I had failed to detect, and for his invaluable suggestions regarding wording and layout. And last, but by no means least, my sincere thanks to Mr Mark Bevan who has expertly handled the format, design, production and publishing of this issue of the book.

Prologue

This book, with the exception of its Epilogue, might well have been written some forty years earlier. At that time all the facts and details included in its pages were known, my memory, eye-sight and energy were undiminished by age, and the original village of Castelnuovo dei Sabbioni in Tuscany still stood uninvaded if already threatened by the expansion of the workings of the local lignite mine.

But forty years ago I had only recently qualified as a Chartered Engineer and was busily engaged for long hours on a number of major projects in order to secure for myself both an interesting and enduring professional career. Thus, the time required to carry out the necessary research and to write was then at a premium. Moreover, the Public Record Office files covering the detailed investigations into the massacres perpetrated by the Germans at Castelnuovo dei Sabbioni and nearby villages were still classified as 'Secret', and would have been difficult if not impossible for me to gain access to.

One might then well ask what eventually prompted me to put pen to paper commencing in the autumn of 1996.

Well! ... Accompanied by my friend Alan Snape, I spent the whole of June, 1994 travelling through Italy with the object of revisiting, perhaps for the last time, many of the places I had passed through during the Italian Campaign. Our journey commenced just after the 50th Anniversary of the Cassino battles at which I was present, and we visited the British Military Cemetery there, as well as those at Arezzo and Orvieto. Also visited was the British Military Cemetery at Bari where Alan Snape's brother, Sgt. Leonard Snape, R.A.F., is buried, having been killed in action in Italy during January, 1944. In addition, our itinerary included a return visit to Castelnuovo dei Sabbioni, where the 4th July, 1994 would see the 50th Anniversary of the massacre of seventy-four innocent Italian men in its Piazza IV Novembre by members of the German armed forces.

As we set off south from Florence on Route 69 we were prevented by road works from forking right on the approach to San Giovanni Valdarno, thereby missing the minor road which passes through Santa Barbara and goes on to Castelnuovo dei Sabbioni. We had reached the outskirts of Montevarchi before we realised the significance of the diversion, but because we had so much travelling before us, decided against retracing our path and making the intended visit.

The following year we were again in Italy, staying at both relatively nearby Lucca and Perugia, but once more omitted to get to Castelnuovo dei Sabbioni.

By the autumn of 1995 I became increasingly uneasy with regard to some of the more significant items missed from the 1994 itinerary. A firm decision was then taken to remedy in 1996 at least some of these omissions, including a return visit to Castelnuovo dei Sabbioni.

As a consequence, in mid June, 1996, this time under the supervision of my son John, the journey was again made south from Florence on Route 69. Without difficulty we forked right at the approach to San Giovanni Valdarno, then turning right to take the road through Santa Barbara with its apartment blocks and power station, which I had seen on earlier visits, and on to Castelnuovo dei Sabbioni.

But when we entered the village I saw that it was not the place I remembered. All the buildings were relatively modern and their configuration quite different from the older ones. It is not unusual when revisiting a place after a long interval of time for it to appear at variance with the image carried in the memory. But nothing which I saw before me was remotely familiar, and I began to harbour grave doubts as to whether we were in the correct location. Then, in a small car park we saw a map of the area which in one corner showed the situation of the nucleus of the old village. Looking on the bearing indicated by the map we saw a few hundred metres away the old church and approach road with its buttressed wall against which the seventy-four villagers had been massacred fifty-two years previously. Making our way down a narrow lane towards the remains of the old village we were faced with a fence and a locked gate. A second route was attempted but this terminated in an even more impenetrable barrier. Retracing our steps, we returned to the locked gate, wriggling through a hole in the fence at its side, and walking down the Via Camonti into the Piazza IV Novembre. Standing again in that Piazza where I had first been nearly fifty-two years earlier was quite overwhelming. The Piazza IV Novembre itself, with the church overlooking it, together with the houses in Via Vittorio Veneto and Via Camonti were all familiar and as I remembered them. But despite the familiarity, the blue sky and the warm summer sun the place seemed quite chill and eerie with its deserted streets and uninhabited houses with their open doors. John and I walked up the ramp to the front of the church, but its door was locked so we could not enter. Looking down from the church we could see where in the Piazza IV Novembre the massacre was carried out. Back in the Piazza we took a protracted look at the shrine erected where the victims of the massacre had been assembled, shot and then incinerated, noting the inscription on its lintel, 'I Massacrati Di Ieri Sono Gl'Immortali Di Oggi'. (The Massacred of Yesterday are the Immortal of Today.) Eventually we opened the wrought iron gate in the surround to the shrine, taking the few steps along the tiled path in order that we could see within. There, on the side walls, were stone plaques detailing the dreadful events of July 1944 and bearing the names of the victims, including those massacred at nearby Le Matole on the 11th July, 1944, together with their photographs. Disturbing and macabre though it was, that moment brought full purpose to the visit. Leaving Castelnuovo dei Sabbioni my son and I continued with our Italian travels. When on the return journey north from Orvieto to Lucca, and skirting Siena, I had the compulsion to visit Castelnuovo dei Sabbioni yet again, and to photograph some of what we had seen there ten days earlier. Without demur we modified our route, passing through the lovely Castellina in Chianti, Radda in Chianti and the beautiful Chianti Mountains before reaching Castelnuovo dei Sabbioni via the small Comune town of Cavriglia. Again, we entered the deserted nucleus of the old village, walking around as much of it as was safe and accessible, familiarising ourselves further with the surroundings and taking several photographs. On departing I had the overwhelming feeling that this would not be my last visit and I would return yet again.

I am uncertain as to how the seed of the idea to put into writing something of those days of more than half a century ago, together with related and subsequent events, was sowed. Suffice it to say that the thought was welcomed and supported by my long-time friend and travelling companion in Italy, Alan Snape, my son John, and later by my dear friend Angela.

So there it is. I too must have thought before starting the work that such a book would be an intellectually rewarding and perhaps useful proposition. And so it has turned out. It has to be said that on occasion I was tempted to abort the venture, and particularly so when a protracted attempt to discover facts and information regarding a specific happening proved fruitless, or when finally unearthed, these failed to be compatible. But such feelings of despair were dispelled by the ease of writing from my own personal experiences, or by such near miracles as the discoveries at the Public Record Office of the War Diary of my own Army unit and the British Special Investigation Branch Reports on the Cavriglia Massacres. On a more pragmatic note, I take the view that if writing this book had been much further delayed, then the inevitable and natural consequence of events would have precluded its appearance indefinitely.

Now that the task is complete, the writer, who will never be entirely satisfied with his efforts, can only hope that the final text makes both a coherent story and an interesting read.

I
From Chiana to Chianti

For the soldiers of British 13 Corps Troops Workshops (13 C.T.W.) the routine of that July morning in Italy in 1944 differed little from many similar mornings. The unit was due to move forward in the wake and close support of the artillery and the fighting formations.

After occupying the afternoon and evening of the previous day with packing up the workshops in preparation for the move, the short and generally uncomfortable night was spent in attempting to catch a few hours of sleep either in or against the side of a truck. Thankfully, the weather was both warm and dry. As usual, reveille was early, at 03.30 hrs., with breakfast and the collection of sandwiches for the midday meal timed for 04.30 hrs. Final packing of equipment and kit on to vehicles, and tidying the site, took place over the next hour, with the leading vehicle of the workshops convoy moving off punctually at 05.30 hrs.

The 'allied trades' group of the workshops was made up of vehicle and general fitters, turners, welders, blacksmiths, instrument mechanics, electricians, joiners and painters, all with their appropriate workshop and machinery lorries. It was around 05.45 hrs. when this group took its place in the convoy.

The electrical section, some twelve craftsmen strong, possessed two machinery lorries. Both were six wheeled Leylands of 1920s design, their driving cabs being without windscreens and having only top and front canvas canopies as protection against the elements. One of these lorries, known as an 'M' type, was equipped to charge batteries and housed its own generating set for so doing. The other, an 'F' type, contained much expensive and sophisticated electrical test and repair equipment. As a consequence, both of these lorries were tail-heavy, with light and uncertain steering.

During unit moves members of the electrical contingent found for themselves a vehicle in which to travel. Some joined mates in other sections of the workshops, and some who were able were recruited to drive a vehicle in the workshops for repair but still roadworthy, while the remainder rode in one or other of the electrical machinery lorries.

On this July morning the 'F' type lorry was driven, as always, by Arthur Paver. He was a Yorkshireman and a vehicle fitter who, prior to war service had worked in the garage of a bus company in his home county. Arthur cared for the 'F' type like a mother cares for her offspring, cranking over its engine by hand every day, conscientiously carrying out the prescribed daily vehicle maintenance 'task', and frequently wiping down the engine, gearbox and transmission gear. Riding in the cab with Arthur Paver were three members of the electrical section: Bob Dempster from Sacriston near Durham, George Edwards who hailed from Nottingham and myself, Maurice Nash from Berkshire.

Bob Dempster at thirty-six was older than most of his peers. He possessed a wealth of electrical knowledge and experience over a wide field, which made him well respected. However, he was difficult to get to know and to deal with, and had no wish to be other than of Craftsman rank. Prior to military service, with which he was acutely unhappy, George Edwards had worked as a maintenance electrician for the Raleigh Cycle Company in Nottingham. He was a competent tradesman, easy going, but openly displayed his discontent with Army life. For myself, I was at this time some six weeks beyond my 21st birthday and had held the rank of Sergeant for just over twelve months. Before joining the services I had been an electrical apprentice with a general engineering firm in my home town of Reading.

The cab of the Leyland lorry in which we four men travelled was not particularly comfortable. With the engine being in the cab the atmosphere was very noisy and conversation almost impossible. But by way of compensation at that early hour, heat from the engine gave a pleasantly warm if somewhat draughty feel to the air. With the help of a few items of kit some small degree of comfort was achieved by the three passengers, one occupying the passenger seat, one sitting on the floor with his back to the direction of travel and the other on the engine casing. Every half an hour or so there was a change round of positions in order to even out the discomforts.

Slowly the convoy left Mugliano and the northern end of the Val di Chiana, eventually joining and going in the direction of Florence on Route 69 at Indicatore, and following the valley of the River Arno. It was just after sunrise as we passed through the small town of Montevarchi, all the rooftops and pavements appearing a vivid red as they reflected the rays of the early morning sun. Seen too on our left were the wooded slopes of the Monti del Chianti, whilst on our right appeared the more elevated and sombre heights of the Pratomagno. Some 61/2 km. beyond Montevarchi the convoy entered San Giovanni Valdarno, military police directing the vehicles to fork left and then turn left into a minor road. 3 km. or so along this road, just past some blocks of flats in the village of Santa Barbara, the convoy of 13 C.T.W. dispersed into a vineyard on the right-hand side of the road that afforded both camouflage and reasonably hard standing in the month of July.

The locations of the machinery and other lorries requiring electrical supplies were decided between myself and Armament Sergeant-Major Chaplin, who was in charge of the 'allied trades' group, so that the diesel generators were in an approximately equidistant position from the major electrical load points. For the remainder of the day work continued with setting up the workshops, together with the peripheral but essential services such as the Orderly Room, cookhouse, stores, and latrines. The electrical section was particularly busy with running out and connecting cables and telephone lines.

Early the following morning I did my rounds to ensure that electrical power was available where required, that the generating sets were operating correctly and the telephone services were all functioning. After satisfying myself that all my electrical crew were gainfully employed I suggested to Bob Dempster that we should venture up into the hills – the Monti del Chianti – to 'see if the natives are friendly'.

Taking a small truck we left the workshop lines, turning right and soon passing on our left a collection of huts and buildings heavy with dust and exuding a smell similar to that of charred wood. We were unable to identify the purpose of the complex at that time, but later came to know it as a lignite mine. As the road rose out of the valley a couple of trees heavy with fruit came into view by the roadside. Bob Dempster and I stopped to examine the fruit but were uncertain as to what it was. We picked half a dozen or so pieces believing them to be peaches and therefore suitable for consumption. However, a positive decision was deferred pending the receipt of further and equally inexpert guidance as to its edibility. In the event a gamble was taken, the fruit being consumed without any adverse effects. The atmosphere became somewhat less oppressive as we gained height. The view behind us over the Valdarno, with the Pratomagno in the background, was quite impressive, while before us we could see the church tower and buildings of a small village, with the heights of the Monti del Chianti beyond.

In 3 km. or so we entered the outskirts of this village, parking the truck and proceeding on foot. Our dress was identical; grey/brown denim trousers with the ankle straps fastened, black boots and khaki drill shirt, but with no headgear. On the upper right sleeve of my shirt were sewn three sergeant's stripes in white tape. Bob Dempster was tall, slightly built, dark and wore a moustache. I am of only medium height, of stocky build and in those days possessed an abundance of fair hair bleached almost white by the Italian summer sun. Moreover, the shape of my head together with my hair gave me a somewhat Teutonic appearance.

Few people were about in the village, but those who we did see walked quickly away or disappeared into their houses. The village was not large, but typical of Italian hill villages, with its church near the centre and at its highest point. Walking through the village we noticed signs of what appeared to be damage caused both by artillery shells and fire alone. Approaching the main square and the church we saw a small gathering of villagers, mostly women, many of whom were wailing or in tears, and nearby, against and on the wall beneath the church, a miscellany of flowers and photographs. Clearly, we had come upon a scene of mourning.

The villagers looked askance at Bob Dempster and me, obviously suspicious as to who we were and what we were doing. After a few minutes of indecision an elderly man left the group and came over to us and asked 'Siete Tedeschi voi?' Although we spoke but little Italian, we readily understood the question being asked, and I replied 'Noi siamo inglesi'. The demeanour of the old man underwent an immediate change. He shook hands vigorously with us, talking to us in rapid and incomprehensible Italian, and then calling to the other villagers that we were not Germans as they had thought and feared, but English. Surrounded by the village folk we were in receipt of much handshaking, followed by an attempt to explain details of the brutal massacres which had recently been carried out by the Germans in that and other nearby villages. In essence, we learned that the village in which we now were was called Castelnuovo dei Sabbioni, and on the 4th July, 1944, in the Piazza IV Novembre where we stood, the Germans had massacred by shooting and then burnt the bodies of some seventy-four local civilian men. A week later a further ten local men had been shot. In addition to the killings, the Germans had also put many buildings to the torch. We were also told that similar massacres had taken place at about the same time at several other nearby villages.

As far as we could ascertain, the Germans, after carrying out this series of massacres had left the area on or about the 15th July, 1944. In the week that followed neither German nor British troops had been in Castelnuovo dei Sabbioni, although British 4th Infantry Division of 13 Corps took Montevarchi on the 18th July, 1944 and San Giovanni Valdarno a few days later. Thus, during the latter part of July, 1944, the inhabitants of Castelnuovo dei Sabbioni were fearful that the Germans might well return, and were together relieved and glad when Bob Dempster and I turned up, quite by chance, in their village, signalling the arrival of British forces. Eventually we said our goodbyes, and I promised to return again soon. On our way back to our workshops unit near Santa Barbara we discussed what we had seen and been told. It all seemed like an horrific nightmare and perhaps in isolation could have been subject to a degree of disbelief. But when at the previous location of 13 C.T.W. near Mugliano we had heard stories of massacres carried out by the Germans at the end of June, 1944 at nearby Civitella in Val di Chiana and San Pancrazio, involving the deaths of more than two hundred innocent men, women and children. Remembering these as yet unsubstantiated stories gave credence to what we had been told had happened at Castelnuovo del Sabbioni. Arriving back at our unit lines I reported to the Orderly Room what Bob Dempster and I had learned at Castelnuovo dei Sabbioni, before picking up and continuing with the duties of the day.

Most probably as a result of my report, which would have been passed on to 13 Corps Headquarters, and similar information transmitted through the Italian authorities, the Special Investigation Branch (S.I.B.) of the British 8th Army, commencing mid-September and through the latter months of 1944 investigated in depth the massacres carried out by the Germans at Castelnuovo dei Sabbioni and other villages in the vicinity.

Before 13 C.T.W. again moved forward in early September, 1944, I made a further visit to Castelnuovo dei Sabbioni, walking the 61/2 km. round trip one evening when I was free of military duties. I took with me in my respirator case a couple of tins of fifty cigarettes, some slabs of army ration chocolate and a few tablets of toilet soap. I called at the house of the elderly man who had first spoken to us in the main Piazza. He and his family were most appreciative of the things I had brought them, and were amused at my insistence that the cigarettes were to be shared amongst the men folk, the chocolate was exclusively for the children and the toilet soap similarly so for the ladies. We all partook of a little of the local wine and toasted one another before I made my way back to my unit near Santa Barbara.

Bob Dempster never returned to Castelnuovo dei Sabbioni, although he and I talked and wrote many times over the years about the significance of our one joint visit there. It was to be another fifteen years before I entered the village again. And never in my wildest dreams did I ever anticipate that fifty-three years hence I would be present at the commemorative ceremony of the massacre held in the very Piazza in which it took place.

2
The decision to invade Italy

T
he first formal proposal to invade Italy was formulated by the British Chiefs of Staff aboard the liner 'Queen Mary' during its voyage to America between the 5th and 11th May, 1943, when the British Contingent, led by Prime Minister Winston Churchill, was on its way to attend the 'Trident' Conference to be held at Washington. It was proposed that an attack on the Italian mainland should follow or perhaps overlap the fall of Sicily, such an attack comprising the seizure of a bridgehead on the toe of Italy followed by a further assault on the heel of Italy, these leading to advances on both Naples and Bari.

At the 'Trident' Conference the proposal was presented to the American Chiefs of Staff as a basis for discussion. Additionally, and in support of the proposals, the Prime Minister said that since the cross-Channel invasion could not take place until during 1944, then the Allies should use their great armies in the Mediterranean area to invade Italy. He continued, saying that in his view a total occupation of that country would not be necessary. With the collapse of Italy the United Nations would control the ports and airfields needed for further operations against Germany, an Italian Government controlling the remainder of the country under Allied supervision.

Despite strong and sustained pressure by the British, no firm recommendation was made by the Combined Staffs at the close of the 'Trident' Conference to invade Italy following the conquest of Sicily. The Americans were of the view that in 1943 the sole objective of the Allies in the Mediterranean area should be the conquest of Sardinia. It was pointed out that such a limited goal would mean that some one and one half million seasoned troops, together with their supporting air and naval power, would be inactive for almost twelve months. At the end of the conference the Prime Minister was acutely disappointed that the American President, Mr. Roosevelt seemed unprepared to press the American Chiefs of Staff to commit themselves to an invasion of Italy.

Since Mr. Churchill intended to visit General Eisenhower in Algiers immediately after the 'Trident' Conference to discuss with him what should happen after the fall of Sicily, it was proposed that General Marshall, the American Chief of Staff, accompany

Mr. Churchill and take part in these discussions. This was agreed, General Marshall travelling by flying boat with Mr. Churchill and his party to Algiers via Gibraltar.

The talks in Algiers took place between the 29th May and the 3rd June. After General Eisenhower had outlined the plans for the capture of the island of Pantelleria and the subsequent invasion of Sicily, the pivotal issue regarding an assault on the Italian mainland was discussed in depth. The general view which evolved was that if the capture of Sicily proved to be relatively easy, then the Allies should immediately proceed to invade the Italian mainland. In support of this view it was argued that there was a requirement in itself to continue to deploy the forces used to liberate the north of Africa and Sicily. But since the cross-Channel invasion was still some twelve months off, there was an additional necessity during this period to take as much pressure as possible off the Russians. A further area of activity in Italy would add to the current difficulties being experienced by the Germans whose forces were already widely dispersed in Norway, Russia, France and the Balkans.

The total current strength in the area was 27 British and British controlled divisions, 4 French divisions and 9 United States divisions. Allowing for casualties in the interim, together with the 9 divisions scheduled to return to the United Kingdom for the cross-Channel operation, left an available strength of 27 divisions for invading Italy.

By the 31st May it became evident that Generals Marshall and Eisenhower were not strongly opposed to the invasion of Italy, but wished to defer making a final decision until progress with the capture of Sicily and the reactions of the Germans became clear. However, both United States Generals agreed that the aim was to see Italy out of the war as soon as possible, and this by the most expeditious route.

While at Algiers General Marshall suggested to General Eisenhower that the latter establish two planning groups to examine both the United States favoured seizure of Sardinia including an assault by the French on Corsica, and the British plans for the invasion of the Italian mainland. These tasks were allocated respectively to the United States 5th Army Headquarters for the Sardinia and Corsica operations and the British 10 and 5 Corps Headquarters for the Italian operation. Initial plans prepared by the two groups envisaged the United States 5th Army landing in the south of Sardinia, with the French landing in the south of Corsica. The British forces would make landings on the toe of Italy in the Gulf of Gioia and on the south of the toe at the port of Crotone, these two British operations being staggered by some four weeks. Because of the likelihood of stiff resistance both by the Italians and the Germans on the Italian mainland, the assaults on Sardinia and Corsica appeared to be the most promising at this stage. No amphibious landing in the vicinity of Naples was considered, although tentative plans were made to take advantage of a possible collapse of Axis opposition in the south of Italy. The Prime Minister on his way home on the 3rd June, again via Gibraltar, still felt disappointed that a firm commitment by the United States to the invasion of Italy had yet to be realised.

The invasion of Sicily commenced on the 10th July. It was carried out by the United States 7th and British 8th Armies, British 13 Corps, as part of the latter force landing in the south-east corner of the island between Pozzallo and Cape Murro di Parco.

At a conference with his senior commanders held on the 17th July, Eisenhower expressed the opinion that, because of the significant progress of operations in Sicily, the Sardinian and Corsican assaults could be left in the hands of the French, with the United States and British forces concentrating on an invasion of the Italian mainland. Arising from this, initial plans were developed that envisaged an assault by the British 8th Army across the Straits of Messina on the toe of Italy, with the United States 5th Army landing on the heel of Italy, east of a line from Taranto to Bari.

General Marshall, now back in the United States, was not impressed with these initial plans. Encouraged by the poor performance of the Italian forces in Sicily, he proposed a major amphibious operation directed at capturing Naples with its extensive port facilities. This proposal was welcomed by the Prime Minister, who saw it as a move by the United States towards his own thinking on Italy and ultimately the Balkans. However, such was not the case, General Marshall being firm in his intention to free the United States forces from having any long-standing involvement in the Mediterranean area. Following General Marshall's proposal, General Eisenhower issued orders on the 27th July to the commander of the United States 5th Army, General Mark Clark, to disregard any thoughts of a landing on the heel of Italy, and to concentrate instead on planning an amphibious assault aimed at taking Naples. Three possible operations were examined: one direct into the Bay of Naples, a second from the north through the Gulf of Gaeta, and the third from the south via the Gulf of Salerno. The various advantages and difficulties associated with each of these three options were studied, including the suitability of the beaches for landing men and armoured vehicles, the overview of the beaches from surrounding hills and the closeness of German formations. Ultimately, the Gulf of Salerno was selected for this major amphibious operation, mainly because this location allowed the best provision of air cover. General Montgomery, the British

8th Army commander, expressed his dissatisfaction with the choice of the Gulf of Salerno for the landings on the grounds that it was too remote from the landings by the British 8th Army across the Straits of Messina, thus preventing any mutual assistance if either operation ran into difficulties. In the event General Montgomery was over-ruled.

On the 16th August General Eisenhower issued firm orders for the invasion of Italy. In essence, these were:

(a)   Operation Baytown across the Straits of Messina between the 1st and 4th September by British 8th Army.

(b)   Operation Avalanche in the Gulf of Salerno on or about the 9th September by United States 5th Army comprising United States 6 Corps and British 10 Corps.

(c)   Operation Buttress in the Gulf of Gioia, date unspecified, by British 10 Corps as an alternative to participation in Operation Avalanche.

(d)   Operation Goblet at Crotone, date unspecified, by British 5 Corps, and kept on hold.

By the following day, the 17th August, the last German soldier had been thrown out of Sicily and the liberation of the island was complete. Equally certain was the invasion by the Allies of the Italian mainland.

3
The fall from power and detention of Mussolini

Mussolini became Prime Minister of Italy on the 29th October, 1922. Nearly 21 years later, in the early summer of 1943, after having exercised absolute control over Italy for that period of time, Mussolini had brought his country to the brink of military defeat. By the 13th May, 1943 the Axis forces had been cleared from the north African shores, and on the 10th July the Allies invaded Sicily. It was abundantly clear to all that once Sicily had been liberated then an attack by the Allies on the Italian mainland was both likely and imminent.

Dissatisfaction with Mussolini's rule had begun at the end of 1942 with covert meetings and conversations involving Officers of the Italian General Staff and members of the Royal Household. There were, however, senior Army Officers who were of the opinion that as well as the removal of Mussolini from being Prime Minister, the King should also be required to abdicate. In April 1943, Marshal Badoglio told a friend that both he and General Ambrosio believed that Italy should terminate its close association with Germany; the Rome-Berlin Axis, either with or without the Monarchy, and this would include the removal from power of Mussolini.

A number of men holding ministerial posts in Mussolini's Fascist Government were also plotting at about the same time to bring about the overthrow of Il Duce, these including Giuseppe Bottai, the Minister of Education, and Dino Grandi, the Minister of Justice. Count Ciano and Roberto Farinacci were also suspected of being disloyal to Mussolini, the latter learning of this indirectly from another Minister, Guido Buffarini-Guidi, through the medium of a letter.

Knowledge of such plotting did not appear to cause Mussolini a deal of concern, with him having dismissed General Cavallero from the post of Chief of Staff on the 31st January because of the military defeats at the hands of the Allies in north Africa, and carrying out a Government reshuffle six days later in which most of the plotters mentioned above either lost or had their appointments changed. One of the seemingly disingenuous new appointments was that of one of the plotters, General Ambrosio, as the Chief of Staff to replace General Cavallero. The aim of such actions was to give a clear signal to the Germans that Italy was firm in its resolve to continue with its prosecution of the war against the Allies.

At long last, and after much vacillation, in early July, the King decided to act on the advice given to him by General Cavallero and the Duke d'Acquarone. This was to have Mussolini detained following one of his weekly audiences with the King at either the Quirinale Palace or the Villa Savoia. The King also approached Marshal Badoglio at this time, asking him if he would replace Mussolini as Prime Minister. To this Badoglio agreed, proposing an administration which included such non-Fascists as Ivanoe Bonomi and Vittorio Orlando.

Concurrently, the Fascist plotters also decided to act by asking for a meeting of the Fascist Grand Council to be convened. The Grand Council had been set up by Mussolini, and was the supreme constitutional authority of the State, but it had not met since the start of the war. Under pressure from several quarters for the Grand Council to meet in order to obtain a report on the war situation as it was presently affecting Italy, Mussolini, although initially refusing, finally relented, and agreed for a meeting to be held on the 24th July.

On the 19th July, Mussolini met Hitler at Feltre in northern Italy. At their meeting Hitler told Mussolini, in essence, that the Italian troops had not fought well, and should now come under German command. Moreover, Hitler continued, the Italian nation had become defeatist, and the civil administration commanded little or no respect. The requirement was to go on fighting the Allies, and to this end stern measures needed to be taken by the Italian Government against traitors, cowards and those who were incompetent. To all of this Mussolini listened without making either comment or reply. In private, Bastianini, Alfieri and General Ambrosio, who were accompanying Mussolini, pleaded with him to reply to Hitler's criticisms, and inform Hitler that Italy could no longer continue the war without substantial German assistance. What passed between Mussolini and Hitler when they were alone will never be known, but certainly Mussolini did not take issue with Hitler when in the presence of his three fellow countrymen. At the airfield at Treviso, when on his way home and when questioned by Alfieri, Mussolini replied saying that he had no need to speak to Hitler in the manner suggested since the Germans would provide any assistance for which Italy asked, as long as such requests were seen to be reasonable.

On his return to Rome, Mussolini reported to the King on his meeting at Feltre with Hitler. But prior to seeing the King, Mussolini had told the Stefani news agency that he believed the Germans could still dam the tide of the Allies, although to do so they required to have control not only of the military situation in Italy, but of all civil administration also. The news agency further learned from Mussolini that the German conditions were unacceptable to himself, the King and the Italian people. Moreover, the King had already heard from General Ambrosio as to what had taken place at the Feltre meeting, and was aware that Mussolini was either unwilling or incapable of presenting to Hitler, or perhaps anyone, the Italian situation as it truly existed. Thus, when Mussolini had his audience with the King, he found the latter to possess a comprehensive appreciation of the situation. While being as equally opposed to the German conditions as Mussolini, the King went on to warn Mussolini of the growing opposition in Italy to him, mentioning rumours of conspiracies both by the military and the civilian administration, but assuring him of his own Royal support and friendship.

Soon after his audience with the King, Mussolini was warned by Farinacci that General Cavallero had in his possession proof that both the Royal Court and Grandi were plotting together to overthrow him and to break the Italian association with Germany. Mussolini also received a warning from Scorza, the Fascist Party Secretary, who told him of an intercepted telephone conversation between the Duke d'Acquarone and Marshal Badoglio in which was discussed his arrest in the near future when he was leaving after an audience with the King. To all of this Mussolini appeared unconcerned, although to all in Rome it was evident in one way or another his demise was imminent.

Three days before the meeting of the Fascist Grand Council, Dino Grandi met with Federzoni, a fellow-Bolognese, and a man who he believed he could trust. Grandi showed Federzoni a draft of the resolution he, Grandi, intended to table at the coming meeting of the Grand Council. After carefully reading through the document Federzoni's response, although not enthusiastic was favourable. He commented, 'We must try anything and everything, even the impossible, in order to save the nation from total ruin'. Following his meeting with Federzoni, Grandi then saw Bottai, Bastianini and Albini, each an influential member of the Grand Council, and all of whom agreed to support his resolution. Of these three, only Bottai was likely to show Grandi open support at the coming Grand Council meeting. The other two men would, no doubt, vote for Grandi's resolution, but would fail to display the same overt support as Bottai. Like the ripples from a pebble thrown into a pond, those who now knew of Grandi's resolution then approached other members of the Grand Council in an attempt to gain support for it. De Bono, De Vecchi, Bigniardi, Count Suardo, Cianetti and De Stefani all expressed agreement to Grandi's resolution, but none were prepared to commit themselves at the 24th July meeting of the Grand Council unless and until the argument there moved in Grandi's favour.

Grandi also showed his resolution to Scorza, who surprisingly, also appeared to support it. Scorza, in turn, as Fascist Party Secretary, put a copy of Grandi's resolution before Mussolini. Il Duce read quickly through it and commented that it was 'inadmissible and contemptible'. Back in his own office Scorza drafted an alternative resolution to that prepared by Grandi, with the intention that this too would be submitted to the meeting of the Grand Council.

Grandi, believing that he now had the support of the majority of his fellow members of the Grand Council, sought an interview with Mussolini in which it was hoped that the latter would make some move that would render unnecessary the meeting arranged for the 24th July. Late in the afternoon of the 22nd July Mussolini received Grandi at the Palazzo Venezia. The meeting was a frosty one with Grandi not even being invited to sit down. Grandi read out his resolution to Mussolini, following its reading with a brief supporting exposition. When Grandi had finished speaking, Mussolini, who had already learned of the contents of the resolution from Scorza, dismissed Grandi, saying 'Now leave me, we shall see one another at the meeting of the Grand Council'.

During the afternoon of the 23rd July, Grandi, Ciano and Bottai met at the home of the latter. It was a long, unsatisfactory and inconclusive meeting with Grandi and Ciano being unable to agree on a common way forward. On one hand Ciano suspected that Grandi wished to depose Mussolini in order to secure a greater degree of influence for Federzoni and himself, while on the other hand Grandi had the impression that, although Ciano might appear to support his resolution prior to the Grand Council meeting, he could well, in the event, give his support at the meeting to Mussolini. Bottai himself was of the opinion that, with Mussolini dismissed, all political and military authority should be with the King, a view with which Grandi and Ciano did not concur.

By the morning of the 24th July, Ciano appeared to have made up his mind to support Grandi, and told Alfieri so. Ciano and Alfieri then called on Grandi at his office, with Ciano telling Grandi he would support the latter's resolution. Alfieri, reading Grandi's resolution for the first time, indicated that he was in general agreement with it, but wished to have some sections clarified. Grandi assured Alfieri that he need have no misgivings with regard to the resolution, then adding Alfieri's name to his list of supporters. But Grandi still felt that Federzoni was the only person on whom he could completely rely for support. He feared being disowned by all his present supporters with the exception of Federzoni, and his subsequent and inevitable arrest.

At 17.00 hours the Fascist Grand Council assembled with Scorza, as Party Secretary, calling the roll. As was customary, Mussolini opened the meeting with a speech in which he attempted to review the current military and political situations of Italy. The speech was together unprepared, protracted and unfocused, and made no prescribed plan for dealing with the dilemma in which Italy presently found itself. There then followed a number of short, contradictory and unconstructive statements by De Bono, De Vecchi and Farinacci, with the meeting showing every sign of degenerating into a petty argument between a few of its members. Bottai then spoke, criticising Mussolini and his régime for getting Italy into its present critical situation.

All eyes and ears were focused on Grandi as he rose to follow Bottai. Grandi said that he would now repeat before the Grand Council what he had said to Mussolini two days previously. He then read out his resolution. This had a long preamble, but went on to say ... 'the immediate restoration is necessary of all State functions, allotting to the King, the Grand Council, the Government, Parliament and the corporations the tasks and responsibilities laid down by our statutory and constitutional laws'. Grandi's resolution continued ... 'to invite the Head of the Government to request His Majesty the King – towards whom the heart of all the nation turns with faith and confidence – that he may be pleased, for the honour and salvation of the nation, to assume, together with the effective command of the Armed Forces ... that supreme invitation of decision which our institutions attribute to him and which, in all our national history, has always been the glorious heritage of our august dynasty of Savoy'. Following the recital of his resolution, Grandi went on to speak for more than an hour, berating Mussolini for his conduct of the war and his imposition of a virtual dictatorship.

Ciano succeeded Grandi with a critical appraisal of the Italo-German alliance, and indicating that Grandi's resolution had his support. In a speech which was almost diametrically opposed to that by Ciano, Farinacci spoke in defence of the Italian alliance with Germany. He invited Mussolini to request the King to take over command of the Italian armed forces in the expectation that the King would readily delegate military authority to the Germans in the person of Field Marshal Kesselring. But Farinacci too required that Mussolini should go.

Throughout the evening hours of the 24th July most members of the Grand Council indicated that they were also of the opinion that Mussolini should no longer be Head of the Government, although a few, including Polverelli, Minister of Popular Culture; Biggini, Minister of Education; and Galbiati, Chief-of-Staff of the Fascist Militia, spoke unconvincingly against Grandi's resolution. But by midnight the meeting had become bereft of direction by degenerating into various personal squabbles and little or no constructive discussion. Mussolini then proposed that the proceedings be suspended, but be continued later that day (now the 25th July), since he felt tired and unwell. But Grandi would not agree to an adjournment of more than ten minutes, telling Mussolini that in the past he had often kept Ministers at meetings until around 05.00 hours to discuss some quite irrelevant issue. In the event, Mussolini conceded to the ten minutes break, this, in turn, having the effect of changing somewhat the tenor of the meeting. With the resumption, Galbiati spoke with passion in support of Mussolini, saying that the entire Italian nation was united around him. Galbiati's words encouraged Mussolini to make a further speech in which he accused many members of the Grand Council of acting dishonestly and amassing for themselves large personal fortunes. Scorza then rose, and in a protracted and rambling speech in support of Mussolini, proposed that Il Duce should hand over command of the armed forces to Marshal Graziani, thus giving him more time in which to deal with his other duties. Then, once again, the meeting degenerated into chaos.

Count Suardo, to the surprise of all those present, announced that he was withdrawing his support of Grandi's resolution, and would vote instead for Scorza's proposal. Ciano too began to feel less sure of the position he had adopted. Cianetti also indicated that he might well support Scorza's proposal, going on to suggest that a commission be established to consider both Grandi's resolution and Scorza's proposal, and distil from them a composite resolution. Cianetti's suggestion was opposed by Bottai who emphasised the need for immediate and resolute action, but he was heard with little sympathy and given a minimum of support. Polverelli interjected whilst Bottai was speaking, saying that he always had been, was now, and always would be Mussolini's man.

Shortly after 02.00 hours Mussolini interrupted the discussions, called the meeting to order and said that Grandi's resolution would be put to the vote. Scorza, as Party Secretary, then called out in turn the names of the twenty-eight members of the Grand Council who were present, the member whose name was called then casting his vote.

Of the twenty-eight, Count Suardo abstained, seven members voted for Scorza's proposal, and Farinacci voted for a resolution of his own, with the remaining nineteen members voting in support of Grandi. When the result of the voting became clear Mussolini immediately left the meeting with the parting comment, 'You have provoked a crisis of the régime'.

Following the meeting, Mussolini was joined in the Sala del Mappamondo of the Palazzo Venezia by Scorza, Polverelli, Buffarini-Guidi and General Galbiati, the latter saying that the traitors who had voted other than in support of Mussolini should be arrested immediately, but Mussolini was disinclined to act, departing to his home at the Villa Torlonia. But by 09.00 hours Mussolini was at his desk in the Palazzo Venezia dealing with routine matters and acting as though the meeting of the Grand Council had not taken place. Later that morning Scorza first telephoned and then called on Mussolini, indicating that several of the members of the Grand Council who had not supported him were beginning to have misgivings, and that he should act at once against them. Mussolini told Scorza that there was no requirement for such action, and he would issue any necessary instructions regarding the miscreants after he had seen the King in the afternoon of that day. During the morning he also received a letter from Cianetti in which the writer withdrew his vote for Grandi's resolution at the Grand Council meeting and offered to resign as Minister of Corporations. Around midday, while travelling back to the Villa Torlonia for lunch in the company of General Galbiati, the latter advised Mussolini, as had Scorza earlier, to have the nineteen dissident members of the Grand Council put under arrest, but again he desisted. He appeared to have no thoughts whatsoever that he was likely to be arrested himself, believing that the worst that could befall was the take over by the King as Commander-in-Chief of the Armed Forces. Indeed, he told General Galbiati that he expected no objections from the King to the appointment of three new members to the Government.

Accompanied by his secretary, De Cesare, Mussolini set off just before 17.00 hours for his audience with the King at the Villa Savoia. Also early on the morning of the 25th July, Grandi reported what had happened at the meeting of the Grand Council to the Duke d'Acquarone, suggesting that the anti-Fascist Marshal Caviglia be appointed by the King as Head of the Government, and that peace negotiations should be opened with the Allies forthwith. Grandi felt thwarted when he learned from the Duke d'Acquarone that the King had already decided on Marshal Badoglio as the new Head of the Government, and promptly departed. The Duke d'Acquarone then acquainted the King with what Grandi had told him regarding the vote by the Grand Council, going on in the company of General Ambrosio to visit Marshal Badoglio to inform him of his pending appointment as Head of the Government. Not having received any firm instructions from the King as to what action to take in respect of Mussolini, Generals Ambrosio and Castellano discussed and agreed that Mussolini should be arrested as he left the Villa Savoia following his audience with the King later that day, since failure to do so then, might well negate any other opportunity. Approaching noon, General Ambrosio went to see the Commander of the Carabinieri, General Clerica, who arranged for a detachment of carabinieri under his command to be at the Villa Savoia some half hour prior to Mussolini's arrival at 17.00 hours. Following his arrival at the Villa Savoia, General Clerica was asked by the Duke d'Acquarone if he required his orders to arrest Mussolini to be issued to him by the King in person. General Clerica, in reply, said he was prepared to act on orders given in the King's name, but he required such orders to be in writing. Prior to Mussolini's arrival at the Villa Savoia, General Clerica was given a written order signed by both General Ambrosio and the Duke d'Acquarone in the King's name to arrest Mussolini that afternoon subsequent to his audience with the King. Several of those members of the Fascist Grand Council who on the 25th July had voted for Mussolini's removal as Prime Minister of Italy also believed that he should be handed over to the Allies immediately following his arrest in order to demonstrate the determination of Italy to withdraw from the war and its alliance with Germany. However, both the King and Marshal Badoglio were disinclined to follow this route for fear of German reprisals, allowing instead their country to continue with the conflict while exploring a favourable means of settlement with the Allies. In the meantime their intention was to hold Mussolini in both secure and secret protective custody.

At 17.00 hours on the fateful 25th July, Mussolini arrived at the Villa Savoia. Unusually, the King, dressed in the uniform of a Marshal of Italy, came down the steps of the villa to greet Mussolini. Equally unusually Mussolini, as he had been requested, was wearing a civilian suit. After some polite conversation about the oppressive climate, the King and Mussolini went into the drawing room of the villa and here the latter reported what had happened at the meeting of the Grand Council. He told the King that the vote taken at the end of the meeting was illegal and thus of no consequence. But the King took issue immediately with Mussolini, saying he was in disagreement with Mussolini's view, since he believed that the Grand Council was a proper organ of State, set up by Mussolini himself, and which had parliamentary approval. Thus, the vote taken by its members earlier that day was highly significant. The King went on to detail the crisis in which Italy now found itself, with the Army demoralised and unwilling to fight, and the country in ruins. He emphasised to Mussolini the magnitude of the vote against him by the members of the Grand Council, saying he must be under no illusion that he was currently none other than the most hated man in Italy. The King ended by telling Mussolini that he need have no fear for his personal safety, and informing him that Marshal Badoglio would be his successor as Head of the Government, since he had the confidence of both the Army and the police. Clearly, Mussolini experienced some difficulty in realising that he was no longer the Head of the Government, but after a short while he composed himself, offering his resignation which the King immediately and unconditionally accepted. With the audience over, Mussolini and the King shook hands, again exchanging words with regards to the oppressive July heat.

As he came out of the Villa Savoia, Mussolini saw that his car was not parked in its usual place, but some distance away, and began to walk towards it. While so doing he was approached by Captain Vigneri of the carabinieri, who said to him, 'Duce, we believe you are in danger, and I have orders to protect you'. Mussolini indicated that he did not consider himself to be at risk, and in any case had his own escort. However, he told Captain Vigneri that in order to comply with the orders he had been given, the officer should accompany him, Mussolini, in his car. Captain Vigneri demurred, saying, 'No, Duce, you must come with me. Such are my orders'.

Captain Vigneri then directed Mussolini to an ambulance parked nearby, the latter noticing as he approached that in its interior was an armed guard. After Vigneri had steered Mussolini along with De Cesare into the ambulance, various other armed police and carabinieri also entered. The doors of the ambulance were closed from the outside and it left the Villa Savoia at speed. At that moment, although it was so, Mussolini did not comprehend that he had been arrested.

After travelling for about half an hour the ambulance stopped at the Podgora Barracks of the carabinieri where he was detained in the Officers' mess for less than an hour. Travelling again in the ambulance, Mussolini was then taken on to the Vittorio Emanuele II Barracks of the carabinieri cadets where he was held under guard for about thirty-six hours in the office of the Commandant. During this period Mussolini received a note from Marshal Badoglio, carried by General Ferone, saying that all that was now happening to him was solely for his own safety, and he would soon be escorted to any place of his choosing. General Ferone then asked Mussolini where he wished to go and suggested Rocca delle Caminate near to his birthplace of Dovia, close to Predappio. In the very early hours of the 26th July Mussolini dictated a letter of reply to Badoglio in which he thanked him for caring for his personal safety, assured him of his co- operation, expressed the wish to go to Rocca delle Caminate, and concluded by saying he was pleased to learn that Badoglio had decided in favour of Italy continuing with the war against the Allies alongside Germany.

In the evening of the 27th July Mussolini left Vittorio Emanuele II Barracks, now being escorted by General Polito, Chief of Military Police. Soon after the car in which they were travelling left the barracks Mussolini noticed that it was not going in the direction of Rocca delle Caminate, but south. Questioning General Polito, Mussolini was told that there had been a change of plan, but Polito did not elaborate. At about 02.00 hours on the 28th July they arrived at the port of Gaeta, being met at the dockside by Admiral Maugeri, Chief of Naval Intelligence. With a minimum of delay the Admiral, General Polito and Mussolini boarded the Italian Navy corvette *Persefone* which almost immediately left Gaeta and set course for Ventotene, a small island some fifty kilometres due south of Gaeta. On its arrival at Ventotene, the *Persefone* anchored a few hundred metres offshore, General Polito making his way to the island in the corvette's launch in order to ascertain the suitability or otherwise of Ventotene as a place of detention for Mussolini. It was Polito's opinion that the island was quite unsuitable for Mussolini's internment, and on the General's return to the *Persefone*, the corvette again set sail, this time for the larger island of Ponza, which is some forty kilometres west of Ventotene. With the *Persefone* dropping anchor just after noon on the 28th July in the Ponza roadstead, General Polito again went ashore in the corvette's launch to survey the island. On his return to the *Persefone*, Polito said that he had requisitioned a house at the village of Santa Maria on the island which was suitable for the detention of Mussolini. Because he did not wish the islanders of Ponza to see him as a prisoner, Mussolini was reluctant to be taken ashore in daylight. Eventually he was taken to Santa Maria in the launch of the *Persefone* at around 22.00 hours. From the beach Mussolini walked up to the house where he was to be detained, and on reaching it was overcome by its miserable appearance and his own fatigue.

The room which was to be his home for the next ten days was comfortless and sparsely furnished. Its walls were whitewashed and it gave all the appearance of a prison cell. But despite the spartan surroundings Mussolini was shown many kindnesses. Carabinieri Sergeant-Major Marini made Mussolini's room as comfortable as was possible and spent much time in conversation with him. And the wife of one of the carabinieri gave him food. On the 29th July, Mussolini's sixtieth birthday, Sergeant-Major Marini made him a present of some peaches whilst some local fishermen and members of the carabinieri called to wish him a happy birthday. Most of Mussolini's time at Ponza was spent in either reading, writing or gazing out to sea, and he rarely left his room. He saw no newspapers, neither was he allowed to attend Mass on the anniversary of his son Bruno's death. It pleased him, however, when he received from his family a box of fruit and two trunks containing clean clothes, together with some letters and money. At about the same time his guard was supplemented by the arrival on Ponza of Lt.-Col. Meoli, Lieut. di Lorenzo and Sergeant-Major Antichi, under whose supervision Mussolini was permitted to go for a swim and to visit various places of interest on the island.

His routine and monotonous existence was abruptly terminated when he was awakened before daylight on the 8th August to be told that he was to be moved immediately to a new location. Collecting together his few belongings, Mussolini was escorted from the house down to the beach and on to a launch which took him out to the *Panthere*, an ex-French naval vessel. Boarding the *Panthere* he was again greeted by Admiral Maugeri, who informed Mussolini that he was being moved to Maddalena Island off the north-east coast of Sardinia.

At the end of a mostly uneventful trip to Maddalena, it was 14.00 hours on the 10th August when a launch drew alongside the *Panthere* with Admiral Brivonesi, the commander of the naval base at La Maddalena, aboard. Mussolini was acquainted with Brivonesi and disliked him. The launch took Mussolini from the *Panthere* on to Maddelena, accompanied by Admirals Maugeri and Brivonesi, where on landing he was escorted to the Villa Weber. The villa, at once remote, well furnished and comfortable, was the property of an Englishman called Weber, and until 24 hours previously had been used as a mess for the officers of the nearby E-boat station.

But Mussolini found the atmosphere on Maddalena bleak and depressing, the days appearing longer than when he was at Ponza, and the solitude more rigorous. During his sojourn on Maddalena he was visited by General Polito. In the course of their conversation Mussolini asked what had become of Badoglio's promise that he could go to Rocca della Caminate. In reply, Polito said it was thought that to go there would put Mussolini in danger, the Prefect of Forlì believing he could not guarantee Mussolini's safety. Mussolini said that he thought this was nonsense, but Polito retorted that it certainly was not so, since throughout Italy there was fierce reaction against the Fascists in general, and against Mussolini in particular.

A German reconnaissance aircraft flew very low over the Villa Weber during the evening of the 26th August, and it was known that German submarines often passed near to the island. These events led to the view that an attempt by the Germans to abduct Mussolini was not only likely but imminent. Thus, in the early hours of the 28th August, after eighteen days on Maddalena, Mussolini was escorted by Lieut. Faiola and Sergeant-Major Antichi from the Villa Weber and put on board a Red Cross seaplane moored in the harbour. One and a half hours after take-off the seaplane alighted on Lake Bracciano, some 36 km. north-west of Rome. At Vigna di Valle, on the southern shore of the lake, Mussolini was transferred to an ambulance, still being escorted by Lieut. Faiola, who had now been joined by police inspector Cueli, the latter having been very recently made Mussolini's principal gaoler.

Leaving Vigna di Valle, the ambulance skirted Rome, speeding in the direction of L'Aquila by way of the Via Salaria, Rieti and the Via Sabina. Passing through L'Aquila and heading north-west towards the Gran Sasso d'Italia, the ambulance reached the village of Fonte Cerreto around noon. At Fonte Cerreto is the base station of the funicular which rises some 1,010 metres to the Campo Imperatore, a plateau 2,130 metres above sea level. Close by the upper station of the funicular is the Hotel Campo Imperatore: the final location at which it was intended to detain Mussolini. For the purpose of holding safe a prisoner the hotel appeared impregnable since it could only be reached by the funicular whose base and upper stations, along with the hotel itself, would be guarded by detachments of the carabinieri.

But on the 28th August the Hotel Campo Imperatore was not ready to receive Mussolini, since all the guests of the hotel had yet to leave. So, for the five days between the 28th August and the 2nd September Mussolini was accommodated at La Villetta, an inn close by the funicular base station. Signora Iurato, the manageress of the Hotel Campo Imperatore came down to La Villetta in order to supervise the preparations there, and saw the arrival of the ambulance carrying Mussolini in the square by the funicular base station. She afterwards said 'From it (the ambulance) emerged a heavily built man wearing a dark suit, overcoat and hat. He no longer had the self assurance of a dictator, but looked anxiously about him as if fearing a trap.' In the event, his brief stay at La Villetta was uneventful, although throughout it he appeared both unwell and depressed.

Finally, on the morning of the 2nd September, and somewhat against his wishes, Mussolini was taken by the funicular up to the Hotel Campo Imperatore. He occupied a small suite of rooms on the second floor having two windows overlooking the front approach to the hotel. Mussolini was treated in the same manner as a hotel guest, being fed as well as his diet permitted, and taking his meals in the sitting room of his suite. Almost every afternoon he took a walk in the company of Sergeant-Major Antichi and then talked with Cueli in his sitting room. After his evening meal he went down to the hotel dining room to play cards with Cueli, Antichi and Faiola, following which he returned to his suite to listen to radio news broadcasts not only of Italian, but also of German and British origin. It was while listening to a broadcast in English from Algiers on the evening of the 8th September that he learned of the armistice between Italy and the Allies, and that included in its terms was the requirement for himself to be handed over to the Allies.

In the silent hours of the following morning Lieut. Faiola was handed a note from Mussolini saying he had heard the terms of the armistice between Italy and the Allies, and asking Faiola to give him his revolver. Although not stated, it must be presumed that Mussolini's intention was to kill himself, and thus thwart the conditions of the armistice. On reading the note Faiola dashed into Mussolini's room where the latter appeared to be about to slit his own wrists with a razor blade. Faiola removed the blade and all other sharp objects from the room, and then, in some distress, told Mussolini that having witnessed British cruelty to Italians in Libya, he would never hand over any Italian to the English. No doubt Faiola's distress was compounded by the immediate fear that he might well have to fulfil his orders to prevent the Germans taking Mussolini alive.

It was from this seemingly impregnable location that the Germans rescued Mussolini in the early afternoon of the 12th September.

4
Armistice between Italy and the Allies

The initial approach for a cessation of hostilities and an armistice between Italy and the Allies came from Italy on the 3rd August, 1943. Its source was the Marquis d'Ayeta, the newly appointed Counsellor of the Italian Legation in Lisbon, and was made to the British Ambassador there. When d'Ayeta, who was acting under instructions from Marshal Badoglio and Guariglia, the new Italian Foreign Secretary, met with the British Ambassador on the following day, he made no mention of an armistice as such, but said that although both the King and Marshal Badoglio wanted peace with the Allies they had to make it appear that Italy was continuing to fight with the Germans in order to prevent a German take-over of Italy.

Two days later a further approach was made by a second Italian diplomat, Signor Berio, to the British diplomatic representative in Tangier. Although Berio asked for a breathing space, he expressed a desire to open meaningful peace negotiations with the Allies, having been authorised to do so by Marshal Badoglio.

The attitude and response of the Allies to the Italians was that they must be prepared to surrender unconditionally, although the British Prime Minister indicated that should the Italians surrender without undue hassle, the Allies ought, in turn, be prepared to accord conditions as acts of grace but not as bargaining counters.

On the 15th August the foregoing tentative approaches to the Allies were overtaken when General Castellano, Chief of Staff to General Ambrosio, the Italian Chief of General Staff called on Sir Samuel Hoare at the British Embassy in Madrid. In essence, General Castellano told Sir Samuel Hoare that, as soon as the Allies invaded the Italian mainland the Italians would change sides to fight with the Allies against the Germans, in addition to disclosing to the Allies all the information they held regarding the disposition of German forces in Italy.

Four days later, on the directions of President Roosevelt and the British Prime Minister, U.S. General Bedell Smith and British General Strong met with General Castellano at the British Embassy in Lisbon. These two senior Staff Officers handed to General Castellano the terms of unconditional surrender, making it clear that they were not prepared to negotiate or to discuss the possibility of Italy taking up arms against the Germans, until the unconditional surrender had been accepted.

Although General Castellano drew on a map the dispositions of both Italian and German forces in Italy, he quickly realised that this did not in any way dilute the requirement by the Allies for Italy to meet in full the terms of unconditional surrender. In consequence, General Castellano returned to Rome taking with him the military terms of surrender for the government of Marshal Badoglio to consider.

There then arrived in Lisbon on the 26th August yet a further Italian emissary. He was General Zanussi, principal assistant to the Italian Chief of General Staff. The purpose of his visit was obscure, although he had been instructed by Badoglio to attempt to get to London, and there to press for the Allies to make a landing in strength north of Rome. Marshal Badoglio might also have feared that General Castellano had acceded too much to the Allies and wished to check on the situation. But since discussions with General Castellano were already under way, General Zanussi was escorted to Algiers, where, at General Eisenhower's headquarters, he disclosed further details of recent German troop movements in Italy.

By previous arrangement U.S. General Bedell Smith, now accompanied by General Zanussi, met again with General Castellano, this time on the 31st August in Sicily. Castellano told Bedell Smith that the Italian Government had studied and now wished to accord with the Allies' terms of surrender, but felt itself unable to do so since the Germans had recently sent more troops into Italy, the country now being under almost complete German occupation. Continuing, he said that it was considered impossible for an announcement of the armistice to be made before the Allied landings on Italy. The Italians pressed to be given details of the intended landings by the Allies on the Italian mainland, since they wished to assure themselves that these would be in sufficient strength and in such locations so as to maintain the continuity of the Badoglio government and the monarchy in Rome. To this end, the Italians made it clear that they expected the Allies to land in strength to the north of Rome.

General Bedell Smith refused to continue the talks with the Italians based on the premise that the armistice would be announced after the landings on the Italian mainland had taken place, and gave Generals Castellano and Zanussi no details of the Allied plans for the landings. Moreover, the Italians were informed without ambiguity that the terms of the armistice were final, and that positive agreement to or rejection of these terms was required by midnight on the 1st September. But such conditions were beyond General Castellano's remit, so he returned to Rome to consult once more with his government.

Since it appeared to the Allies that the Italians lacked the courage to sign the armistice until certain that the Allied landings on Italy would be in overwhelming strength, General Eisenhower proposed to General Castellano, through the medium of a secret radio link set up earlier, that an Allied airborne force be landed near Rome to secure that city. The despatch of this airborne force was conditional on the signing and announcement of the armistice as required by the Allies, in addition to the seizure of all airfields and the cessation of all anti-aircraft fire by the Italians in the vicinity of Rome, together with armed action by them against all German forces in the Rome area.

Having consulted again with the Badoglio Government in Rome, General Castellano returned to Sicily, and acting on their behalf signed the armistice with the Allies in an olive grove close to Syracuse during the afternoon of the 3rd September. U.S. General Bedell Smith signed on behalf of the Allies.

Before first light on the day the armistice was signed British 8th Army crossed the Straits of Messina to set foot on mainland Italy. The British force, which was essentially British 13 Corps, comprised 13th and 17th Infantry Brigades of British 5th Infantry Division, and the 3rd Canadian Brigade of Canadian 1st Infantry Division, landed just north of Reggio di Calabria.

On the 7th September U.S. General Taylor, who commanded the U.S. 82nd Airborne Division, made a secret visit to Rome in order to arrange with the Italian General Staff for the seizure by his force during the night of the 9th September of the airfields in the vicinity of the Italian capital. But the Germans had already acted decisively in the Rome area and had taken possession of the airfields. The Italians now feared that the announcement of the armistice signed on the 3rd September would provoke the Germans into occupying Rome and overthrowing the Badoglio Government. In the early hours of the 8th September General Taylor met and spoke with Marshal Badoglio who pleaded for the announcement of the armistice to be delayed, having already contacted the Allied authorities in Algiers to inform them of the occupation of the airfields around Rome by the Germans. As a consequence of the prevailing military situation in the Rome area, the assault by the U.S. 82nd Airborne Division scheduled for the night of the 9th September was cancelled. However, a combined U.S. and British force was due to land around and south of Salerno before dawn on the 9th September. In view of the imminence of this operation General Eisenhower refused to consider any further arguments put forward by the Italians to delay the announcement of the armistice, broadcasting its terms from Algiers at 18.00 hrs on the 8th September. From Rome, Marshal Badoglio made a similar broadcast an hour or so later. Thus, the surrender by Italy to the Allies became an established and publicly known fact.

Following the announcements of the armistice, German forces commenced to surround Rome. But during the early hours of the 9th September, and in order to avoid being taken by the Germans, a small convoy left Rome in haste for the port of Pescara on the Adriatic coast, the party including the Italian Royal Family and General Ambrosio together with Badoglio and some members and senior officials of his Government. The party sailed from Pescara to Brindisi on board two corvettes of the Italian navy, arriving there on the morning of the 10th September. Shortly afterwards the basis of an anti-Fascist Italian Government was set up to administer under Allied supervision territory recently liberated by British forces.

Some sporadic fighting took place in and around Rome between units of the Italian army together with local Partisans and the German forces during the 9th and 10th September. But by the 11th September a military truce brought all Italian resistance to an end, the Germans thereby being able to occupy and move through Rome without restriction.

Following the announcement of the armistice the U.S. and British landings in the vicinity of Salerno took place on the 9th September as planned. The progress of these landings and those made by the British on the toe of Italy on the 3rd September are covered elsewhere in the book.

A crowning achievement of the armistice was the surrender of the Italian fleet. During the 8th and 9th September its ships sailed from Genoa, La Spezia and Taranto for Malta, and although the battleship *Roma* was lost and the battleship *Italia* was damaged as a result of German action, by the 11th September the remainder of the entire Italian fleet was anchored at Malta.

5
Rescue of Mussolini from the Campo Imperatore by a German glider-borne force

During the 25th July, 1943 reports reached Hitler that his friend and ally, Mussolini, had been deposed, and that Marshal Badoglio had been appointed by the King to replace Mussolini as Prime Minister of Italy. In the evening of the same day Hitler learned that following an audience with the King at which he had resigned as Prime Minister, Mussolini had been arrested and was being held prisoner at some secret location. As a result, the Germans laid plans to rescue Mussolini, to reinstate him as Head of the Government in Italy, and to prop up the Italian Fascist regime.

Accounts of Mussolini's rescue from the Campo Imperatore by German forces on the 12th September have been well told elsewhere. However, it is not inappropriate for the rescue mission, an outstanding military operation in its own right, to be reiterated briefly here.

On the 26th July, after lunching with a fellow Viennese at the Hotel Eden in Berlin, S.S. Hauptsturmführer Otto Skorzeny was summoned to Hitler's headquarters, the Wolf's Lair, near Rastenburg in East Prussia. Late in the evening of that day, at Hitler's headquarters, Skorzeny was assembled with five other officers, all of whom were to be interviewed by the Führer.

After a considerable delay the six officers were escorted into Hitler's presence, Hitler passing along the line to stand in turn before each officer who gave a brief resume of his career. Hitler then asked 'Who of you is familiar with Italy?', to which question only Skorzeny replied, saying he had twice travelled as far south in Italy as Naples by motor-cycle. There followed a second question, 'What do you think of Italy?'. The other five officers gave varying replies but Skorzeny merely said 'I am Austrian, mein Führer'. There was then a long silence which was eventually broken by Hitler saying, 'I have to speak further with Haupsturmführer Skorzeny. The other officers may withdraw.'

Alone with Skorzeny, Hitler told him that his friend and ally Mussolini had been betrayed, the King of Italy having had him arrested. Continuing, he said that the Badoglio Government would soon desert Germany both politically and militarily, and as a result would hand Il Duce over to the Allies. Hitler then charged Skorzeny with the mission of finding and rescuing Mussolini in as short a time as possible, emphasising both the urgency and secretive nature of the task. Before dismissing him, Hitler informed Skorzeny that he would be attached to the Luftwaffe and under the command of Generalleutnant Student for this specific mission.

Subsequent to leaving Hitler, Skorzeny telephoned his second-in- command Untersturmführer Radl at Friedenthal where their unit was based, instructing him to select a total of fifty volunteer officers and soldiers for a special and hazardous mission, and to have them kitted out with paratrooper uniforms. There followed further instructions to Radl over the teleprinter detailing equipment and arms required for the operation.

On the morning of the following day, the 27th July, Skorzeny flew to Rome with Generalleutnant Student, Skorzeny acting ostensibly as Student's operations officer. For this flight the plane was flown by Hauptmann Gerlach, Generalleutnant Student's personal pilot, who was later to play a significant part in Mussolini's rescue. A base for the special mission was set up at Frascati in the Alban Hills some 25km. south-east of Rome, with men from Skorzeny's own unit and reinforcements from 1 Fallschirmjäger Division assembling next to the airfield at Pratica di Mare on the coast just south of Rome.

After following many misleading rumours and much deceptive scheming by the Italians, Skorzeny was no nearer to discovering where Mussolini was being held. Then the carabinieri barracks to which Il Duce had first been taken after his arrest was identified. Around mid-August the interception of a love letter from a member of the carabinieri on the island of Ponza to his girlfriend on the mainland revealed that Mussolini was being held there. This, in turn, was followed by idle talk from an Italian naval Lieut. being overheard, during which he said that Mussolini had been taken aboard his ship from Ponza to the naval base at La Spezia.

Through the German liaison officer to the Italian harbour master of the fortified part of the island of Maddalena off the north-east coast of Sardinia, it was established on the 10th–11th August that Mussolini had been moved from Ponza during the night of the 7th– 8th August and taken by ship to Maddalena via La Spezia, and was being held in a house on Maddalena known as the Villa Weber.

Rescue of Mussolini from the Campo Imperatore

On the 18th August, Skorzeny, accompanied by Untersturmführer Warger, who spoke fluent Italian, flew from Ciampino near Rome to Vieno Fiorita airfield on Sardinia in a Heinkel III. Travelling on by road the 80 km. to Palau in the north of the island, the commander of the two German flak battalions stationed there told Skorzeny that Mussolini was ill and had been taken from Maddalena to the monastery hospital at Santa Maria, a small village through which Skorzeny and Warger had just passed. Skorzeny thought it odd that if what the German flak commander had told him was in fact so, that no carabinieri presence or activity was evident in the vicinity of this village.

After returning to Vieno Fiorita, Skorzeny asked the pilot of the Heinkel III to fly over Maddalena and to take photographs of the whole island and its coastline in preparation for any rescue attempt of Mussolini that might have to be made. During this flight the port engine of the aircraft failed as a result of the inferior Italian fuel it had taken on at Vieno Fiorita, the plane nosing into the sea. No one on board the Heinkel III was lost, although Skorzeny broke three ribs and damaged his right arm. All the occupants of the plane were rescued from a small rocky island by an Italian auxiliary cruiser, with Skorzeny eventually landing late that night at Bonifacio on Corsica and arriving back at Frascati on the 21st August.

At Frascati Skorzeny learned that Edda Ciano, Mussolini's daughter, had written to her father at Maddalena, which gave further confirmation of his presence there. Thus, a mission to rescue Mussolini was planned, with a flotilla of motor torpedo boats, on one of which would be Skorzeny, entering Maddalena harbour on the 27th August, this being followed the next day by a flotilla of mine sweepers carrying Skorzeny's main force led by Radl, the combined group rescuing Mussolini from the Villa Weber on the latter day, the 28th August. Further confirmation that Mussolini was being held on Maddalena then arrived at Frascati from Untersturmführer Warger who had remained on the island since the 18th August. Warger had made a bet with a market gardener who supplied the Villa Weber that Mussolini had escaped or was dying. In order to win the bet the market gardener took Warger as close as it was possible to get to the villa to point out Mussolini walking on its terrace.

It was on the 23rd August that Skorzeny and Radl flew in a Heinkel III from Pratica di Mare again to Vieno Fiorita, travelling on by road to Maddalena. Commander Hunäus, the German liaison officer to the Italian harbour master at Maddalena, was, of necessity taken into the confidence of Skorzeny and Radl and told of the proposed rescue of Mussolini planned to be carried out in the near future. Skorzeny and Radl then returned to their base at Frascati to organise the rescue operation in detail with the co-operation of the Kriegsmarine and the approval of Generalleutnant Student.

At Frascati a conflicting set of orders was received. They originated from Admiral Canaris, the German secret service chief, directing that since Mussolini had been found to be held on a tiny island off Elba, Skorzeny was to indicate the earliest possible date for a mission to effect his rescue. In the light of the positive identification by Warger of Mussolini at the Villa Weber on Maddalena, Skorzeny convinced Generalleutnant Student that the intelligence from Admiral Canaris was in error. As a result Student and Skorzeny flew again to Hitler's headquarters on the 26th August where they presented their evidence to the Führer, Goering, Keitel, et al., which showed that Mussolini was in fact on Maddalena. This evidence was accepted by Hitler, who then shook hands with Skorzeny, withdrew the orders to assault the tiny island off Elba, and had Skorzeny describe in detail how it was proposed to carry out the rescue mission at Maddalena.

After Hitler and those of his senior commanders who were present had approved Skorzeny's plan, Hitler warned Skorzeny that should he fail then he would be dismissed, since Italy and Germany were still nominally allies. Hitler went on to explain how he would say that Skorzeny had acted without orders, his conduct being prompted by excessive zeal and possibly ambition. Moreover, Hitler said, if he failed, then Skorzeny must not defend himself against public repudiation. Finally, Hitler put his hand on Skorzeny's shoulder and told him 'But you will succeed'.

On the 27th August, the day prior to that scheduled for the actual rescue of Mussolini, Skorzeny was on one of the six motor torpedo boats which were dressed over-all and entered the harbour at Maddalena, ostensibly on a naval courtesy visit. Still feeling somewhat uneasy about the operation Skorzeny, accompanied by Warger, both dressed in the uniform of naval ratings, carried out a last reconnoitre close to the Villa Weber on the morning of the 28th August. They talked with a guard who was taking a parcel to a local laundry, saying that they believed Mussolini had recently died. The guard insisted that Mussolini was still alive. Warger then told the guard that he had spoken with a doctor who was present at Il Duce's demise. Such was not, of course, true, but the remark prompted the guard into telling Warger that he was a member of the escort party which only that morning, the 28th August,[1] had taken Mussolini from the Villa Weber to a Red Cross seaplane moored in the harbour, the seaplane subsequently flying off with Mussolini on board. Skorzeny was fortunate in having sufficient time to call off the rescue operation, thus saving himself the embarrassment of storming a prison which held no prisoner.

Back again at his base at Frascati, Skorzeny attempted to discover the new whereabouts of Mussolini. During a tour of inspection with Generalleutnant Student in the Rome area it came to light that a white coloured seaplane, possibly an ambulance, had recently landed on Lake Bracciano, some 36 km. north-west of the capital city. This clue was then followed by the interception of a coded message to the Italian Ministry of the Interior which stated 'Security measures around the Gran Sasso complete', and was signed by Cueli, an inspector general of police who had recently been made responsible for Mussolini's safety. The message had been intercepted and passed to Skorzeny by S.S. Obersturmbannführer Herbert Kappler, head of the Sicherheitsdienst (S.D.) in Rome, and who later, in March 1944, was heavily involved in the massacre of 335 Italians at the Ardeatine Caves near Rome.

The Gran Sasso d'Italia is some 100 km. north-east of Rome, with peaks approaching heights of 3,000 metres. Skorzeny found that maps of the area contained only scant detail. However, a tourist leaflet together with information from a German living in Italy who had recently taken a holiday in the vicinity identified a winter sports complex, including a hotel, that had been built in the mid 1930s at the eastern end of the Campo Imperatore at a height above sea level of 2,130 metres. The hotel, known as the Hotel Campo Imperatore, could only be reached by funicular from Fonte Cerreto some 1,010 metres below.

1 In his memoires Skorzeny gives the 29th August as the date on which Generalleutnant Student and himself flew on the second occasion to Hitler's headquarters in East Prussia, this time to convince Hitler that Mussolini was being held on the island of Maddalena off north-east Sardinia rather than on a tiny island off Elba.

Since Mussolini was taken by Red Cross seaplane from Maddalena to Lake Bracciano, near Rome, on the morning of the 28th August, with Skorzeny learning of this flight later that morning and calling off the mission to rescue Mussolini, Skorzeny would not on the following day, the 29th August, have been seeking to convince Hitler that Mussolini was being held in Maddalena.

Moreover, since Skorzeny entered Maddalena harbour on the 27th August, it seems likely that the date of his and Generalleutnant Student's visit to Hitler's headquarters was on the 26th August as given in the text. It is, however, acknowledged that the visit in question could have taken place one day earlier on the 25th August.

It appeared to Skorzeny that this hotel would be an ideal location at which to hold a prisoner. Using agents variously disguised to probe the approaches to Fonte Cerreto it became clear that the roads leading to the Gran Sasso were blocked off and guarded, all of which reinforced Skorzeny's suspicions that Mussolini was being detained at the Hotel Campo Imperatore.

On the 8th September Skorzeny and Radl flew over the area at a height of 5,000 metres in a Heinkel III. The automatic camera fitted to the plane failed to function so photographs were taken using a heavy hand held and cranked camera. The pictures so obtained were of poor quality but showed clearly the hotel at which it was thought Mussolini was held, the upper station of the funicular and a small sloping plateau on which it appeared a landing could be made.

During the evening of that same day Skorzeny and Radl began to draw up their plans for the rescue mission. These took into account the fact that the Hotel Campo Imperatore could only be reached by the funicular from Fonte Cerreto, and since there was telephonic communication between the base and upper stations of the funicular and the hotel, all element of surprise would be lost if the funicular was attacked. Moreover, any attack by ground forces and not involving the use of the funicular would involve a large number of troops, and these could quite possibly incur heavy losses, in addition to giving good warning of their approach to Mussolini's captors, who might well then kill him in order to prevent him being taken alive. A parachute drop was considered but ruled out because in the rarefied atmosphere at that altitude the paratroops would descend at too great a speed and also be widely dispersed. Helicopters were thought to be the ideal solution, but the helicopter base at Erfurt could not provide the machines required. Thus, the only possible means of attack left was by gliders.

The intention was to land on the small plateau adjacent to the Hotel Campo Imperatore with twelve type DFS-230 gliders, each carrying nine armed men and its pilot. Generalleutnant Student and his staff were sceptical of the possibility of landing safely in the thin air at a height of about 2,000 metres, forecasting likely losses of 80%. This might mean that only just over twenty combat troops would be opposed by an estimated one hundred and fifty to two hundred carabinieri, most likely well armed with automatic weapons, machine-guns and mortars. Additionally, Generalleutnant Student expressly forbade any crash landings by the gliders. Following the objections made by Generalleutnant Student and his staff to the proposed glider borne assault, Skorzeny said that he had been ordered personally by Hitler to rescue Mussolini, and was prepared to consider any alternative plan for so doing as long as it was an improvement on his own. Since no such alternative plan was forthcoming Generalleutnant Student withdrew his objections and authorised the glider borne operation.

An initial decision to carry out the rescue mission at noon on the 11th September was made by Generalleutnant Student. He informed Skorzeny that operations in the valley to secure the base station of the funicular and possibly subsequently the airfield at L'Aquila would be undertaken by members of a parachute battalion commanded by Major Mors, requesting Skorzeny to visit Mors in order to brief the latter on the overall details and objective of the mission.

Skorzeny, accompanied by Untersturmführer Schwerdt, then met with Major Mors. From Skorzeny Mors learned that the intention of the operation was to rescue Mussolini from the Hotel Campo Imperatore, and to accomplish this ninety men from the 2nd Company of his parachute battalion together with four officers and twelve N.C.O.s from Skorzeny's own unit would land by glider on the Campo Imperatore under the command of Skorzeny himself and his Leut. Berlepsch. Meanwhile, Major Mors and the remainder of his unit would advance into the valley under the Gran Sasso by means of the side roads, barricading the valley and cutting the telegraph and telephone lines. The force commanded by Major Mors was then to occupy the base station of the funicular, this action being synchronised to coincide with the landing of the first glider on the Campo Imperatore above.

Radl then came up with the brilliant idea of taking with the glider borne troops an Italian officer who was reasonably well known to the carabinieri guarding Mussolini at the Hotel Campo Imperatore. It was thought that the presence of such an officer would cause a degree of confusion amongst the carabinieri, making them hesitate to react immediately to the arrival of the paratroopers by using some form of violence against Mussolini. The Italian officer selected, General Soleti, was invited to meet with members of the German force who were to carry out the rescue operation, together with Generalleutnant Student, at Pratica di Mare, the latter persuading Soleti, against his better judgement, to accompany the glider borne troops on to the Campo Imperatore.

D-day for the operation was finally set for the 12th September with a take-off time for the first towing plane and its glider of 06.00 hours. News was then received that the gliders could not reach Pratica di Mare before 11.00 hours; thus, take-off time was finally fixed at 13.00 hours, giving a landing time on the Campo Imperatore of 14.00 hours.

During the late morning of the 12th September, the twelve glider pilots and group commanders were addressed by Generalleutnant Student who emphasised the necessity to make smooth landings, this being followed by a briefing from Skorzeny which included giving the landing place for each glider. Flying times, altitudes and distances were then covered by Hauptmann Langguth, the Parachute Corps Intelligence Officer who had piloted the Heinkel III on the photographic reconnaissance flight of the 8th September, and who was, therefore, familiar both with the route and the landing zone.

Despite a British air raid on the airfield at Pratica di Mare at around 12.30 hours which had cratered the runway, the armada set off on time at 13.00 hours. But two machines had been damaged in the raid, and during the flight the two leading towing planes with their gliders went astray. This left Skorzeny with only eight gliders and seventy-two men.

Approaching the destination of the force, and recognising L'Aquila from the air, Skorzeny, who had now taken over the leading position, sought out the small plateau adjacent to the Hotel Campo Imperatore on which it was intended to land. As he got closer, Skorzeny saw that not only did the surface of the plateau have on it pieces of outcrop rock, but it sloped steeply with its edge remote from the hotel falling away almost vertically into the Campo Imperatore valley below. Skorzeny quickly decided that to land on the plateau was an impossibility, and disregarding Generalleutnant Student's orders instructed the pilot of his glider to make a crash landing as close as possible to the rear of the hotel. The landing was decidedly rough since the ground was littered with rocks and boulders. But these, together with the glider's parachute brake, halted the machine some 50 metres from the right-hand rear of the hotel, the glider being almost completely wrecked.

Skorzeny leapt from his glider, passed a mesmerised carabinier, and went towards the first doorway in sight. In the room in which Skorzeny found himself was an Italian operating a wireless set which Skorzeny smashed with his weapon. But the room had no other exit and did not lead into the interior of the hotel as Skorzeny hoped that it would. Leaving the room, he turned right around the rear of the hotel, closely followed by his men. Here he was hoisted up onto a terrace some 2 1/2 metres above ground level, continuing on it clockwise around the hotel to reach a raised forecourt. From this Skorzeny saw Mussolini at a second-floor window and shouted to him to go back out of sight into his room. Reaching the main front entrance of the hotel he saw it was guarded by two machine-guns which his men promptly kicked off their stands, Skorzeny him-

self forcing his way through the confusion of carabinieri in and around the hotel entrance and foyer to reach and ascend the staircase in the right-hand corner of the entrance hall. On the second floor he opened a door to face Mussolini in the company of
two Italian officers and a civilian. Untersturmführer Schwerdt, who was close behind
Skorzeny, hustled the three men with Mussolini out of the room. The faces of Unter-
scharführers Holzer and Benzer then appeared at the window of Mussolini's room, with
them having climbed up the face of the building by way of the lightning conductor. Entering the room by its window the two men left by the door to guard the corridor outside.

From, the window of Mussolini's room Skorzeny saw Radl and his group approaching the front entrance of the hotel from where their glider had landed. Skorzeny
shouted to Radl that all was well so far and ordered him to secure the situation at ground
level. Still looking out from the window of the room Skorzeny watched gliders 4, 5, 6
and 7 all land safely, but was much concerned to see glider 8 caught in a gust of wind
and crash on to a rocky slope. Although the crash gave the appearance of being disas-
trous, the ten men in the glider were recovered and treated for their injuries by both
German and Italian medics, none being very seriously hurt.

Skorzeny then opened the door of the room and shouted for the Italian commander
to present himself without delay. In a short time the commander, a colonel, arrived at
the door of the room. He was given just one minute by Skorzeny to surrender his forces
and thus avoid any bloodshed. During the one minute interval Radl appeared and was
present when the Italian colonel returned to surrender to the Germans and offer to Skorzeny a glass of red wine which he accepted. A white bedspread was then hung from the
outside of an upper front window of the hotel to signal the surrender to those below.

Turning to Mussolini and addressing him in German, Skorzeny said, 'Duce, the
Führer has given me orders to set you free'. Embracing Skorzeny, Mussolini replied
that he knew his friend Adolf Hitler would not abandon him. It then came to light that
the civilian in Mussolini's room when Skorzeny first entered it was Cueli, the inspector general of police whose responsibility was Mussolini's safety, and whose coded
message referring to the Gran Sasso had been intercepted by S.S. Obersturmbannführer
Kappler.

The Italian garrison at the Hotel Campo Imperatore was then disarmed by Skorzeny's men. Although a brief skirmish had developed when the Germans captured the
base station of the funicular, the Italian force defending it suffered only minor casual-

ties. Major Mors, who commanded the paratroop formation in the valley, then asked if he could come up to the Hotel Campo Imperatore by means of the funicular. In doing so he confirmed to the Italians at the hotel that the funicular was in German hands and that German forces were present in the valley below.

There remained the essential task of getting Mussolini from off the Campo Imperatore and to Rome. It was considered unlikely that Mussolini would reach Rome safely by road from the base station of the funicular, since the area through which he would have to be taken was largely unoccupied by German forces. Thus, the decision was made for German paratroops to take and hold the airfield at L'Aquila for such time as it took to escort Mussolini there from the base station of the funicular, and for three Heinkel IIIs to land and then take-off, one plane carrying both Mussolini and Skorzeny with the other two planes giving protective cover. Although wireless contact with Rome earlier had informed the headquarters of the Parachute Corps of the success of the mission so far, it proved impossible to re-establish this contact, so the plan involving the Heinkel IIIs was abandoned. A second plan for a Fiesler Storch light aircraft to land in the valley near the base station of the funicular, pick up Mussolini and fly with him to Rome was initiated. The plane, whose landing in the valley was watched by Skorzeny through his binoculars, suffered damage to its undercarriage on touch-down which could not be readily repaired.

There remained the third and final possibility: to land a Fiesler Storch close to the Hotel Campo Imperatore and to fly Mussolini off from there to Rome. A strip of the small sloping plateau adjacent to the hotel was cleared of boulders with the help of the Italians, a green flare signal being given to the pilot of the plane, Hauptmann Gerlach, that it was safe for him to land, which he then accomplished with great skill. After the plane had landed Skorzeny told Gerlach that it was the intention for a take-off to be made from the plateau with both himself and Mussolini as passengers. Gerlach protested vigorously at the proposal, maintaining that it was an impossibility in view of the weight of the passengers together with the hazardous take-off path. It is not recorded exactly what was said to Gerlach by Skorzeny when the latter took Gerlach aside, but it proved sufficiently forceful to persuade Gerlach to attempt his impossible. With Gerlach and his two passengers on board, the revolutions of the plane's engine were increased to the maximum, the plane itself being restrained by twelve paratroopers. At a signal from Gerlach the Fiesler Storch was released and catapulted across the plateau, hopping over a drainage ditch, tipping over to its left, touching the ground again and finally disappearing over the edge of the plateau into the airspace of the valley of the Campo Imperatore. Gradually, and with great skill Gerlach brought the plane under control, levelling out some fifty metres or so above the floor of the valley and flying on towards Rome. At Pratica di Mare airfield Gerlach brought the Fiesler Storch down with a perfect two point landing made necessary in order to compensate for the damage to the plane's landing gear caused during the difficult take-off from the Campo Imperatore. The time spent at Pratica di Mare was brief and sufficient only for Mussolini and Skorzeny to transfer to one of the Heinkel IIIs scheduled to take part earlier in the rescue operation, this plane then departing for Vienna escorted by the two other similar aircraft.

Darkness had fallen when the planes reached Aspern airfield at Vienna, from where Mussolini and Skorzeny were taken to the prestigious Hotel Imperial. Just before midnight on that memorable day, the 12th September, Skorzeny was visited by the Chief of Staff of the Vienna Corps headquarters, who, on behalf of the Führer presented Skorzeny with the Knight's Cross of the Iron Cross. Then, amongst a confusion of congratulations and explanations, a personal telephone call was received by Skorzeny from the Führer. In it Hitler told Skorzeny that he had not only carried out an operation unique in military history, but had returned to him a friend. He continued, 'I knew if anyone could carry this out it was you. You are immediately promoted to Sturmbannführer of the Waffen S.S. and awarded the Knight's Cross. I know that you are already wearing this decoration, for I ordered that it should be presented to you immediately.' Mussolini meanwhile had gone to bed.

The following day Mussolini and Skorzeny flew on to Riem airport at Munich where Mussolini was reunited with his wife Donna Rachele, his son Romano and his daughter Annamaria. He then spent two days with his family at the Karl Platz, the German government guest house in Munich, before both he and Skorzeny travelled again by air on the 15th September to Rastenburg airfield near to the Führer's headquarters in East Prussia. At the airfield Hitler awaited Mussolini's arrival, greeting him on the tarmac with great warmth.

Later in the day Skorzeny had the opportunity to relate to the Führer a detailed account of the entire operation. As part of it he told the Führer that he thought the total losses in men were of the order of 30%, but in the event only ten were lost. Skorzeny also took the opportunity to recommend to Goering that both Hauptmann Gerlach and Leut. Meier-Wehrer be awarded the Knight's Cross, as well as recommending decorations for the volunteers from his own unit, including Radl, who was also promoted to the rank of Hauptsturmführer. These recommendations were all approved by Hitler. But there have always been misgivings that the contribution to the success of the rescue operation by Major Mors passed unrecognised.

Skorzeny was involved in many other exploits before he surrendered to U.S. forces on the 20th May, 1945. He escaped from Darmstadt Camp on the 27th July, 1948, and in 1952 was finally declared 'denazified in absentia'.

After living the remainder of his life partly in Madrid and partly in Curragh, Ireland, he died in Madrid on the 5th July, 1975 at the age of 67. Following his death his remains were taken to his native Vienna for interment.

6

The Salò Republic

Mussolini's experiences immediately following his rescue from the Campo Imperatore on the 12th September, 1943 are detailed in the previous chapter. After journeying via Rome, Vienna and Munich he joined Hitler at his headquarters in East Prussia on the 15th September.

Initially, Mussolini told Hitler that he had no desire to create and head a new Italian Government. But after discussions with some of his former Fascist supporters, including Pavolini and Farinacci, he acceded to Hitler's wish that he should do so. After leaving the Führer's Headquarters on the 17th September, Mussolini spent a further ten days in Germany, going first to Munich and then moving on to Schloss Hirschberg near Barmisch. In a broadcast to the Italian nation on the 18th September from Munich he announced that he had resumed the leadership of Italian Fascism and would immediately establish a new Republican-Fascist Government and administration in German-occupied Italy. Mussolini went on to say that the new state would again take up arms as an ally of Germany, and that he intended, with the help of loyal Italians, to purge Italy of the traitors who had voted him out of office on the 25th July.

Leaving Germany on the 27th September, Mussolini returned to Rocca delle Caminate where a number of the members of his new Government came to be sworn in. His own preference was to go on to Rome, but the Germans did not intend that he should head an Italian Government with any real authority, and certainly not in the capital city. Instead, Mussolini was permitted to live in the Villa Feltrinelli at Gargnano, a small town on the west bank of Lake Garda, taking up residence there on the 5th October. His various government departments, from which he was effectively isolated by the German presence, were established at Salò and other nearby towns, all being within a short distance of the main German Army headquarters in Italy. In fact, Mussolini could accomplish very little without the consent of the German Ambassador Rahn and the German S.S. General Wolff who, to all intents and purposes, governed and were responsible for controlling that part of Italy not yet taken by the Allies. To monitor all that Mussolini said and did, Hitler appointed Col. Jandl, together with a staff of Italian-speaking German officers, who established themselves in a house next door to the Villa Feltrinelli.

So close was the supervision of Il Duce that one of Col. Jandl's junior officers actually lived in the Villa Feltrinelli. This then was the scenario for what became known as the drama of Mussolini's Hundred Days.

Also during September 1943, Pavolini revived the Fascist headquarters in Rome at the Palazzo Wedekind, but he had great difficulty in persuading any of the former Fascist politicians to join the new administration. Buffarini-Guidi did so as Minister of the Interior as did Tamburini as Chief of Police. These two men, along with Pavolini, held extreme Fascist views and possessed violent and fanatical dispositions. Pavolini in particular, who was Mussolini's second-in-command and Secretary of the Republican-Fascist party, was strongly opposed to the Partisan movement, and had ordered that ten anti-Fascist Partisans be killed for every Fascist killed by them. He also formed his own militia, known as the 'republican guard', which often acted in conflict with the carabinieri, and operated outside the jurisdiction of the courts. In this atmosphere many squads emerged to suppress and terrorise the population at large, such squads being tolerated and encouraged by the occupying Germans. But in contrast Mazzolini, a generally recognised sound and hard-working politician, joined the new Government as Foreign Minister, while the veteran Field Marshal Graziani was persuaded by German Ambassador Rahn to become Minister of War. This latter appointment particularly pleased Mussolini.

On his arrival at the Villa Feltrinelli in the initial days of the Salò Republic, Mussolini learned that on the 10th September Germany had annexed that part of Italy which had originally belonged to the Hapsburg Empire. The area taken over embraced the provinces of Belluno, Bolzano, Friuli, Gorizia, Ljubljana, Quarnaro, Trento and Trieste, and was controlled by two German Gauleiters. Mussolini appealed to Hitler to rescind this occupation but was ignored. The rebuff gave a clear indication of how Germany intended to treat the new Salò Republic, and had Mussolini been told of the annexation when he met with Hitler on the 15th September he might well have refused to establish a new Republican-Fascist government.

It was at the Villa Feltrinelli that Donna Rachele learned of her husband's long-standing association with Clara Petacci. As a result of her disapproval and jealousy Donna Rachele made life extremely difficult for Mussolini who, at one particularly tempestuous juncture, suggested to the Germans that they might find somewhere else for his wife to live. But the Germans, with some guile, established Clara Petacci in a house near to the Villa Feltrinelli, provided her with a personal S.S. guard, and received in return copies of Mussolini's private correspondence as well as details of such secret information as he discussed with her. Although Mussolini became aware of these deceptions, it appears that this had little or no influence on his relationship with Petacci.

Arising out of a Fascist Congress held at Verona on the 14th November, the new Republican-Fascist administration issued a policy document known as the 'Verona Manifesto'. This promised, among other things, greater freedom for the trades unions, a free press, restoration of the independence of the judiciary, and an elective means of choosing both the members of parliament and the head of state. By its very nature the manifesto was critical of many of the principal features of the previous Fascist administration. But the 'Verona Manifesto' was never put into effect, the Salò Republic being as much an authoritarian regime as its predecessor.

At the Fascist Congress a debate was held as how best to treat those who had voted against Mussolini at the meeting of the Fascist Grand Council held on the 25th July. By a unanimous vote the Congress authorised a Special Court to be set up to try all those in the hands of the Republican-Fascists who had called for Mussolini's dismissal. Although the vote against Mussolini taken by the members of the Grand Council was legal, he had enacted a retrospective law which allowed the Special Court to pass the death sentence on anyone found guilty of betraying the Fascist ideology.

The most prominent person likely to appear before the Special Court was the ex-Italian Foreign Minister and Mussolini's son-in-law, Count Ciano. The Republican-Fascist party wanted Ciano to be put on trial immediately, a view supported by the then Minister of Justice, Tringali-Casanova. However, at this juncture Tringali-Casanova died, his successor, Pisente, taking a contrary view and opposing Ciano's trial. Indeed, Pisente advised Mussolini that the vote against him by the Grand Council on the 25th July was perfectly legitimate, and Ciano had no case to answer.

At a meeting of Fascist Ministers held on the 24th November Pavolini put forward and had accepted a motion to establish the Special Court. The President and the other judges comprising the Special Court were all Fascist extremists who, on the 19th January, 1944 sentenced five of the six accused to death. The five condemned were Marshal de Bono, Ciano, Gottardi, Marinelli and Pareschi. The sixth accused, Cianetti, received a sentence of thirty years' imprisonment, avoiding the death penalty through having withdrawn his vote for Grandi's resolution at the Grand Council meeting of the 25th July on the following day. Even prior to their trial, Mussolini ordered that those accused be found guilty, since he wished to avoid being considered weak and indecisive or culpable of showing clemency towards his son-in-law. After much indecision as to who would confirm the death sentences, Mussolini ordered the executions to proceed, with General Vianini, Head of the National Guard at Verona, eventually being persuaded to sign the death warrants.

The executions were carried out at 08.00 hours on the 11th January at Verona, being filmed for posterity by a Fascist propaganda unit. The shootings themselves were chaotic, no less than three rounds of firing being required, followed by the final despatch of each man by a pistol shot to the head.

This barbarous act at Verona was followed by the arrests of many former Fascist officials who had co-operated with Badoglio's first government. Initially, Mussolini wanted all these officials to be executed, but eventually relented. However, many of his former Admirals were apprehended and either executed or given protracted prison sentences.

One of the main aims of Mussolini's new regime, in order to enhance its status and authority, was to establish a new army. To this end Marshal Graziani, the new Minister of War, visited Mussolini at the Villa Feltrinelli on the 3rd October with plans for a small volunteer force. Mussolini was in full agreement with Graziani's ideas, and in order to advance them arranged for Graziani to visit Hitler a week later to discuss the formation of this new army.

Meanwhile, Pavolini continued to operate his 'republican guard' and Mussolini appointed Renato Ricci to re-establish and head up the Fascist militia or 'black brigades'. In previous times these had been military type formations controlled by the Fascist party, and which acted quite independently from the army. Not surprisingly, both Pavolini and Ricci were opposed to Graziani's plans to establish a new army, since this would not be directly controlled by the Republican-Fascist party. Graziani took the further view that a strong and well disciplined army would undoubtedly strengthen Italy's hand in any possible future armistice negotiations with the Allies. In all of this Mussolini gave Graziani his full support.

During his meeting with Hitler, Graziani asked that some twelve divisions of the new Italian army be formed from the 600,000 or so Italian soldiers who, after the signing of the armistice between Italy and the Allies in September 1943, had been taken to Germany to work there as forced labour. Graziani's request was flatly rejected by Hitler, since the German military considered that such a force would be both unreliable and ineffective. Indeed, Hitler would not allow Graziani to visit any of the labour camps at which the Italian soldiers were held, Hitler believing that the purpose behind such visits would be to obtain volunteers for the new army and to raise hopes amongst the Italians of a return to their native land. But Hitler did inform Graziani that sympathetic consideration would be given to the training in Germany and the equipping of four divisions for the new army.

In the light of this indication by Hitler, Mussolini issued a Conscription Order for men between eighteen and twenty years of age, coupled with an energetic campaign directed at raising a sufficient number of volunteer recruits to fill the ranks of the proposed four new divisions. These efforts were a dismal failure, since only about 40% of the estimated possible total answered the call. General Canevari was then appointed by Mussolini to negotiate with the Germans to obtain the most advantageous deal he could from them for producing the new divisions. In the event, an agreement was reached between Canevari and Keitel that not more than four divisions would be trained and equipped by Germany, but that the personnel required for these divisions would come from conscription and recruitment in Italy. As the result of a direct appeal to Hitler by Mussolini, some 12,000 volunteer officers and N.C.O.s were released from forced labour in Germany to join the new army, while by Christmas 1943 a further 50,000 men had been raised in Italy through the mediums of conscription and the recruitment campaign.

Much military confusion existed in German-occupied Italy at the end of 1943. The Germans were recruiting ex-Fascists into the Italian S.S., these units coming under German orders and having senior officers who were Germans. Even after the armistice between Italy and the Allies several units of the Italian army maintained their loyalty to Mussolini and fought alongside the German forces. And following an appeal by Graziani in the autumn of 1943, a great many Italian soldiers reported back to their barracks. Thus, by the year-end, some 200,000 to 250,000 Italian troops were under the authority of the Germans, being employed for the most part as working parties.

A great deal of discussion and bargaining took place between Graziani, Ambassador Rahn and Field Marshal Kesselring at this time. Graziani continued to argue for the release of at least some of the 600,000 Italian soldiers interned in Germany to serve in the four new divisions, but the Germans persisted in their rejection of this proposal. Graziani demonstrated that, even allowing for the large numbers of Italian soldiers employed in German working parties, there remained sufficient numbers from which to form the four new divisions. Out of these discussions Kesselring acceded to the proposal that a few thousand troops from Ricci's 'black brigades' be transferred to the new divisions as would the Italian S.S. Huntziger Division. Italian forces fighting the Allies alongside the Germans earned a great deal of praise from the latter for their courage and determination. Both at Salerno and Anzio the Italian formations distinguished themselves, which led to the Germans adopting a more acceptable attitude towards them. This was followed, in turn, by the Italians being supplied with increased quantities of German materiel, and gaining a higher level of support from the Germans for the formation of the four new Italian divisions.

Early in 1944 Graziani reported to Mussolini that the Salò Republic had armed forces totalling just over 200,000, of which some 50% were under German orders. He also reported that he now had about 35,000 men available for the new divisions, with roughly one third of these already under training in Germany. At about this time Graziani visited a number of locations in Italy where many recruits for the new divisions had been enrolled and found there considerable support for the Salò Republic and its new army. The spring months of 1944 saw the new Italian divisions being trained and equipped at the German army training centres of Paderborn and Grafenwohr. On the 24th April, after a meeting with Hitler two days earlier at Klessheim, Mussolini visited the new San Marco Division at Grafenwohr. Here he presented the battalions of this division with new flags, these being in the Republican-Fascist rather than the Royal colours. Mussolini received an enthusiastic welcome from the Italian soldiers at Grafenwohr, and after he had delivered an inspiring speech, they responded with the most rapturous applause.

When in early June 1944 the Allied forces were approaching Rome, Mussolini was displeased to learn that Kesselring had declared Rome an 'open city', withdrawing the German forces north of the capital city in order to spare it from suffering severe damage. Mussolini had neither forgotten nor forgiven the Romans for their pleasure at his demise almost a year earlier, and wished for them to suffer the horrors of protracted street fighting between the Germans and the Allies. He made a strong appeal to Hitler to have the decision making Rome an 'open city' reversed, but this Hitler declined to do.

As dealt with elsewhere in this work, military operations by the Partisans against the German forces reached a peak in June and July of 1944. In order to help combat this threat, Field Marshal Kesselring gave consideration at this juncture to the return to Italy of two of the divisions of the new Italian army under training in Germany. At the same point in time Mussolini too believed the Partisan movement to be a threat to his Republican-Fascist Government, and urged the return of all the four divisions in Germany to Italian soil to assist in dealing with the Partisans. To this end he also actively encouraged an increase in the number of Ricci's 'black brigades' who were violently opposed to the Partisans. Both the Ministry of the Interior and the Ministry of War were displeased at the proliferation of these groups, many of whom committed some of the worst atrocities of the time, and whose activities were considered by the Germans to be self-defeating.

Following the agreement between Graziani and Kesselring that, in order to raise their morale, a further visit to the four divisions of the new army by Mussolini was desirable, he set off for Germany on the 16th July. Mussolini first visited the Monte Rosa Division at Munsingen on the 16th July, following this on the two succeeding days by visits to the Italia Division at Paderborn and the San Marco and Littorio Divisions at Grafenwohr and Sennelager respectively. At all of these venues the Italian troops welcomed Mussolini with enthusiasm and responded warmly to his speeches.

After visiting the divisions in his new army, Mussolini went on to meet Hitler at Rastenburg during the afternoon of the 20th July. It was to be the last time that the two men would meet. Earlier that day there had been an assassination attempt on Hitler as a result of which he had received some not too serious injuries, and had avoided being killed as was the intention. Pleased with himself because of the welcome he had been given by the soldiers of his new divisions, Mussolini was further gratified when he learned of the attempt on Hitler's life, since this demonstrated to Mussolini that the German military were plotting to remove Hitler from power as the Italian monarchists had removed him some twelve months earlier. In a remark to Marshal Graziani, Mussolini said at the time, 'We no longer have a monopoly of treachery'.

A concurrent meeting held at Rastenburg between Marshal's Graziani and Keitel resulted in an undignified shouting match between the two men when the latter said that he required three out of the four new Italian divisions to be deployed on the Russian front. Graziani told Keitel without equivocation that such a decision would signal the collapse of the Salò Republic. But Hitler, who was anxious for Mussolini to depart in order that he could make progress with identifying, arresting, bringing to trial and condemning to death those who had plotted against him and been responsible for the recent attempt on his life, overruled Keitel, and assured Mussolini that all four of the new Italian divisions would be returned to their native country once their training and re-equipping had been properly completed. Moreover, he promised Mussolini that those Italian soldiers interned in Germany would henceforth be treated in a better manner than heretofore, and that no further deportations of Italians to Germany would take place.

But for the 600,000 or so Italian soldiers taken to Germany after the 8th September, 1943, the date on which the armistice between Italy and the Allies was announced, nothing changed. They continued to be treated harshly, including beatings, inadequate food, protracted hours of work and executions. The camps in which the Italian soldiers lived were primitive in the extreme and lacked the proper facilities for the men to keep themselves clean and free from parasitic infection. Much of this hardship and suffering was frequently witnessed and subsequently documented by a member of the Roman Catholic church in Berlin, Monsignor Orsenigo. Those of the 600,000 who managed to survive their brutal treatment at the hands of the Germans returned to their homeland after the European phase of World War II ended in May, 1945. They had undergone insufferable privations as a result of a remote political decision over which they had no influence, and because they had obeyed the orders of their King on the 8th September, 1943. The crimes by the Germans against these 600,000 Italian soldiers are as great as those committed against the Italian civilian population as reprisals for Partisan activities. However, and in contrast, the labour camps for Italian civilians who had volunteered to work in Germany prior to the 25th July, 1943, the date of Mussolini's dismissal from power, together with those forcibly recruited and deported to work in Germany after the 8th September, 1943, were of a reasonable standard, and considering the current and general dearth of food in Germany, provided the men living in them with adequate rations.

By the beginning of August, 1944 the Allied forces were approaching the Arno Line which was the last German defensive position of any significance before the formidable Gothic Line. The Arno Line ran along the course of the River Arno from Pisa eastward through Florence and then across the Apennines to just south of Fano on the Adriatic coast. On the 4th August the Germans began their withdrawal from the Arno Line to the Gothic Line, retreating north of Florence after having blown-up all the bridges across the River Arno in Florence with the exception of the Ponte Vecchio, which they blocked at both ends, and leaving the remainder of the city virtually intact. As when the Germans withdrew north from Rome some two months earlier, Mussolini was again displeased at this German retreat. He expressed the view that the Germans ought to have fought a determined rearguard action in Florence in order to delay for as long as possible the northward advance of the Allies, and thereby gaining additional time for the deployment of Hitler's then secret flying bomb and rocket weapons. Mussolini believed that every inch of Italian soil should be contested with no concern being shown for the preservation of Italy's cultural and artistic heritage.

In accordance with the promise given to Mussolini during their meeting at Rastenburg on the 20th July, Hitler ordered that two of the new Italian divisions, the San Marco and the Monte Rosa, be returned to Italian soil without delay. But at the onset of autumn of 1944 Mussolini learned that Keitel intended to disband one and probably both of the new Italian divisions remaining in Germany, deploying the men in Flak units on the Russian front. The Italians had already supplied some 10,000 men for such duties and many thousands more to work for the Todt organisation on construction work. Mussolini appealed both to Hitler and Reichsmarschall Goering to abstain from disbanding the two divisions in question, emphasising that to do so would lead to a decided weakening of the authority of the Salò Republic in northern Italy. In the event, one of the two divisions, the Littorio, returned to Italy in late October, 1944, thus giving Mussolini three out of his required four new divisions.

The remaining division, the Italia, then became a pawn in a power game between the Germans and the Salò Republic. Although the division had completed its training, was fully equipped and ready to return to its home country, the Germans continually threatened to break it up. They used this ploy in order to obtain the immediate transfer to Germany of a further 25,000 men. In parallel with this situation, Mussolini and his Government were acutely aware of the appalling conditions of the 600,000 Italian soldiers taken to Germany in September, 1943, and hoped that sending further manpower to Germany would help to alleviate the suffering of those unfortunate soldiers. There is no doubt that the men forced to go to Germany in the autumn of 1944 were certainly shown better treatment than the soldiers taken there twelve months earlier. Indeed, the majority of able-bodied Italian men who chose not to join the Partisans were sent to work in Germany, the Germans with Mussolini's albeit unwilling agreement, treating Italy as they did any other occupied country.

Much of the foregoing illustrates the impotence of the Salò Republic brought about by the Germans strictly limiting its authority and influence, this being achieved in part by denuding it of its manpower.

By the end of November, 1944, the Italia Division had been returned to Italy in response to the manpower demanded by and despatched to Germany from the Salò Republic. These four new Italian divisions made a minimal contribution to the war against the Allies. As soon as they reached Italian soil many of the soldiers from the new army promptly deserted, either to go home or to join the Partisans. As a result of these desertions morale began to decline. The San Marco Division was first deployed along the coast of the Gulf of Gaeta between Genoa and Savona, whilst the Littorio Division relieved German forces in the Maritime Alps and along the French border. Neither of these new divisions was involved in any significant actions against Allied forces. The Monte Rosa Division was stationed in the vicinity of Piacenza in November, 1944. Initially it was well disciplined, but close association with the civilian population and exposure to Partisan propaganda soon began to take its toll, resulting in a large number of desertions. In one instance almost a complete battalion of this division refused to accept orders from a higher authority, going on to desert and join the ranks of the Partisans. In the wake of the departure of the Monte Rosa Division, the Littorio Division was also stationed near Piacenza. Again, despite showing excellent discipline at the outset of its stay in the area, morale soon declined and wholesale desertions began.

When reports about the conduct of his new army reached him, Mussolini soon came to realise that any likely prestige of the Salò Republic would only be impaired by the army's current performance and reputation. With this in mind Mussolini appealed to Kesselring to use some of the new Italian divisions in action against the Allied forces. In spite of his better judgement to the contrary Kesselring ordered that the Monte Rosa Division be deployed in a limited operation in the valley of the River Serchio at the western end of the Gothic Line. In this operation, which took place over the Christmas period of 1944, German and Italian forces assaulted and occupied the small town of Barga situated about 4 km. east of the River Serchio itself. Shortly afterwards the town was recaptured by units of Indian 8th Infantry Division of British 13 Corps. However, this small and short-lived victory gave Mussolini's own morale a much needed up-lift. As a consequence he paid a visit in appalling weather conditions to troops of the Italia Division then deployed in the mountainous area near Pontremoli. He found this division to be grossly deficient in both arms and suitable clothing, and became personally involved in obtaining and transporting to them adequate quantities of the latter. But a general lack of equipment and supplies, coupled with low morale made the new army unusable in the front-line, so that by the spring of 1945 all four divisions were engaged principally against their fellow countrymen, the Partisans.

At the termination of the Italian Campaign, Graziani surrendered the army of the

Salò Republic to the Allies, and was indeed fortunate to have his soldiers dealt with as prisoners-of-war.

There is perhaps one aspect of the Salò Republic for which some qualified credit should be given, and that is in its treatment of Italian Jews. From the late 19th century onwards Jews became prominent in Italian commerce and society. Following the persecution of the Jews in Nazi Germany, anti-Semitic laws were passed in Italy in 1938, and although these laws were not rigorously enforced, many of the less prosperous Jews in the country suffered as a consequence.

Until the armistice between Italy and the Allies, signed on the 3rd September, 1943, Jews both in Italy and the areas of those countries under Italian occupation were shielded by the Italians from the excesses of the Germans, and led generally normal and unpersecuted lives. But after the date of the armistice and the German occupation of Italy, there commenced a determined persecution of Italian Jews. In late September, 1943, S.S. Obersturmbannführer Kappler, head of the Sicherheitsdienst (S.D.) in Rome, was ordered to round-up and send for extermination in Germany all Jews living in and around Rome no matter what their nationality, sex, age or profession. To carry out this order Kappler needed the assistance of additional German troops, and this Kesselring refused to sanction. To circumvent this refusal Eichmann, on Himmler's instructions, sent an S.S. unit specialising in Jewish deportations to Rome, Kappler providing this unit with a list of all Jewish families living in the Rome area that he had taken from the central Roman synagogue. But Pope Pius XII, through Molhausen, the senior German diplomat in Rome, and Weizsacker, the German Ambassador to the Holy See, learned of the German intentions, and arranged for some 5,000 Jews from the Rome area to be secreted in the Vatican itself and in the convents and monasteries in and around Rome. Nevertheless, on the 16th October, the S.S. deportation unit seized a large number of people, mainly Jews, living in or close to the Jewish ghetto in Rome. Following a strong protest from Pope Pius XII those arrested who were of the Christian faith were released, but over a thousand Jews were transported to Auschwitz where most met their death in the gas chambers.

At the end of November, 1943 the Salò Republic enacted a further set of anti-Semitic laws which were much more severe than those passed in 1938. It was forced to do so under pressure from Hitler who was determined to rid of Jews all that part of Italy ostensibly under the authority of the Salò Republic, but in reality under German control. These new laws laid down that all of those Jews living in the Salò Republic were to be

49

arrested, irrespective of nationality, their goods and property being confiscated. Following arrest they would be held in specially prepared concentration camps. The main Italian-run concentration camp was near Modena, whilst the Germans built their own camp near to Trieste. Those arrested were taken either to one of these principal camps or to one of a number of smaller camps, from where the majority went on to Auschwitz and almost certain death. For those of mixed Jewish blood the new laws established a special surveillance system.

To his credit, Buffarini-Guidi, Minister of the Interior, delayed a public announcement of the new laws, thus providing a brief opportunity for those Jews who were able to do so to avoid arrest either by going into hiding or leaving their known whereabouts. Moreover, because of shock and concern at the barbarous treatment of his fellow Italians by the Germans, Buffarini-Guidi pleaded with Mussolini to intervene to halt such treatment. But Mussolini was well aware that he had no authority in these matters. Indeed, early in January, 1944 a further anti-Semitic law was enacted by the Salò Republic sequestrating all Jewish assets. And in the same month, at Hitler's insistence, Mussolini appointed Preziosi as Minister for Jewish Affairs in his Government.

Preziosi was a fanatical anti-Semite of the worst possible and most extreme kind. He was an ex-Neapolitan journalist and one-time Priest who took the view that all those with any trace of Jewish blood of whatever age, sex, nationality or state of health should be exterminated. During his period in office Preziosi proposed a new set of anti-Semitic laws to be introduced by the Salò Republic, these laws being based on the German (Nuremberg) laws of 1935. Because Preziosi had both Hitler's ear and approval, Mussolini went along in principle with Preziosi's thoughts and proposals, but worked with Buffarini-Guidi to avoid at all costs the total institution of such anti-Semitic intolerance in Italy. Buffarini-Guidi, who was always at variance with Preziosi, made a strong protest to the Germans in January, 1944 with regard to what he considered to be the wrongful deportation of Italian Jews, at the same time requesting Italian concentration camp commanders not to hand over Italian Jews in their charge to the German S.S. His pleas were, however, largely ignored.

In March, 1944, Caruso, the Fascist Police Chief of Rome, contributed the names of 78 Jews to S.S. Obersturmbannführer Kappler for inclusion in the 335 massacred in the Ardeatine Caves. And by the time that Rome fell to the Allies in early June, 1944, Caruso had handed over a further almost 1,100 Jews to the Germans for transportation to the death camps. Caruso was put on trial for his activities and found guilty, as a result of which he was executed by an Italian firing squad on the 21st September, 1944.

It was indeed fortunate that in Italy the general population was tolerant of the Jews and sympathetic towards them. Although the Germans insisted that the Fascist police should aid them in arresting Jews, their normal reaction was one of non-co-operation. Little can be said to the credit of the Salò Republic, but its resistance, albeit passive, to the German effort to exterminate the Jewish population of Italy must show in its favour. But it was the Italian people at large who prevented the major part of the Jewish community in that country from perishing in the German death camps.

By March, 1945 Mussolini had come to realise the hopelessness of his situation. He attempted to establish negotiations with the Allies through the medium of the Roman Catholic church, advancing the view that both the Salò Republic and Germany would, before long, become associated with the Allied cause in an attempt to staunch the spread of Communism throughout Europe. The Vatican, which was then in something of a cleft stick, could see that the Allies were unlikely to move away from their declared policy of 'unconditional surrender', and wished to avoid appearing to favour the Anglo-American wing of the Allies whilst opposing the Russian Communist faction. In April, 1945, having received no positive response from the Roman Catholic church, Mussolini resuscitated his plan for a 'fight to the last bullet stand' against the Allies. He deluded himself into believing that if he moved with his Government to near the Swiss and Austrian borders, in the vicinity of Sondrio, surrounding himself with loyal Republican-Fascist troops supported by German armour, he could then negotiate a favourable settlement with the Allies. After protracted discussions in mid-April involving Graziani, the German Ambassador Rahn and S.S. General Wolff, no firm decision evolved. In part, this was due to the fact that Mussolini's proposals cut across the German plans to surrender to the Allies in Italy, the German plans not having been revealed to Mussolini.

Under German escort Mussolini left the Villa Feltrinelli for the Milan Prefecture, arriving there on the evening of the 19th April. Over the next few days he met with various factions and advisers to discuss whether or not to surrender to the Allies or to pursue his 'fight to the last bullet' policy. At a meeting on the 25th April with Cardinal Idelfonso Schuster the Archbishop of Milan and the Communist dominated C.L.N.A.I. he discovered that S.S. General Wolff had already been in contact with both the Americans and the C.L.N.A.I. regarding the surrender of the German forces in Italy to the Allies.

With U.S. armoured spearheads fast approaching Milan and the control of the city by the Partisans imminent, Mussolini decided to depart without further delay for Como. This action effectively brought to an end the life of the Salò Republic.

The end of life for Mussolini himself then came swiftly. In the leading vehicle of a convoy containing German S.S. troops and a car carrying his mistress Clara Petacci together with members of her family, Mussolini set off for Como. The German S.S. troops, despite Mussolini's protests, were ostensibly acting as escorts, although their orders were to guard him closely and prevent him from crossing the state border into neutral Switzerland. Late in the evening of the 25th April Mussolini arrived at the Prefecture in Como. Here he waited expectantly for a few hours for the arrival of Pavolini accompanied by some 3,000 loyal Fascists who would support him in his 'fight to the last bullet' stand in the vicinity of Sondrio. But Pavolini and the Fascists failed to arrive, and around 04.30 hours on the morning of the 26th April, still under German escort, Mussolini travelled up the western side of Lake Como to Menaggio. Here he went to the house of the local Fascist leader to rest, being joined at the house by Clara Petacci. After spending a few hours at Menaggio, Mussolini took the road towards Lake Lugano, turning off this road to go to the Miravalle Hotel at Grandola. At the hotel he was accompanied by Clara Petacci and three of his Fascist Ministers. Later that day Mussolini and Clara Petacci were prevented by their German escort from leaving the hotel by a rear door. It was at the Miravalle Hotel that Mussolini also learned that two of three other Fascist Ministers had been taken prisoner by frontier guards as they attempted to cross the border into Switzerland, and that his wife Donna Rachele had been turned back into Italy at the Italian-Swiss border town of Chiasso.

On the morning of the day following, Pavolini caught up with Mussolini at Grandola where the latter learned from his second-in-command that all hope of a 'fight to the last bullet' stand had faded, since the Fascists at Como had surrendered to the Partisans. In desperation, Mussolini arranged through his German escort for his party to join-up with a Luftwaffe unit travelling north up the western side of Lake Como, this unit having as its ultimate destination Innsbruck in Austria. Still early on the 27th April, Mussolini, together with his German escort, returned to Menaggio, there turning north to proceed up the side of Lake Como. At a road block set-up at a bend in the road known as Rocca di Musso there was an exchange of fire between the armoured car in which Mussolini was now travelling and the Partisans manning the obstruction. After a Partisan was killed a truce was called during which the Partisan leader told the Germans that they could pass unhindered, with the proviso that the vehicles in the convoy were searched for Fascists when they reached the small town of Dongo some half a kilometre further on. Because of this condition the German officer in charge of the convoy persuaded Mussolini to don as disguise a German helmet and greatcoat. Although at first he refused, Mussolini eventually complied, also transferring from the armoured car to the back of a lorry.

It was mid-afternoon when the German vehicles, together with a car bearing Spanish number plates and in which Clara Petacci was travelling, drew-up in the main square of Dongo. Mussolini had already been identified by a passing cyclist when the convoy was halted at Rocca di Musso and the Partisans told of his presence. Thus, the Partisans in Dongo were very confident of discovering and apprehending Mussolini. In a search of the vehicles comprising the convoy he was identified by the deputy political commissar of the Partisan 52nd Garibaldi Brigade and taken from the German lorry in which he was found to the local Prefecture. Following Mussolini's detention the German convoy was permitted to continue on its journey to Innsbruck, the Partisans now holding Mussolini reporting his capture to the C.L.N.A.I. in Milan.

In order to foil any attempt to rescue Mussolini, the Partisans first moved him from Dongo to the mountain village of Germasino. Shortly after he had retired to bed in the upstairs room of a customs post the Partisans holding him received instructions to move Mussolini to a villa at Blevio on the east bank of Lake Como and some 6 1/2 km. north of the town of Como. This transfer was to take place in part by boat from Moltrasio to Blevio so as to avoid passing through Como town. In the small hours of the 28th April Mussolini was taken from Germasino under Partisan guard for Moltrasio, meeting up en route with a car carrying his mistress. When Moltrasio was reached no boat had arrived to carry Mussolini and Clara Petacci to Blevio. Moreover, artillery fire could be heard from the direction of Como town. In the light of the prevailing circumstances the decision was taken by the Partisans guarding Mussolini to travel back up the western shore of Lake Como as far as Azzano near to which, at Mezzegra, was a farmhouse whose resident was sympathetic to the Partisan movement. It was approaching 04.00 hours on the 28th April when Mussolini and Clara Petacci finally retired to spend together what remained of their last night on this earth alive.

During the evening of the 27th April the C.L.N.A.I. in Milan debated whether or not Mussolini should be handed over to the Allies in accordance with the terms of the armistice between Italy and the Allies. Arising from this meeting, Walter Audisio, a Communist liaison officer, was detailed to fetch Mussolini from Mezzegra and bring him back to Milan, although Togliatti, the head of the Communist party in Italy, had already issued orders that both Mussolini and Clara Petacci were to be executed imme-diately following their positive identification.

Leaving Milan early on the morning of the 28th April, Audisio, accompanied by Aldo Lampredi, Vice-Commandant General of the Partisan Garibaldi Brigades, arrived at Dongo in the early afternoon of that day, believing Mussolini to be held there. By 16.00 hours Audisio and Lampredi, now joined by Michele Moretti, a Partisan Brigade Commander, reached the farm at Mezzegra where Mussolini and Clara Petacci had spent the previous night. Audisio and his two companions burst into the room at the farmhouse occupied by Mussolini and Clara Petacci, telling the couple that they had come to effect their rescue and hurrying them outside into Audisio's car.

The car was driven a few hundred metres along the road towards Azzano, as far as the gates of the Villa Belmonte, where Mussolini and Clara Petacci were ordered out of the vehicle and informed by Audisio that they had both been sentenced to death. Aud-isio first shot and killed Clara Petacci with a sub-machine-gun, then turning to fire at Mussolini with the same weapon. Finding Mussolini to be still breathing after he had been shot, Audisio finally despatched Mussolini with a pistol shot to the heart.

Together with the bodies of fifteen other Fascists shot dead on that day at Dongo, in-cluding those of Pavolini, Bombacci, Mezzasoma, Zerbino and Gatti, Mussolini's and Clara Petacci's corpses were taken to Milan in the back of a commandeered removal van late on the 28th April, to be deposited outside a garage in the Piazzale Loreto. During the morning of the next day the bodies of Mussolini and Clara Petacci were shot at, kicked, trampled underfoot and urinated on by members of the public before being strung up by the feet from the steel frame supporting the garage roof.

It was indeed a brutal, ghastly and ignominious end.

7

Journey of British 13 Corps from Africa through Sicily to Italy

The Invasion of Sicily

On the 13th May, 1943 the Tunisian Campaign ended in victory for the Allies. Some 150,000 German troops were taken prisoner during the final phase of the campaign, together with over 1,000 artillery pieces, of which 200 were the legendary 88mm. gun, many trucks and around 250 tanks.

Within two months of this magnificent feat of arms the invasion of Sicily was to follow. The Sicilian enterprise, known as 'Operation Husky', was sanctioned at the Casablanca Conference held in January 1943. As has been recently pointed out by no less a person than Sir Alec Guinness, the significance of 'Operation Husky' lay in the fact that it was the initial invasion of Europe by the Allies, preceding the cross-Channel invasion by almost a year.

The 15th Army Group commanded by General Alexander had overall responsibility for the operation, having under its direction British 8th Army and United States 7th Army commanded by Generals Montgomery and Patton respectively.

The initial task of British 8th Army was to assault in the south-east corner of the island between Syracuse and Pozzallo, and to establish itself on the general line Syracuse-Pozzallo-Ragusa. British 8th Army comprised British 13 Corps commanded by Lt. General Dempsey and British 30 Corps commanded by Lt. General Leese, with British 46th and 78th Infantry Divisions in reserve.

British 13 Corps, with whom we are principally concerned, had as its immediate objectives the capture of Syracuse, followed by Augusta and Catania. For the assault the Corps had under its command the following main formations, all of whom were British: 5th Infantry Division, 50th Infantry Division, 1st Airborne Division, and 4th Armoured Brigade.

Most of the troops of British 13 Corps embarked at Suez on the 32 ships that were to take them to Sicily, the fast assault convoys with their troops going to and finally sailing for Sicily from Port Said and Alexandria on the 6th July. Vehicles and support forces

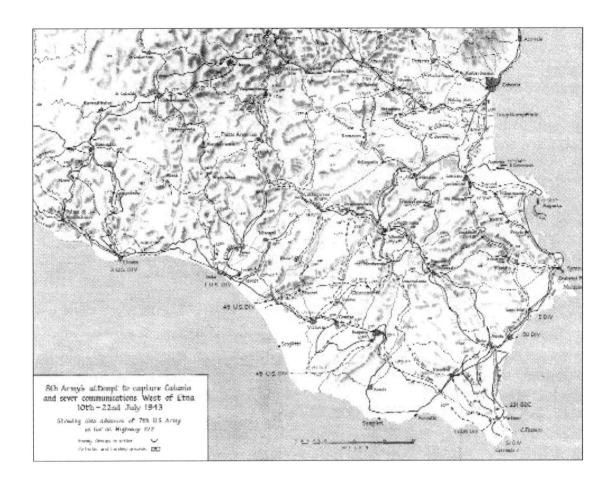

8th Army's attempt to capture Catania
and sever communications West of Etna
10th – 22nd July 1943

Showing also advance of 7th US Army
as far as Highway 117

Enemy forces in action
Airfields and landing grounds

were loaded into a further 60 ships distributed between Haifa, Beirut, Alexandria and various other small ports along the African shore from Tripoli to Beirut.

The principal sailings of the ships carrying British 13 Corps took place over the period 3rd July to the 9th July, British 5th Infantry Division landing in the vicinity of Cassibile at around 00.35 hours on the morning of the 10th July, only 20 minutes later than scheduled. But due to strong winds and a choppy sea British 50th Infantry Division made landfall near Avola in scattered groups with its units intermingled and some 60 minutes late. However, by soon after 06.00 hours on the 10th July all the assault troops were ashore. Although the landings were made difficult by the bad weather this, in turn, caused the defending Italian forces to relax their vigilance, allowing the landings to take place virtually unopposed.

The airborne forces were less fortunate. Between one third and one half of the gliders carrying the British 1st Air Landing Brigade were cast off prematurely by the aircraft of the United States forces towing them, most of these gliders descending into the sea with their occupants being drowned. The remainder of the force was scattered across south-east Sicily, with only a dozen gliders landing near the Ponte Grande bridge over the Anapo River just south of Syracuse that they were targeted to reach and then hold until relieved by British 5th Infantry Division.

The build up from vessels at sea of equipment and stores was confused, much either going astray or arriving in an incorrect order. Nevertheless, by the end of 'D' day, troops of British 13 Corps had captured Syracuse, and three days later, on the 13th July, had also taken Augusta.

British 13 Corps Main Headquarters was established at Syracuse also on the 13th July, with 100 Field Maintenance Centre opening up just north of Syracuse on the 18th July, and moving on the 50km. to Lentini during the last week of July.

British 13 C.T.W. moved from Palestine into Egypt in various groups between mid-May and early June 1943, some travelling by road and others by sea. The Forward Party comprising four officers and seventy other ranks sailed from Alexandria on H.M.T. K119 in D+3 Convoy on the 9th July, arriving and disembarking at Syracuse on the 13th of July. Three days later the Forward Party moved from the assembly area near Syracuse to Priolo, some 14km. north up the coast, opening up there the workshops and recovery sections. Then on the 22nd July the Gun Shop, together with the Instrument and Wireless Transmitter sections, moved some 40km. from Priolo to just north-east of Lentini in order to more readily service the medium artillery regiments. The Rear Party of British 13 C.T.W., the balance of the unit, also embarked on H.M.T. K119 at Alexandria, sailing in D+14 Convoy on the 20th July. They arrived off Syracuse on the 24th July, sailing on to Augusta and disembarking there on the same day. It was two days later that the Forward and Rear Parties of British 13 C.T.W., excluding the Gun Shop and the Instrument and Wireless Transmitter sections, joined up with each other and became fully operational at Carlentini, just south of Lentini.

After much hard fighting and being held by the Germans at the Hauptkampflinie some 8km. south of Catania, troops of British 13 Corps entered that city and port on the 5th August. Their advance continued northwards, both along the coast and inland although east of Mount Etna, British 5th Infantry Division taking Paterno and Belpasso on the 6th August, and then following the inland route through Milo and Francavilla, with British 50th Infantry Division taking the coastal route by way of Acireale, Fiumefreddo and Taormina.

On the 4th August General Montgomery announced that British 13 Corps would be

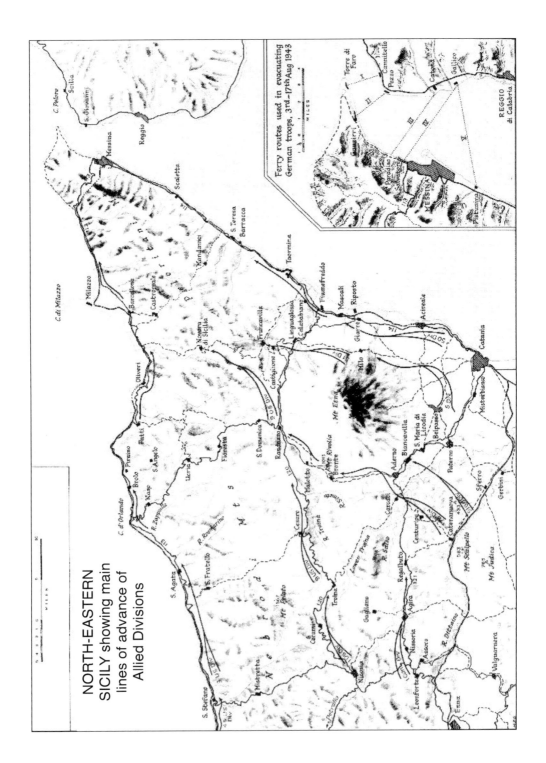

NORTH-EASTERN
SICILY showing main
lines of advance of
Allied Divisions

Ferry routes used in evacuating
German troops, 3rd-17th Aug 1943

required to prepare for the invasion of mainland Italy. As a consequence, on the 10th August, he directed that when British 13 Corps reached the line Taormina-Linguaglossa-Francavilla the control of operations to clear Sicily of German forces would pass to British 30 Corps, British 13 Corps Headquarters being disengaged in order to plan and prepare for the invasion of the Italian mainland, this major undertaking having been finally agreed between the British and the Americans on the 22nd July.

The 9th and 10th August saw the component sections of British 13 C.T.W. move forward from north-east of Lentini and Carlentini respectively to Misterbianco, just west of Catania, remaining there and continuing to be fully functional during the final phase of operations against the Germans in Sicily, while preparing to cross the Straits of Messina to Italy in the first week of September. By the 12th August troops of British 13 Corps had reached the general line Riposte-Milo, halting there and taking no further part in the Sicilian campaign.

The island of Sicily was cleared of German forces on the 17th August, the final Allied operations being executed by units of the United States 7th Army and the British 78th Infantry Division that had but recently arrived in Sicily from Tunisia to join British 30 Corps. The piece de resistance of the last days of the campaign occurred when United States units entered Messina on the 16th August, a little ahead of their British comrades-in-arms, and to the consternation of General Montgomery.

The Invasion of Italy

Such was the progress of operations in Sicily that, as indicated above, General Eisenhower and his senior commanders could properly decide on the 22nd July to proceed with the planning necessary for the invasion of the Italian mainland. Moreover, General Montgomery, some two weeks later, announced that British 13 Corps would be required both to plan and prepare to carry out this invasion.

Following the signing of the Short Armistice between Italy and the Allies on the 3rd September a British force, part of British 13 Corps and comprising British 5th Infantry Division and Canadian 1st Infantry Division crossed the Straits of Messina to land just north of Reggio di Calabria. This operation bore the name 'Baytown'. The Canadian 3rd Infantry Brigade had taken Reggio di Calabria by noon on 'D' day, and within a week of the initial landings British forces had reached the Catanzaro neck, an advance of some 160km. After concentrating its forces in the area of Catanzaro and Nicastro, British 13 Corps began a more general advance on the 14th September, British 5th In-

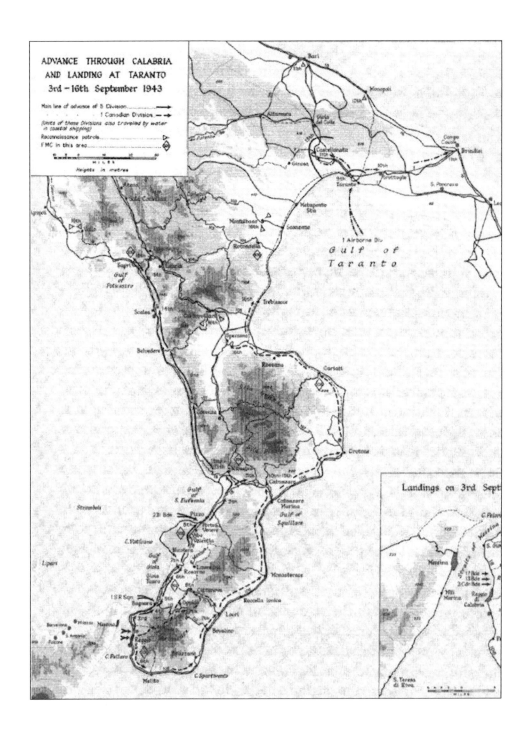

ADVANCE THROUGH CALABRIA
AND LANDING AT TARANTO
3rd – 16th September 1943

fantry Division reaching Sapri and the Canadian 1st Infantry Division approaching Spezzano by the 16th September.

Leaving Misterbianco in Sicily on the 5th September, British 13 C.T.W. moved to Santa Teresa and then on to the embarkation assembly area at Mili Marina. From there the unit crossed the Straits of Messina in two parties on the 9th and 10th September, going north along the Italian coast to Palmi some 32km. from Reggio di Calabria. Two days later there was a further move on to Nicastro where British 13 C.T.W. set up operations that continued until the 29th September. There followed a series of frequent moves from Nicastro to Cosenza, Scanzano, Castel del Monte and San Sevro over the next five days, the unit establishing itself and fulfilling its essential operational functions at San Sevro until the 28th October.

While at San Sevro Major C. M. Hunter replaced Major Rundle as Officer Commanding British 13 C.T.W., the former remaining as such until mid-July 1944 when he was promoted to Lt.-Col. and tranferred to British 13 Corps Headquarters as Corps Royal Electrical and Mechanical Engineer (C.R.E.M.E.).

Meantime, British 13 Corps continued its northward advance, with the Canadian 1st Infantry Division taking Potenza on the 20th September and British 5th Infantry Division, on the left of the Canadians entering Aulette by the following day. By this stage of operations British 13 Corps could not be properly sustained through its over-stretched lines of supply and communication, this situation resulting from the speed and extent of its advance. Thus, any further substantial move forward had to be delayed until circa 1st October.

Indeed, much difficulty was experienced in the early days of the Italian Campaign in setting up and operating long lines of supply and communication in Calabria in order to service British 13 Corps. At this period of time the Corps possessed a fighting strength of around 58,000 men. Initially there was a phase of maintenance from ships offshore across the beaches controlled directly from British 13 Corps Headquarters. This arrangement was soon superseded by an area headquarters being established at Reggio di Calabria to control a sequence of Army Road Heads together with Field and Divisional Maintenance Centres. In fact, during the first fortnight of the Italian Campaign no fewer than six Field Maintenance Centres were set up, with sea transport being used for both trans-Mediterranean supply as well as in the coastal waters. Demolition by the Germans prohibited use of the rail network and caused grave problems in supplying British 13 Corps by road. Remedies for overcoming these difficulties included the provision of a

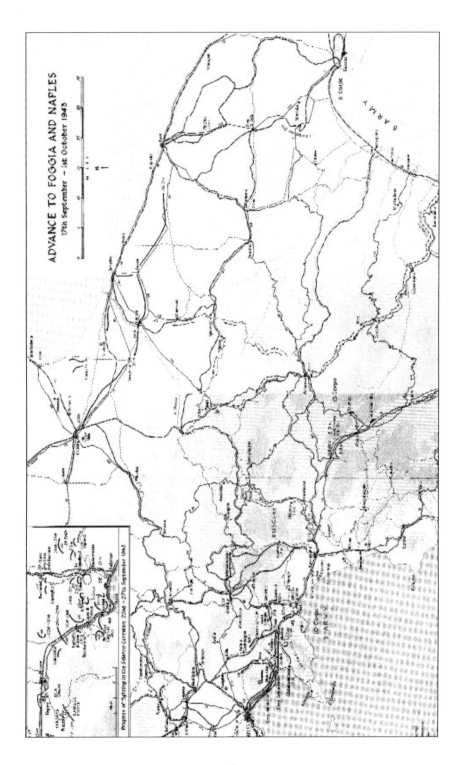

significant increase in maintenance transport, additional Field Maintenance Centres and opening up new forward ports. With effect from the 16th September, British 8th Army was allocated additional landing craft to assist in dealing with its supply problems. As a result, from that date, British 13 Corps had control and use of five more tank landing craft (L.C.T.s) on the Italian west coast, four more L.C.T.s on the east coast, and a General Transport Company (G.T.C.) on each of its several main road supply routes.

The second set of landings on the Italian mainland took place before the dawn on the 9th September in the vicinity of Salerno. The operation was code named 'Avalanche' and was under the direction of United States 5th Army. The Allied forces involved included British 10 Corps, comprising the British 46th and 56th Infantry Divisions, the United States 6 Corps, comprising the U.S. 36th (Texas) Division with U.S. 45th Division in reserve, together with units of British Commandos and U.S. Rangers.

On the same day as the Salerno landings the British 1st Airborne Division of some 6,000 men was put ashore at Taranto from British warships, their landing being completely unopposed.

At Salerno the Allied landings were strongly contested by the Germans. The United States 6 Corps having landed and crossed the beaches made good progress, advancing some 15km. both south and inland by the night of the 11th September. British 10 Corps met stiffer opposition than their American comrades-in-arms, but soon took both Salerno and Battipaglia, along with the nearby airfield of Montecorvino. But this facility could not be used by the Allied fighter aircraft since it remained under German artillery fire. German troops attempting to prevent the advance of British 8th Army from Calabria northwards were redeployed against the landing at Salerno, as were the major parts of three German divisions from further north in Italy.

The critical phase of the Salerno battles took place between the 12th and 15th September. British 56th Infantry Division abandoned Battipaglia, and although suffering heavy losses, prevented the Germans from reaching the sea. The Germans identified and exploited the thinly held area between the United States 6 Corps and British 10 Corps, crossing the River Sele and threatening to reach the beaches in the rear of the U.S. forces. Only sustained and resolute action by the U.S. artillery saved the day. In the event, Allied reinforcements were quickly brought to bear, including the U.S. 45th Division, the U.S. 82nd Airborne Division and the British 7th Armoured Division. The British 8th Army too moved with all possible speed up the west coast of Italy so as to make urgent contact with the beleaguered United States 5th Army.

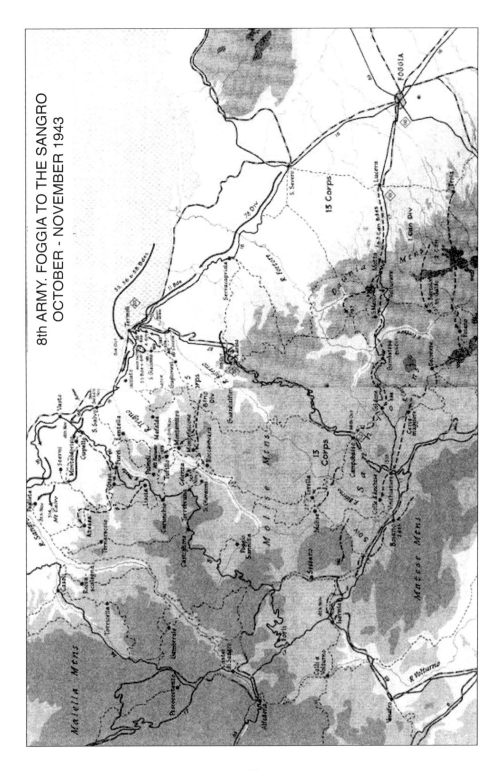

8th ARMY. FOGGIA TO THE SANGRO
OCTOBER - NOVEMBER 1943

By the 14th/15th September the Salerno battle tipped in favour of the Allies, and on the following day the German General von Vietinghoff called off the fight, withdrawing his forces on to the high ground above Salerno. On the 16th September also, units of British 5th Infantry Division from British 13 Corps joined up at Vallo with units of United States 5th Army. Thus, the Salerno battle was over, ending in victory for the Allies.

Subsequent to the Salerno conflict the United States 5th Army, with British 10 Corps and United States 6 Corps on the left and right respectively, pushed back the Germans who fought determined rear guard actions at the Cava defile and Altavilla. After moving up strong British and U.S. reinforcements the route through the Chiunzi Pass was opened and Nocera was taken on the 27th September. Progress was then made past the ruins of Pompei, around Mount Vesuvius and on to Naples. U.S. 23rd Armoured Brigade reached the outskirts of Naples on the 1st October, the city being completely in Allied hands four days later.

After joining up with units of United States 5th Army at Vallo on the 16th September, British 13 Corps continued its northerly advance, the Canadian 1st Infantry Division reaching Malfi on the 27th September and pushing on with light forces towards Foggia. Meantime, British 78th Infantry Division, which had recently joined British 5 Corps, entered Bari on the 23rd September, continuing forward through Andria and Cerignola to take Foggia on the 27th September.

From the area of Foggia British 13 Corps spearheaded the advance on the Adriatic front with Canadian 1st Infantry Division heading westward and entering Campobasso on the 14th October and taking Vinchiaturo on the day following. Concurrently, British 78th Infantry Division, now also part of British 13 Corps, made their long advance through San Severo and Serracapriola to take Termoli on the 3rd October, aided by a seaborne Commando landing.

Because of the diverging lines of attack of the two divisions of British 13 Corps, General Montgomery decided to regroup his forces, with British 13 Corps operating inland and comprising Canadian 1st Infantry Division and British 5th Infantry Division, and British 5 Corps advancing along the Adriatic coast with British 78th Infantry Division and Indian 8th Infantry Division.

Continuous rain delayed any further advance by British 8th Army on the Adriatic front until the night of the 2nd/3rd November. During that night British 5 and 13 Corps attacked side by side across the River Trigno, with 5 Corps nearest to the Adriatic Coast.

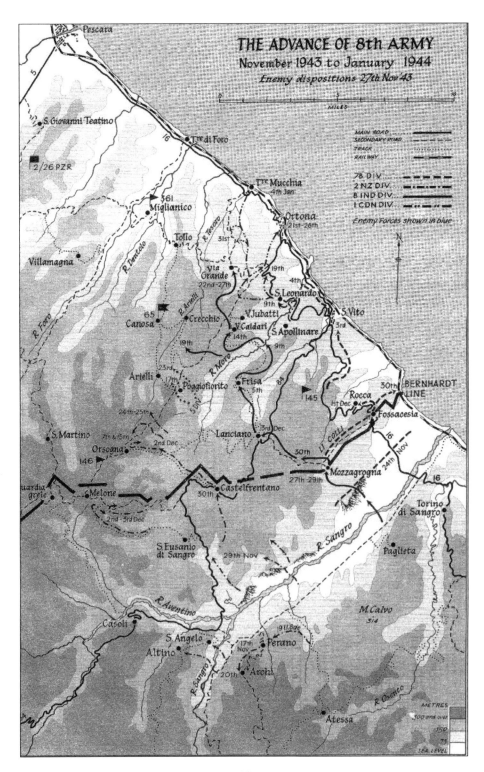

THE ADVANCE OF 8th ARMY
November 1943 to January 1944
Enemy dispositions 27th Nov 43

After heavy fighting along the coast British 78th Infantry Division reached the River Sangro on the 8th November. Indian 8th Infantry Division advancing inland on the left of British 78th Infantry Division, made slower progress than the latter division, but closed up to the River Sangro at Pagliata by the 17th November. Further inland, British 13 Corps made good progress despite the many bridges demolished by the Germans, entering Isernia at the intersection of Routes 17 and 85 on the 4th November.

Some 3km. behind the River Sangro the Germans had constructed part of a formidable defence line. In its entirety this defence line, known as the Gustav Line, ran inland from just south of Ortona on the Adriatic coast and parallel to the River Sangro, then across the spine of Italy and through Cassino to the mouth of the River Garigliano on the Tyrrhenian coast. Because of bad weather the initial assault against that section of the Gustav Line behind the River Sangro and between the Adriatic Coast and Casoli was deferred to the 28th November.

The principal units of British 5 Corps involved in this attack were British 78th Infantry Division and Indian 8th Infantry Division, together with the New Zealand 2nd Infantry Division. British 78th Infantry Division again advancing along the coast took San Vito on the 3rd December and reached the River Moro the following day. Indian 8th Infantry Division, some 7km. inland from the Adriatic coast, also made fair progress, finally securing Mozzagrogna by the 29th November, taking Lanciano on the 3rd December and Frisa on the 5th December, and reaching the River Moro by the 9th December. Further inland still, New Zealand 2nd Infantry Division found the going hard due to bridges having been damaged by enemy action and mud bound exits from river crossing points. However, by the 30th November the Division had taken Castelfrentano, and by the 3rd December was attacking both Orsogna and Melone, although in the event neither place was then wrested from the Germans. As a diversion to the attacks by British 5 Corps, British 13 Corps began an advance from Isernia towards Castel di Sangro on the 24th November. But following the capture of Alfedena that day, and the taking of Molise and Torella on the 27th November, the operations were called off pending the following changes by General Montgomery in the deployment of British 8th Army forces.

Nearest the Adriatic coast, British 78th Infantry Division was relieved by Canadian 1st Infantry Division who, together with Indian 8th Infantry Division on its left came under the direction of British 5 Corps. Next inland, on the left of Indian 8th Infantry Division, British 5th Infantry Division entered the line with New Zealand 2nd Infantry Division on its left, these two latter divisions coming under the orders of British 13 Corps. Finally, and because of its protracted period in continuous action, British 78th Infantry Division transferred into the mountains to fulfil the somewhat less arduous duty of protecting the left flank of British 8th Army.

Following this reorganisation, Canadian 1st Infantry Division attacked across the River Moro on the 8th December with the objective of cutting the Ortona-Orsogna road and turning towards the Adriatic coast to take Ortona. Because of the most determined German resistance the Canadians did not reach the outskirts of Ortona until the 20th December. There followed a further eight days of intensive street fighting before the town was finally cleared of German forces. Other units of Canadian 1st Infantry Division reached the River Riccio some 3km. north-west of Ortona by the last day of 1943, whilst Indian 8th Infantry Division captured Villa Grande on the 27th December and reached the approaches to the River Arielli just north of the town of Arielli by the 19th December.

British 5th Infantry Division and New Zealand 2nd Infantry Division of British 13 Corps made a further attempt on the 23rd December to take Orsogna and reached Route 81, the main road north from Casoli to Chieti. Despite being subjected to heavy artillery and air attacks the German defenders did not yield, and when heavy rain fell on the 25th December, the operation was ended.

At the termination of these last efforts by British 5 and 13 Corps, General Montgomery reviewed the situation on the Adriatic front. He concluded that there should be no further major offensives until the weather improved in the spring of 1944, and this, in turn, determined the final position on the Adriatic front of the Allied line. A broader assessment of the Italian Campaign during the last days of 1943 made it abundantly clear that the Allies' best prospects of reaching Rome lay on the United States 5th Army front and the west coast, since on the Adriatic coast the plain at British 8th Army's front led on only as far as Ancona, whilst on British 8th Army's left rose the formidable central Apennines. As a consequence of the foregoing, the United States 5th Army was instructed by General Alexander to move in force against Cassino and Frosinone in order to attract German forces that might otherwise be used against the Anzio landings, scheduled for the 22nd January. United States 5th Army was to attempt to breach the German defence lines and link up with the Anzio landings, thus threatening the rear of the German 14 Panzer Corps. The overall objective was to reach an approximate line Civitavecchia-Viterbo-Terni. In the meantime British 8th Army was ordered to maintain pressure on the Adriatic front so as to prevent German forces being transferred from there to oppose the United States 5th Army operations.

During a period of relative inactivity, General Montgomery relinquished command of British 8th Army on the 30th December to return to the United Kingdom in order to prepare for the coming cross-Channel invasion. To replace General Montgomery, General Leese was recalled from the United Kingdom, having served under General Montgomery as commander of British 30 Corps in Sicily.

We left British 13 C.T.W. in San Severo at the end of October. During the following two months the unit made a number of moves in order to service and render support to the combat units comprising British 13 Corps. Thus, on the 28th October British 13 C.T.W. moved from San Severo west into the mountains to Gambatesa, operating there for nine days. On the 7th November there followed a further move westward to Vinchiaturo, a village some 650 metres above sea level and near to Route 17. At this time the weather began to deteriorate with the arrival of much heavy rain that made engineering work in the open both difficult and uncomfortable.

While at Vinchiaturo, on the 16th November, a tragedy struck 13 C.T.W. Three men were killed instantly and three other men sustained severe injuries when an oxygen cylinder exploded in a blacksmiths' shelter in the Gun Shop. It was thought that the oxygen cylinder, which was being moved, was dropped on to a mine, causing an initial explosion that, in turn, fractured and caused the oxygen cylinder to explode.

Because of continuing heavy rain the Gun Shop, Armourers, Instrument and Wireless Transmitter sections were moved over the 19th and 20th November to higher ground so as to keep clear of the increasing mud and flooding. But by the 23rd November the weather had so deteriorated that all personnel of the unit were moved into permanent buildings from their customary tents, canvas lean-to shelters at the sides of the workshop lorries and the like.

The 27th November saw the Gun Shop move some 80km. north to Archi, just south of the River Sangro and about 22km. inland from the Adriatic coast so as to more readily service the artillery units in action in that area. Three days after Christmas Day 1943 the remainder of British 13 C.T.W. also moved north, but to Gissi, some 16km. southeast of Archi, here occupying the whole of the street areas as hard standing for the workshops equipment and lorries. New Year's Day 1944 saw a very heavy snowfall which blocked all roads in and out of Gissi, and drastically reduced the volume of work carried out by the workshops. Within a few days, when the roads became passable although with difficulty, the Recovery section of 13 C.T.W. was called up to carry out a great deal of vehicle recovery work on the roads around Gissi under the most arduous and adverse weather conditions.

As part of a redeployment by General Leese of British 8th Army forces during the first six weeks of 1944, British 13 Corps moved from the left of the Adriatic front to its central sector, with British 78th Infantry Division and Indian 8th Infantry Division under its command. Resultant from this redeployment, all sections of British 13 C.T.W. moved to Atessa on the 20th January. This small village stands about 470 metres above sea level and is located some 25km by road south-east of Archi from where the Gun Shop had to travel, and about the same distance by road north-west of Gissi, the previous location of the remainder of the unit. Following the moves to Atessa, an improvement in the weather allowed the output from the workshops to return to normal. But on the 9th February, after a heavy snowfall, all work had to be abandoned except by those fortunate enough to obtain cover or to work in a machinery lorry. In due course the weather again improved, normal working again becoming possible. Indeed, during the third week of February, and in addition to its normal duties, the workshops produced for the Mountain Warfare School a total of ten sledges manufactured from skis and standard stretchers. This achievement required work by several craftsmen on a number of days until 23.00 hours.

Because of bad weather and the related general stalemate of the Adriatic front, British 13 C.T.W. remained at Atessa until the 18th March, when it moved again to Vinchiaturo, where it had been during the previous November. At Vinchiaturo the unit came temporarily under command of the newly formed New Zealand 2 Corps, moving on the next day the 70km. to Pietravairano, which is 5km. east of Route 6, the main approach road to and through Cassino, the latter being some 34km. distant. British 13 C.T.W. became fully operational at Pietravairano where it remained before moving forward a further 16km. on the 2nd April to Presenzano, returning to British 13 Corps command on the 25th March. Over the next six weeks the unit was heavily engaged in preparations for the last battle for Cassino in which British 13 Corps played a major role.

8

Quae cum ita sint

The Royal Corps of Electrical and Mechanical Engineers (R.E.M.E.) came into being on the 1st October, 1942. Its personnel was sourced from the Royal Army Ordnance Corps, the Royal Army Service Corps and the Royal Engineers, the preponderance being from the first of these. Thus, by the start of the Italian Campaign, R.E.M.E. had been in existence for a little under 12 months.

The task of R.E.M.E. during the Italian Campaign was to recover, repair and return to use weapons, vehicles and other equipment which had become unserviceable due either to enemy action or wear and tear. To fulfil this task R.E.M.E., by the end of the Italian Campaign, possessed a strength of circa 29,000 British all ranks supported by some 24,000 Italian civilians, the latter being employed mainly in base workshops.

By far the major part of day to day repair work was carried out by Brigade, Division, Corps and Army Troops Workshops. These were fully mobile field units which were deployed and controlled on an area basis. It is a truism that these mobile workshops could not undertake any repair work while on the move; yet frequent moves were necessary in order for them to maintain close contact and give support to the combat units. During advances, the general modus operandi was to close down the rearmost workshop and then move it forward as far as it was possible and safe so to do. This resulted in a series of leapfrog moves that required a great deal of co-ordination with regard to meeting the engineering work load.

Although the tank was undisputedly the most important fighting vehicle, in Italy it was the ordinary wheeled vehicle which was used in the supply role, and driven over badly paved and twisting roads almost to destruction, which required the highest priority from R.E.M.E. Indeed, more tanks were available than could normally be deployed, since, because of the terrain, these could only be used in a limited number. For the ordinary wheeled trucks and lorries, gearboxes, chassis, springs and half-shafts all called for high rates of repair. A particular difficulty which came to light during the Italian Campaign was the absence of a separate provision to handle Army Group Royal Artillery (A.G.R.A.) equipment. This omission led to the Gun Shops of Corps Troops Workshops being frequently overloaded due to work from their associated A.G.R.A.

Recovery of damaged vehicles and guns was an important role played by R.E.M.E. units, including Light Aid Detachments (L.A.D.s) and Recovery sections of the field workshops. These operations called for a high degree both of ingenuity and tenacity, and such was their success that over the period of the entire campaign 78% of all equipment casualties were returned to their user units within 48 hours.

But life with a field workshop, and British 13 C.T.W. with whom I served during the Italian Campaign in particular, was neither enlightening nor inspiriting. One day passed on to the next with monotonous regularity, each day seeming exactly the same, so that no one knew or cared which day of the week it was in fact.

The work of repairing and servicing a great variety of military hardware was arduous and had to be carried out under less than ideal conditions; generally outside and either in the heat of summer or the cold and wet of winter, with at best the limited protection of a canvas lean-to at the side of a machinery lorry. Materials and spares were always at a premium, so much of the work was done on a 'make do and mend' basis, wrecked and damaged equipment being sought and cannibalised for parts. Nonetheless, the standard of craftsmanship and ingenuity employed were of a high order and source of a modest and unexpressed pride. It was also clearly understood that the life and limb of other British soldiers might well rest with the proper operation and reliability of equipment passing through the workshops.

Food too was insufficient and of generally poor quality, being prepared and dispensed with minimal imagination. For months on end the midday meal, 'tiffin',[1] consisted on a 3-day repetitive basis of either a slice of corned beef, or half a tin of fish such as pilchards or sardines, or a quadrant of processed cheese, with one slice of bread and a knob of margarine. Rice pudding frequently found its way on to the evening meal menu, and was readily distinguished by its containing many black specs. These specs were, in fact, tea leaves originating from 'compo rations', the only sugar source available to sweeten the rice and constituting an inseparable mixture of both sugar and tea leaves intended solely for use in making the ubiquitous brew of tea. On numerous occasions, as a result of doing a favour for a unit we serviced through by-passing the military bureaucracy, and promptly repairing and returning a truck or an armoured vehicle, I would receive some tins of corned beef or evaporated milk or sardines. In part, such

---

1 'Tiffin' is an Anglo-Indian word meaning lunch, and much used by the British 8th Army, along with other words and phrases of similar origin.

items were consumed by members of the electrical section to supplement our inadequate supply of food, the balance being used to bargain with, say, the local field bakery for additional loaves of bread, or the quartermaster for tins of fruit.

My monthly ration of either a bottle of whisky or gin was also a most useful bargaining counter, especially when dealing with our American cousins, who were not permitted such luxuries. I recall one instance when, for a bottle of Gordon's gin, costing 6 shillings and 6 pence (32 1/2 p), I obtained a brand new American combat jacket and a camp bed!

To achieve a reasonable standard of personal hygiene presented every soldier with a problem since the unit possessed no washing, bathing or laundering facilities. Most men washed themselves down daily with cold water from a bowl or a tin, the water itself being obtained from any nearby source. Laundering clothes was equally difficult. On occasion a small group of men would pool efforts and resources to heat a large receptacle of water, washing their clothes therein with the aid of a combined soap issue. Sometimes, if near a village, the ladies living there would offer to wash clothes free of charge on condition that they were given and did not have to return any unused part of the soap provided. This situation was always welcomed. It was not until the last months of the campaign that British 13 C.T.W. was visited by a mobile bath unit which provided hot water showering facilities and an exchange of underclothes, socks and shirts.

Little was available by way of entertainment. Many read or listened to one of the few radios in the unit during their off duty hours. But others continued with their everyday work in order to occupy themselves. Most devoted some of their spare time to letter writing. Occasionally, the local Army Kinema Unit, which was part of the Royal Army Ordnance Corps, managed to borrow a film from the Americans for showing in the open after dark during the warmer evenings, or half a dozen seats were allocated to the workshops unit for viewing a film in a nearby and usually derelict cinema. These were significant events, the competition for places being vigorously contested.

The soldiers of British 13 C.T.W. slept where best they could. In the summer months most did so in tents or in the open covered only by a mosquito net. In the spring of 1944 we were issued with a new type of mosquito net embracing a wooden bar rather than a metal hoop suspension. Because they were new and white in colour, the nets showed up clearly after dark, and particularly so when there was a moon, thus being visible to an observant enemy. To overcome this problem it was decided that all mosquito nets should be camouflaged by submerging them in a solution of permanganate of potash, which was purple in colour, and mepacrine, an anti-malarial tablet which produced a brilliant yellow solution when dissolved in water. It was a decidedly messy but ultimately successful operation. Even during the wet and cold of winter some soldiers still chose to remain in their tents to sleep. Others laid their heads down either inside or beneath the canvas lean-to of a machinery lorry. But on several occasions when the winter weather became severe, the soldiers moved into nearby buildings such as railway stations or houses, the Italians being given the option either of moving over or moving out. They usually chose the former.

The general attitude regarding the progress of the war, and particularly so prior to the cross-Channel landings on the 6th June, 1944, was one of resigned cynicism. It was thought that the worldwide conflict would continue indefinitely, so that even if and when the Italian Campaign was concluded, British 13 Corps would be transferred elsewhere, probably to the Far East, to continue life in the same way as it then seemed to have existed for as far back as anyone could remember. Our world was circumscribed by our workshops and the equipment we handled, and although its location changed, life within it remained the same. To us the past was a blur and the future undefined. The only time was the present: it had always been like this and would ever remain so.

Yet despite all that they experienced and thought, the soldiers of British 13 C.T.W. realised how fortunate they were compared with their compatriots in the infantry regiments but a short distance to their front who went frequently into action against the Germans, and whose only hope of immediate relief was a non-lethal bullet or shrapnel wound.

As for the United Kingdom, this, despite its own sufferings, was regarded as some sort of Arcady, and equally remote.

All service units possess their characters who either generate or withstand the brunt of much ribaldry. British 13 C.T.W. was no exception, the happenings and tales involving such characters, a selection of which follows, doing much to leaven the monotony of daily life and maintain morale at a reasonably buoyant level.

George Edwards, a member of the electrical section who has been mentioned earlier, had a most pronounced dislike of army life. George was a pleasant enough fellow, but was also something of a 'Jonah'. During the early days of the Italian Campaign, George heard a rumour to the effect that the Dental Officer at a nearby field hospital was quite liberal in his attitude to dental treatment and the provision of false teeth. It so happened that George had a dental plate with several false teeth, but believed that if one additional tooth was removed – a perfectly sound one – this would then clear the way for him to have a much more extensive and to him infinitely better dental plate made and fitted. Permission was granted for George to visit the Dental Officer who proved to be quite agreeable to George's proposal. Indeed, there and then he injected the required anaesthetic around the sound tooth destined for extraction, then asking George to wait outside the dental truck for such time as it took the anaesthetic to become fully effective. Alas, during this wait the medical orderly assisting the Dental Officer inadvertently mixed up his patient/treatment records so that, in the event, instead of extracting the specified and anaesthetised tooth the Dental Officer removed a different but equally sound tooth from George's mouth, doing so without the benefit of an anaesthetic. Surprised and shaken, and still in the dentist's chair, George told the Dental Officer in no uncertain manner of his displeasure at what had occurred. The latter, in an attempt to compensate for the error, then offered to extract the correct tooth. But George would have none of it, returning to his unit completely thwarted in his initial aim, in pain, with a rapidly swelling cheek and blood trickling from the corner of his mouth. Back at the workshops, George related the tale of woe to his peers, who thought the episode to be quite hilarious, whilst George remained in pain and totally unamused.

Another workshops character was Ted Sutton, the senior blacksmith. He was normally a jovial man, but could turn ugly if provoked or when having imbibed to excess. Ted was of average height but rotund of shape, appearing almost as broad as he was tall, with his large hands reaching down to just above his knees. His roundness was accentuated by the leather apron which he invariably wore when working. Any approach to Ted to have a job of smithying done almost always met with protests as to the difficulties involved, and the virtual certainty of failure. A subsequent visit to his workshop to enquire how the job was progressing would be rewarded with a piece of perfect workmanship, infinitely better than was hoped for and expected, and a tale of how simple such jobs were to accomplish if only one knew, as Ted did, what to do. We all understood Ted, and how best to humour and get what was required from him.

At one location British 13 C.T.W. was set up close by a farm complex, the owner of which had sometime earlier secreted away a large and potentially valuable quantity of olive oil, only to have this discovered and confiscated by the authorities at about the time the unit arrived nearby. In an attempt to equal up the score the farmer, a disagreeable man, who for some reason disliked the British, removed the muzzle from his large and ferocious alsatian dog which threatened to attack all, but British soldiers in particular.

One morning, following the muster of 'allied trades', a senior non-commissioned officer (N.C.O.), myself, in fact, on this particular morning, as was customary, marched the group some 50 yards away from the muster area, ordering it to 'Halt!', and then 'Advance, right turn!'. This manoeuvre left Ted Sutton in about the centre of the rear rank. The farmer's alsatian dog, his curiosity obviously aroused by the activity, approached the rear of the soldiers unseen and stood behind Ted. On the command 'To your duties, dismiss!', Ted, in common with his colleagues, turned smartly to the right prior to falling out. Alas, the dog, no doubt frightened by the rapid movement in front of him, was misguided enough to nip Ted's right calf.

Together surprised and displeased, Ted released a flow of invective, and to the amazement of all, especially the alsatian, grabbed each side of its collar and with the bottom of his boot forced the dog's head through the collar. Clearly, the alsatian's head underwent a significant change of shape as it was pushed through the leather hoop, with one of its ears being partly torn off. Yelping with pain the dog turned to make off with Ted, still cursing, planting a well directed kick on its rear end and throwing the collar in the alsatian's general direction.

There were rousing cheers for Ted which accompanied the recognition that only someone of his unusual physical shape could have accomplished such an act. Moreover, during the remainder of the brief stay of British 13 C.T.W. at that particular location the alsatian was a changed character and a friend of all British soldiers, allowing himself to be patted, fussed over and fed at each and every opportunity.

As for the farmer, he remained disagreeable and never understood how and why his dog had coincidentally slipped its collar and undergone a fundamental change in personality.

I was not without my own difficulties. During the early summer months of 1944 I contracted diarrhoea: a common complaint amongst troops in Italy and thought to be spread by flies via the food. For me it manifested itself in an urgent need to evacuate my bowels immediately after waking. On the first two mornings after the complaint struck I managed to make it to the latrines without mishap. But on the third morning, while attempting to concentrate my mind on anything other than my immediate need, I tripped over a railway line when crossing rail tracks to the latrines, fell, dislocated my right thumb, simultaneously discharging my bowels and literally filling my boots. News of the incident soon spread, becoming a source of much hilarity and amusing if somewhat cruel and crude comments.

In the absence of washing facilities, both personal and for clothing, cleaning up presented something of a problem, but in a relatively short time I got myself back into reasonably good order.

Not wishing the mishap to be repeated, I decided to report sick on the following day. Now, reporting sick was designed by the Army to be as difficult and tortuous a process as could be devised in order, it was said, to deter malingerers. For any soldier persisting in reporting sick the objective appeared to be to ensure that he really was sick by the time he was seen by a Medical Officer (M.O.), even if he was not so at the outset. In British 13 C.T.W. the arrangement required the soldier reporting sick to register his intention at the Orderly Room by the late afternoon of the preceding day, to pack his kit in a prescribed manner, depositing it with the unit storekeeper – on the possibility that the soldier might be detained in hospital, and parading at 06.30 hours, complete with small pack and essential items of personal kit such as razor and spare pair of socks on the appointed day.

All the foregoing I complied with, eventually being transported in the back of a truck to a nearby Field Hospital and having my essential details recorded by a medical orderly. 'What's your problem, then?' I was asked. 'I have an acute looseness of the bowels and difficulty in controlling their movement' I replied. 'You mean you have the shits?' responded the orderly. 'Just so' said I.

After a considerable wait I was called and presented myself before an M.O. seated behind a blanket covered table in a tent. As I approached I heard the orderly say to the M.O. sotto voce 'This N.C.O. has the shits, Sir!'.

'How long have you been like it?' asked the M.O. 'Nearly four days, Sir', I replied. 'Then you ought to have come to see me sooner' said the M.O. I concurred.

The medical orderly then produced a box and from it took a dozen round white pills, each about half an inch in diameter and similar in appearance to an old fashioned moth ball. 'Take these' instructed the M.O. 'and on your return to your unit swallow half of them with plenty of water. They might just make you feel dizzy or slightly deaf but that will soon pass'. 'And the effect on the diarrhoea?' I asked. The M.O. looked up somewhat quizzically, appearing surprised by my question, and said 'Without any compensating medication, after having taken those six pills, you will never shit again'.

A bottle containing liquid – probably castor oil – was then produced by the orderly and placed on the table with the pills. Concurrently the M.O. added '3 days after taking the initial 6 pills you are to take a prescribed dose of the liquid. This will loosen your bowels, and after a movement you will take a further 3 of the pills which will again bind you. Repeat the treatment alternatively with the liquid and the pills until all the latter have been consumed, ending with a dose of the liquid.' He ended, 'With some luck 10 to 14 days from now should see you converge back to an even keel'.

Stepping forward, I picked up the pills and the bottle of liquid, stuffing them into my pockets. Then, with just the barest hint of sarcasm in the voice that I was unable to suppress, I said 'Thank you, Sir. Sounds most scientific.' I then saluted, turned about and departed the tent, just catching the medical orderly commenting 'Cheeky sod!'.

The cure worked within the time period indicated, although the amusement and ribald remarks generated by the incident persisted for long afterwards.

A second story concerning George Edwards requires some background detail to be sketched in as a preliminary to the tale proper.

It has to be appreciated that the provision of latrines in the field for a large number of men is no simple task. For British 13 C.T.W., with a strength of about 250, it was achieved by digging 2 or 3 rectangular section pits in the ground some 5 feet deep, over each of which was positioned a substantial wooden box type construction having 3 holes side by side in its top, each hole being provided with a heavy lid so designed that it was impossible to leave its corresponding hole uncovered, thus preventing access to the pit below for flies and the like. These wooden structures were affectionately known as 'Thunder Boxes'. Dependent upon the degree of privacy of their locations these latrines were sometimes surrounded by a hessian screen, but had no top cover to protect the users from the elements.

The digging and final filling of latrine pits, together with the movement of 'Thunder Boxes' was effectively executed by a small group of general duties men headed by a Lance-Corporal Pickford. The group was always referred to as 'The Shit House Squad', Lance-Corporal Pickford being known to all as 'Mary' (after the famous actress). Each day, punctually at 10.00 hrs., Pickford and his squad added a quantity of petrol to the contents of the pit beneath each 'Thunder Box', then igniting the petrol with a paper torch, the objective being to burn the toilet paper therein and to destroy any flies who had managed to gain access. The ignition operations were all carried out almost simultaneously and were accompanied by muffled but distinctly audible explosions, whereupon all those possessing time pieces adjusted them to 10 o'clock. This was done in a most serious vein: it was indeed as ceremonial an occasion as the firing of the 'Noonday Gun', and a significant feature of our daily lives.

It is also necessary to reveal that George Edwards, like so many soldiers at that time, was a cigarette smoker. This was a vice positively encouraged by the Army, who issued free each week to every soldier serving overseas a 50 tin of either Player's Medium Navy Cut, Churchman's No. 1, or Capstan Full Strength cigarettes. No half measures there!

On this particular day George made his way to the latrine a few minutes after 10.00 hrs, taking with him both cigarettes and matches. With no one else in residence George lowered his denim trousers, sat down, propping up the latrine lid with his back, and prepared to indulge in the pleasure of carrying out one of life's natural functions. And to further enhance the joy of the moment he lit a cigarette. He could not have had even the remotest thought that a pocket of unignited petrol vapour was present a few feet below him, otherwise he would not have lifted an adjacent latrine lid to drop through the hole so exposed a lighted match.

There was an immediate second explosion as the petrol vapour ignited which caused some confusion to those who had checked and adjusted their timepieces a little earlier. As for George, it is unclear as to whether he jumped or was blown off the 'Thunder Box', and if he had completed that which he had initially set out to accomplish. With regard to the latter, the pundits declared that he had, in fact, completed, but because of the pressure of circumstances went on to perform an encore.

Immediately afterwards and in something of a daze, George staggered back to the electrical section. In recounting the incident he said that 'It felt as if a bloody blowlamp had been played on my ring, my knackers, and halfway up my bleeding back'. He also described how a tongue of flame appeared between his thighs from below. As with the tooth extraction episode related above, George's peers thought the 'Thunder Box' job the pinnacle of hilarity; an attitude which afforded him neither comfort nor sympathy.

In the event, no permanent damage was done, although stories circulated for quite a while that George was now 'less his wedding tackle', and that his voice tone had moved up a couple of octaves. Directly following the occurrence the singed parts were anointed with an appropriate lotion by one of the unit first-aid men and then wrapped by George himself in a copious quantity of mutton cloth. It was said that he was excused coming to and standing at attention for 10 days, but this was never confirmed.

George did not give up smoking cigarettes, but thereafter arranged his visits to the latrine for the mid-afternoon.

British 13 C.T.W. was blessed with having a number of fine officers during the Italian Campaign. Between early October 1943 and mid July 1944 Major C. M. Hunter was the Officer Commanding. He was some 32 years of age, a Scot, and Chartered as both an Electrical and a Mechanical Engineer. An excellent Officer Commanding, reserved and compassionate in nature, he was liked and respected by all ranks. On occasion Major Hunter gave me sound technical advice and guidance. (I was but 20 years of age when we first met, and it was to be a further 11 years before I too achieved Chartered Engineer status. My technical knowledge and experience therefore had many gaps. But despite my relative immaturity I was responsible for all day to day electrical matters in British 13 C.T.W.)

Major Hunter relates the story of a despatch rider who went absent, taking his motor cycle with him. The man was eventually apprehended, less his machine. When the matter came to the notice of the most senior authorities, Major Hunter was hauled up before the 8th Army Commander, General Leese, who took the view that the loss of the motor cycle was the responsibility of the despatch rider's Officer Commanding; thus Major Hunter was ordered to pay for the machine's replacement. Because of the sympathy and generosity of a fellow officer, Major Hunter had only to find about one half of the cost of the replacement motor cycle, but regarded the ruling by General Leese as being unjust and something of an imposition.

Major Hunter and I maintained contact over the years, with him acting as one of my Proposers when I made successful application for Corporate Membership of the Institution of Electrical Engineers in 1954. I visited Lt.-Col. Hunter, as he later became, at his home in Edinburgh in 1995. It was a happy and memorable occasion. During the preparation of this book, for which he would gladly have written the Foreword, I was much saddened to learn of his death in May, 1997.

The Gun Shop was under the authority of Dick Wall, an ex-boy soldier who, at the outset of the Italian Campaign was a Warrant Officer Class 1.

Around the time of the Cassino battles many of the large calibre guns, 4.5, 5.5 and 7.2 inch, suffered prematures, when the shell, after being fired, would explode in the barrel of the gun. This would usually burst the barrel, splitting it and leaving it looking like a part-peeled banana, and injuring or killing members of the gun crew. Sgt. Major Wall, at great personal risk, went into the gun pits while the guns were being fired in action, eventually identifying the cause of the prematures (related to faulty driving bands fitted to the shells during their manufacture), initiating the identification, withdrawal and replacement of the faulty ammunition, and thus eliminating the costly and sometimes fatal incidents. For his endeavours he was promoted in the field on the 30th April, 1944 to the rank of First Lieutenant, and on the 22nd September, 1944 was awarded the British Empire Medal (B.E.M.). Both promotion and award were richly deserved and roundly applauded by all.

It is unfortunate, but perhaps not surprising, that so many of the incidents that were a source of amusement to the soldiers of 13 C.T.W. and troops in general had a lavatorial slant. There was, in truth, little else to be amused by or to laugh about.

A further tale concerning myself is so biased, as was the earlier one. The story opens with the day following my having had a one day leave pass to Rome, and discovering that while in the Eternal City, I had inherited a dose of 'crabs'. These are a minute parasitical insect which infects humans, adhering to the flesh with crab like tentacles (hence their name) and laying their eggs in great profusion in the pubis region. They are regarded by soldiers as something of a joke, but are very unpleasant, causing much irritation and discomfort, and spreading with great rapidity.

By the end of the day following my return from Rome I took decisive and drastic action by removing with the aid of a pair of nail scissors and a razor my pubic and nearby hair. This proved to be a less than simple operation, resulting in my nicking myself in several places with the razor and finding myself unable to remove hair from the places I could not see. In order to overcome this latter problem I requested the assistance of my Corporal, James Candler.

James, who considered life to be one huge and continuous joke, expressed his willingness to help. As the operation progressed he asked me to hold my testicles to one side or the other while bending over, or to form my anus into a particular shape which James Candler would demonstrate with his mouth. All this was accompanied by peels of laughter from James and a high level of apprehension on my part. I suffered particular concern when James indicated that the razor had slipped and irreparably damaged an essential part of my anatomy. But eventually the operation was completed by the application of a liberal quantity of 'Dettol' antiseptic to the affected area.

I also decided that I should report sick, following the procedure detailed earlier, ultimately ending up before an M.O. attended by an orderly who, as I presented myself before the M.O. said to him 'I'm afraid that this N.C.O. has crabs, Sir'.

As was general practice when reporting sick in the services, whatever the symptoms, the M.O. ordered me to drop my trousers, exhibiting mild amusement at my absence of pubic hair and the numerous small razor cuts. He went on to examine the vital areas, front and rear, with an illuminated magnifier, remarking as he did so, 'You seem to have got rid of them quite successfully'. Of course, I felt greatly relieved. 'Have you shaved yourself elsewhere?' asked the M.O., to which I replied in the negative. 'I think a shave-off would be advisable in the circumstances' said the M.O., 'particularly so since you have already done a fair bit towards it'. He then told the orderly to get some-one to take me into a treatment tent to effect his instructions. To my absolute astonish-ment I had to strip completely and was shaved from head to foot using an open razor, the main mass of the hair on my head initially removed by the use of a pair of clippers.

The amusement generated when I returned to my unit and was seen to be hairless knew no bounds. In addition to the many and varied indecent suggestions as to how the 'crabs' had first been caught, there were offers of polish to put a shine on my bald pate, together with proposals for various concoctions to serve as 'knacker lacquers'.

Moreover, at about this time there was a change in head dress from forage caps to berets. Despite always having my hair worn short, my new beret size was 3/8 inch less than that of my forage cap immediately subsequent to my being shaved off. As a party trick, I could, when wearing my old forage cap, execute a smart 'about turn', leaving the forage cap pointing in the same direction while I turned through 180° beneath it.

A new 'allied trades' workshops officer, Lieut. 'Pip' Page joined British 13 C.T.W. in the summer of 1944. He was a tallish, well built and quite good looking man in his late twenties. It was said that he had been a Sergeant in the Royal Corps of Signals dur-ing the campaign in the Western Desert, but had transferred to R.E.M.E. on receiving his commission. Mr Page possessed a charming manner and a particularly cultured speaking voice, being amenable and easily approachable under normal circumstances. However, when on occasion he over imbibed, he became somewhat irrational, wild in his behaviour, and difficult to constrain.

At lunchtime on Christmas Day 1944 Lieut. Page, who had taken a few drinks, was responding to encouragement by some of the troops to relate a selection from his fairly extensive repertoire of risqué stories. 'Pip' Page, warming to the occasion, had just em-barked on a second tale when the assembled company, unseen by most of those pres-ent, and certainly not by Mr Page, was joined by the then Officer Commanding 13 C.T.W. and the 13 Corps Padre.

The story itself concerns a bull giraffe at London Zoo standing with his rear end against the bars of the cage in which he was housed. Two rather demure young ladies were admiring the animal, the bolder of the two girls urging the other to reach up and tweak the giraffe's testicles. After some encouragement from her companion, this the other girl eventually does, the giraffe as a consequence emitting a startled bellow and setting off at a canter around his cage. Unbeknown to the two young ladies, the episode had been witnessed by the giraffe's keeper who was approaching with a meal for the animal. On reaching the giraffe's cage, he set down the food he was carrying and removed his trousers, saying to the two girls 'Now you'd better pinch my balls so I can catch the sod, because it's his feeding time!'.

Of course, the assembled soldiery thought the story hilarious, and called for yet a further tale. However, as Orderly Sergeant (I took the duty on Christmas Day and combined it with the operation of generating sets and the like) who had noticed the arrival of the Officer Commanding and the Padre, I tactfully brought their presence to the attention of Lieut. Page who, somewhat reluctantly it must be said, then withdrew.

Shortly afterwards a then contrite Lieut. Page was marched back and forth through the workshop lines in the company of a senior Officer from British 13 Corps Headquarters, simultaneously being given a severe verbal chastisement. Whether this had a long lasting effect on the behaviour of Lieut. Page is doubtful – but that's another story.

9

The first three Battles of Cassino

Although British 13 Corps was not directly involved in the first three battles of Cassino, its role in the fourth and final battle was both major and crucial. Moreover, just after the commencement of the third battle on 15th March, 1944, elements of British 13 Corps, including my own unit, 13 C.T.W., moved on the 18th March from the Adriatic front to support and come under the command of New Zealand 2 Corps on the Cassino front. It is, therefore, necessary to cover, albeit briefly, the first three battles of Cassino, before dealing in greater detail with the fourth.

The initial intention of the Germans was to withdraw to north of Rome and hold only the northern part of Italy. But Hitler was persuaded by Field Marshal Kesselring in October 1943 to fight and defend as far south in Italy as was practicable. The southern defence line selected became known as the 'Gustav Line', which ran from between S. Vito Chietino and the River Sangro on the Adriatic coast, across the Italian peninsula to between Minturno and the River Garigliano in the Gulf of Gaeta, having Monte Cassino as one of its strongest and most significant features. To the south-east of that part of the Gustav Line between Castel di Sangro and S.M. di Mortola on the River Garigliano the Germans also established the 'Bernhardt Line', known to the Allies as the 'Winter Line'. This additional line consisted of a series of defensive positions located around the Mignano defile through which Route 6, the road to Rome passed, via Cassino, being dominated by the surrounding heights of Monte Sammucro, Monte Lungo and Monte Rotundo to its north, and Monte Maggiore, Monte la Difesa and Monte Carmino to the south. The main purpose of the Bernhardt Line was to give the Germans sufficient time to carry out the necessary work, mainly engineering, in the Cassino area of the Gustav Line so as to render it virtually impregnable.

It was through the Bernardt Line that the United States 5th Army fought from the beginning of December 1943 to mid-January 1944 before reaching the outposts of the Gustav Line.

The First Battle of Cassino
The first battle of Cassino was not even recognised as such by the Germans. It was not

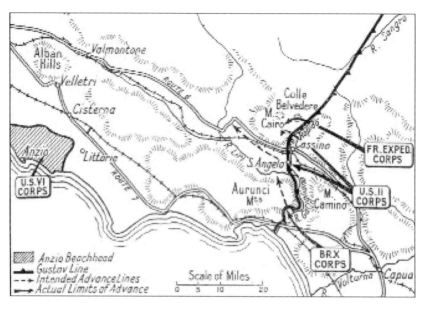

First Battle of Cassino
General offensive on main front combined with seaborne landing at Anzio.

a planned attack by the Allies against the Gustav Line, but a piecemeal continuation of a protracted and tiring advance during which the Allies had taken heavy casualties and the weather conditions had been quite dreadful. This poorly organised attack arose out of the date of the 22nd January, 1944 being fixed for the Anzio landings, this date, in turn, being determined by the scheduled dates on which the landing craft to be used in the Anzio operation needed to be returned to the United Kingdom in preparation for the coming cross-Channel invasion. Additionally, Mt Trocchio, some 5km. south-east of Cassino, and behind which the American units who were to attempt to cross the River Rapido formed up, was not captured until the 15th January. Thus, nowhere near sufficient time was available to plan the initial attack on this most formidable of defence systems.

The first battle of Cassino proper did not start until the 20th January, continuing until the 12th February. There were, however, three preliminary attacks. The first of these was by the French Expeditionary Corps which, on the 12th January crossed the upper River Rapido between Valvori and Cardito, moving towards Mt Carella into the trackless terrain north of Cassino. The second attack, by the British 5th and 56th Infantry Divisions of British 10 Corps, was made across the River Garigliano some 24km. south of Cassino and towards San Lorenzo and Castelforte. Both of these attacks achieved some success, but neither was able to make any significant progress against the flanks of the German defenders. Lastly, British 46th Infantry Division attacked on the 19th/20th January at a point just south of the confluence of the Rivers Liri and Rapido towards San Ambroglio. The aim was to reach high ground near San Angelo and thereby to afford protection to the coming activities of the United States 36th (Texas) Division on the right flank of British 46th Infantry Division. This last operation was a complete failure: the attack was anticipated by the Germans who repulsed it, while most of the assault craft were swept away by the strong current of the River Garigliano.

The initial main assault of the first battle took place on the night of the 20th January when the United States 36th (Texas) Division attempted to cross the River Rapido north and south of San Angelo with their 141st and 143rd regiments. The approach to the river was across open and flooded meadows sown with enemy mines and under observation from the heights held by the Germans. Moreover, immediately prior to the start of the approach to the river a thick fog developed. To protect the advancing troops a heavy artillery barrage was put down by the Americans. The German defenders, who were well dug in, were virtually unaffected by the American fire, but responded in kind. Hence, the American units suffered heavy casualties in their approach to the river, the tapes marking the supposedly mine-free paths were blasted away or lost in the mud, and many of the assault craft were damaged by shrapnel, making them quite useless for the job at hand. On reaching the River Rapido the leading American infantry could no longer be protected by its own artillery bringing down fire on the Germans, since the latter were only some 80 metres away on the opposite bank. Thus, the river crossings were attempted without artillery support and in the face of close and concentrated fire from a skilful and well dug-in enemy.

Although the Americans persevered throughout the next day, by mid-afternoon of the 22nd January it became clear that the operation was a total and costly failure. The United States 36th (Texas) Division had lost 1,681 men in less than 48 hours, more than half of whom were missing. At that point in time the division effectively comprised only one regiment, the 142nd, which had been held in reserve.

But only two days after the debacle of the River Rapido crossing, on the 24th January, the battle was renewed using the United States 34th Division, which now included the 142nd Regiment, late of the United States 36th (Texas) Division, and the French Expeditionary Corps. In this new operation the Americans had to approach the River Rapido north of Cassino across some 3km. of open marshland made so by the Germans flooding the valley as a result of their destroying a dam on the upper reaches of the river. Having forded the River Rapido, the Americans would be met not only by wire entanglements, minefields and a well-entrenched enemy, but almost vertical mountains immediately behind the river and running south to Monte Cassino some 2½ km. away. If they overcame these obstacles and fought their way up into the mountains behind the River Rapido, the United States 34th Division was then to turn south and bear down on Monte Cassino from its surrounding higher peaks.

The 133rd Regiment of the United States 34th Division ran into immediate difficulties, one battalion being stalled by a minefield only 200 metres beyond their start point. The two other battalions reached the River Rapido but failed to cross it in the face of heavy fire from the Italian barracks just across the river. And because of the terrain it was impossible to deploy tanks in support of the infantry.

By late on the 25th January a small bridgehead had been made across the River Rapido and a company of the 133rd Regiment had reached the outskirts of Cassino town, but had there been repulsed by the Germans. The Americans continued to attack through the 26th and 27th January, the 168th regiment passing through the 133rd Regiment to spearhead the advance. Eventually, four tanks managed to cross the River Rapido, destroying much of the wire entanglements and minefields. These tanks were themselves destroyed, and a further squadron of tanks attempting to follow became bogged down, thus preventing any further tanks from making the river crossing. But the use of the tanks enabled the small bridgehead to be widened, and such gains as had been made to be consolidated.

Using wire and steel mats, such as those used by the air forces to provide temporary runways on soft ground, the Engineers worked under heavy artillery fire to make tank lanes across the quagmire leading to the river. By the 29th January these tank lanes were ready for use, both tanks and infantry using them to cross the River Rapido in strength. The following day saw further limited gains by the Americans, and on the 31st January they captured the strategically important village of Caira, some 4km. north of Cassino town, and also took the headquarters of the German 131st Grenadier Regiment together with many prisoners.

Concurrent with the operations of the United States 34th Division, the French Expeditionary Corps, 3km. north of the Americans, attempted to turn the German left flank between the River Rapido and the village of Terelle. On the morning of the 25th January the French attacked, capturing both Colle Abate and Colle Belvedere during the following day. In determined counter attacks the Germans recaptured Colle Abate on the 27th January, but the French retained Colle Belvedere. In an attempt to maintain the momentum of progress by the French Expeditionary Corps, the 142nd Regiment, late of the United States 36th (Texas) Division, was put into the line between the French and the 168th Regiment of the United States 34th Division, to move through the mountains to support the latter in their attempt to thrust in a southerly direction, also through the mountains, towards Cassino and Route 6, the Via Casilina, and the road to Rome. In the event, this operation was not successful.

As at the 31st January the French Expeditionary Corps could make no further progress, but constituted a threat to the German left flank. Similarly, near the Tyrrhenian coast, British 10 Corps could progress no further after two weeks of hard fighting in their attempt to extend their bridgehead over the River Garigliano. But like the French Expeditionary Corps, British 10 Corps now posed a threat to the right flank of the German defences.

There was to be one final attack in the first battle to take Cassino by United States 34th Division. This was to take place in the mountainous area north and north-west of Cassino. On the 1st February, the 135th Regiment attacked the hill masses of Maiola and Castellone, moving along Snakeshead Ridge towards Colle San Angelo. By the 3rd February two battalions had reached the foot of Point 593. This feature, which overlooks the Monastery, and is some 1,250 metres north-west of it, was recognised by the Germans as being the most important strategic height in the Cassino defence system, and they fought resolutely to retain it. Between the 4th and 7th February a battalion of the 135th Regiment reached and took Colle San Angelo, but was ejected from it by the Germans. At the same time a battalion of the 168th Regiment took Point 445, a hill just below the Monastery, and only some 400 metres distant. It appeared at this time as if one last supreme effort by the American forces would capture the Monastery. But the soldiers of the 168th Regiment were caught in a deep ravine on the edge of the northern slope of Point 445 and subjected to heavy machine-gun fire from the numerous and surrounding German positions, eventually retiring, having taken heavy casualties.

From the area between Monte Castellone and Colle San Angelo the Americans now overlooked Route 6 after its exit from Cassino towards Rome. But they were unable to break through to reach this highway, and thereby cut off the German defence system around Monte Cassino, since they were checked by the determined action of the German Schultz Battle Group fighting with their backs to the edge of the steep slopes down to the valley along which lay Route 6 and the road to Rome.

The 11th February saw the Americans make one last attempt to capture both the Monastery and Cassino town below. A heavy artillery bombardment and driving snow accompanied the attacks, but little progress was made. The 141st Regiment of the United States 36th (Texas) Division was held near Massa Albaneta, a farm complex converted into a formidable strong point by the Germans, and located close to the track leading up to the Monastery from their rear. In making a further attempt to capture Point 593, the 142nd Regiment, also of the United States 36th (Texas) Division, was badly mauled, and by the day end both units ceased their efforts, having only sufficient fit men available to hold on to their then present positions. Similarly, the attack towards Monte Cassino and the Monastery by 168th Regiment of the United States 34th Division made little progress due, in part, to a lack of artillery and air support made impossible by the inclement weather.

Thus, by the 12th February the first battle of Cassino was over. British 10 Corps had achieved a shallow bridgehead over the River Garigliano near the coast of the Gulf of Gaeta which had cost them 4,000 casualties. The French Expeditionary Corps had taken Colle Belvedere, but with no fresh force available to take over from them to exploit their success, further progress proved impossible. Losses by the French totalled 2,500. The United States 34th and 36th Divisions suffered an aggregate of 4,200 casualties, but had gained a substantial bridgehead in the mountains above Cassino. But by the 12th February both divisions were completely exhausted having fought magnificently. When they were finally relieved, many men were so numbed by cold and exhaustion that they were unable to walk without assistance. Some of these soldiers were carried from their positions on stretchers, and with the supreme irony of warfare, some were killed by shellfire while on the long journey down from the mountains to shelter and safety.

The Americans were relieved by the New Zealand 2nd Infantry Division and the Indian 4th Infantry Division, both of these divisions being transferred from the British 8th Army front at the end of January 1944, and with effect from 4th February becoming the New Zealand 2 Corps, under the command of Lt.-General Sir Bernard Freyberg. Shortly afterwards British 78th Infantry Division joined the newly-formed New Zealand 2 Corps, but they saw no action against the Germans until during the third battle. The initial purpose behind the transfers was to exploit any successes achieved by the Americans, but in the event this requirement did not arise. However, New Zealand 2 Corps was to play the major role in both the second and third battles at Cassino.

For the Germans, the first battle was an undoubted victory. The Gustav Line withstood all the assaults made on it, and any weak points that had been exposed were reinforced either by additional troops or engineering works in preparation for the further attacks that would inevitably follow.

The Second Battle of Cassino

As with the first battle, prevailing circumstances allowed insufficient time for the second battle to be properly planned. Because of the imminence of a major offensive by the Germans at Anzio, aimed at driving the Allied forces from off the beachhead and back into the sea, the commencement of the second battle had become a matter of urgency. Such time as was available to plan the operation would have taxed to the utmost a full team of Corps Staff Officers. The New Zealand 2 Corps possessed no such asset, having to rely on a hastily established headquarters comprised mainly of New Zealand 2nd Infantry Division Staff. There was a real need too for the Staff Officers of the newly-constituted New Zealand 2 Corps to have a sympathetic liaison with the Staff Officers of the United States 5th Army. This arrangement failed to develop as it should have done, due mainly to the attitude of General Mark Clark, commander of the United States 5th Army, who General Alexander had failed to consult regarding the formation and transfer of the New Zealand 2 Corps into the United States 5th Army. General Clark's resentment was accentuated by the fact that the commander of New Zealand 2 Corps, Lt.-General Sir Bernard Freyberg, was older and much more experienced in warfare than General Clark.

The hurriedly contrived plan for the second Cassino battle was effectively a development of the first battle. From the mountain bridgehead secured at such great cost by the United States 34th and 36th (Texas) Divisions, the Indian 4th Infantry Division would take Point 593, and from there attack and take Monte Cassino, including the Monastery itself. Simultaneously, the New Zealand 2nd Infantry Division would advance from behind Mt Trocchio, crossing the River Rapido and moving towards Cassino railway station by way of the causeway carrying the tracks of the Naples–Rome main railway line. Should both attacks succeed, then all of Cassino would be surrounded and capable of being pinched out both by the Indian 4th Infantry Division moving down to Route 6 from the heights above and beyond the town, and the United States 1st Armoured Division moving through the New Zealand 2nd Infantry Division and into the valley of the River Liri.

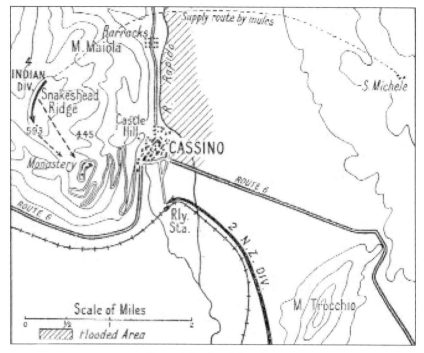

Second Battle of Cassino:
Pincer attack from north and south by 4th Indian and 2nd NZ Divisions.

Both Lt.-General Freyberg and Major-General Tuker, the commander of Indian 4th Infantry Division, came under intense pressure to commence their assaults during the period between the 12th and 15th February. General Freyberg assessed the chances of success for the Allies in the second battle to be no greater than fifty-fifty. General Tuker, after studying the situation and terrain personally and in detail, arrived at the conclusion that the Monastery building itself was the key to success, and it was necessary first to destroy it.

There is no doubt that the view from the Monastery dominated the entire battle area at Cassino, and all the Allied soldiers within its sight believed themselves to be under continuous observation as a result. Following consultation at the highest military levels, and much heart searching, the decision was reached to destroy the Monastery by aerial bombardment. In order to determine the degree and type of bombs to be delivered, the intelligence services having no useful information on the subject, a subaltern on the staff of General Tuker visited Naples, and in one of that city's second-hand bookshops discovered a book giving the principal dimensions and main details of the construction of the Monastery. Because of its massive proportions, the main walls being some 50 metres in height and of solid masonry, and no less than 3 metres thick at their base, it was considered necessary to employ blockbuster type bombs for its destruction.

During the afternoon of the 14th February leaflets were fired by the artillery in propaganda shells which fell near to the Monastery. The leaflets informed the Italians that so far every effort had been made to avoid bombarding the Monastery. But because the Germans had taken undue advantage of this, and because the fighting had gradually become closer and closer to the sacred building, the time had now come when the Monastery itself was open to bombardment. The leaflets went on to urge the occupants of the Monastery to leave without delay so as to avoid putting their lives at risk, for the warning was urgent and for their own good. After some difficulty, the 80 years-old Abbot-Bishop of Monte Cassino, Gregorio Diamare, met with a junior German officer, suggesting to the latter that he and his monks be allowed to move towards the Allied lines, whilst the numerous refugees in the Monastery went to the German rear. This suggestion was rejected, but the German officer indicated that his Commanding Officer would agree to all the occupants of the Monastery moving down a path towards the German rear in the early hours of the 16th February. The old Abbot-Bishop protested that this time might well be too late, but was told by the Germans that this was the best arrangement that could be made.

On the cold but clear morning of the 15th February, just a few minutes after 09.30 hrs., the bombing of the Monastery began. The operation was opened by B-17 Fortress bombers and continued throughout most of the morning. Although the bombing by the B-17s was not particularly accurate, the interior of the Monastery was completely wrecked, as were the cloistered courtyards, the high altar, and the ancient and famous Catarinozzi organ. In the early afternoon Mitchell and Marauder medium bombers continued and completed the bombing, totally destroying the west wall of the building. In total, over a period of about 4 hours, 255 aircraft had dropped some 450 tons of high explosive bombs on the Monastery.

After the bombing had ended the Abbot-Bishop and his monks dug themselves out of their refuge, distributing what little food was to hand and doing what they could to comfort the injured. But with the early fall of darkness they were subjected to the dangers of collapsing masonry and Allied artillery fire now being directed on the building. While considering when and how to vacate the ruined Monastery, the junior German officer, with whom the Abbot-Bishop had spoken two days earlier, reappeared. He told the Abbot-Bishop that Hitler, at the request of the Pope, was to ask the Allies for a truce that night in order that the Abbot-Bishop, his monks and the refugees could leave the Monastery in relative safety. The Abbot-Bishop was then requested to sign a declaration that no German soldiers had ever occupied the Monastery prior to its destruction by the Allies. This he did, although the truce and evacuation failed to materialise.

The only enlightenment for the Abbot-Bishop and his monks was the knowledge that the cell used by St Benedict himself, and preserved for 14 centuries, had survived the bombardment. Of even greater wonder, had they then known of it, was that a large calibre shell had landed adjacent to St Benedict's tomb and failed to detonate.

Early on the morning of the 17th February, Abbot-Bishop Diamare gathered together the surviving monks and refugees at the great entrance arch of the Monastery, which still stood intact, and gave absolution to all. Bearing a large wooden crucifix, he led the party of some forty souls through the rubble of the building and along a track towards the German lines. Eventually, with the Abbot-Bishop nearing collapse, the party reached a German medical post set up in a remote cottage. The Germans rendered first aid to those injured, advising the party to continue its journey to the rear in small groups in order to minimise further injuries from shelling. The groups moved off as advised, finally leaving only the Abbot-Bishop and his Sacristan at the medical post. By an interchange of messages, the location of the Abbot-Bishop became known to General von Senger, commander of the German 14 Panzer Corps, who ordered that the Abbot-Bishop be cared for until such time as he could be collected by an ambulance. Following their collection, the Abbot-Bishop and his Sacristan spent the night at General von Senger's headquarters. During their overnight stay the Abbot-Bishop was persuaded to conduct a discussion with General von Senger about the wanton destruction by the Allies of the Monastery, this being recorded and broadcast. After the broadcast, arrangements were made to convey the Abbot-Bishop and the Sacristan to the centre of the Benedictine Order at Sant'Anselmo in Rome. During the journey the Abbot- Bishop was intercepted by agents of the German Ministry of Propaganda and induced to make a further broadcast statement as dictated by the German propagandists. Yet another broadcast statement having a political propaganda bias was then demanded by representatives of the German Foreign Ministry. Abbot-Bishop Diamare broke down under such pressure, refusing to make any further statements about the bombing of the Monastery and coming to the realisation that he was to all intents and purposes now a prisoner of the Germans.

The destruction of the Monastery of Monte Cassino gave rise at the time to great controversy, and continues to do so. With hindsight, the issue of whether or not to destroy the venerable building was a simple one. But immediately prior to the bombing the debate was clouded by the uncertainty as to the occupation of the Monastery or otherwise by the Germans. After the event it was firmly established that the Germans only occupied the ruins of the Monastery subsequent to the bombing, and did not use it for military purposes whilst it was intact. But, as Fred Majdalany points out in his book Cassino: Portrait of a Battle, this is an irrelevance.

The Monastery, and Monte Cassino on which it stands, were part of the German defence line, the mountain itself being fortified and the location of a large number of observation posts giving it a clear and uninterrupted view of the valley and battlefield below. The Monastery had been converted into a fortress during the 19th century and was an ideal place from which to observe the movement of Allied forces beneath it. And those believing themselves to be so observed had no reservation in being persuaded that the building was occupied by the Germans.

General Alexander, in his final report on the Italian Campaign stated, 'This famous building had hitherto been deliberately spared, to our great disadvantage, but it was an integral part of the German defensive system, mainly from the superb observation it afforded.' Moreover, in his Memoirs, written some 18 years later, the then Field Marshal Alexander said,

> When soldiers are fighting for a just cause and are prepared to suffer death and mutilation in the process, bricks and mortar, no matter how venerable, cannot be allowed to weigh against human lives. Every good commander must consider the morale and feelings of his fighting men, and what is equally important, fighting men must know that their whole existence is in the hands of a man in whom they have complete confidence. How could a structure which dominated the field of battle be allowed to stand? The Monastery had to be destroyed.

With absolute inevitability, the ruins of the Monastery were occupied by the Germans immediately following its destruction, adding to rather than diminishing the problems of the Allied forces in the vicinity.

In the early morning of the 15th February, the day the Monastery was bombed, the Indian 4th Infantry Division were beginning their third day in the mountains. Soldiers of the 1st Royal Sussex were on Snakeshead Ridge, just short of Point 593, which was occupied in strength by the Germans, while the 4th/16th Punjabis were down the slope to their left, with the 1st/2nd Gurkha Rifles in reserve a few hundred metres to the rear. The alternative routes to the Monastery from Snakeshead Ridge were all equally difficult, but on balance it was believed that the best route was via Point 593, which meant wresting this essential feature from the Germans, an issue whose problems were not properly realised by New Zealand 2 Corps headquarters.

While the details of such an attack were being settled and without any prior warning to the troops of Indian 4th Infantry Division, the bombing of the Monastery commenced, 24 hours earlier than they had been advised. Many of the bombs fell close to the soldiers of Indian 4th Infantry Division causing a number of casualties, and this confusion was compounded when orders were received that an attack had to be made on Point 593 that coming night in order to clear the route to the Monastery.

After dark on the 15th February, C Company of the 1st Royal Sussex moved on Point 593 astride Snakeshead Ridge, the attack only being possible on a single company front because of the terrain. After advancing in silence and with great care for about 50 metres they were met with sustained machine-gun fire and hand grenade attacks. Despite efforts to move around the flanks of the enemy no progress was made, and before daybreak C Company was ordered to withdraw having lost 2 officers and 32 men out of an initial complement of 3 officers and 63 men.

Notwithstanding their losses, the 1st Royal Sussex were ordered to make a further attempt to dislodge the Germans from Point 593 on the following night. Lt.-Colonel Glennie, the Commanding Officer of the 1st Royal Sussex, on receiving this order made an immediate and firm request for a large supply of hand grenades, since these were required more than any other weapon for the virtual hand-to-hand fighting amongst the rocky terrain. At midnight on the 16th February this second attack opened, having been delayed in order to allow the required hand grenades to be delivered, although only in reduced quantity. Artillery fire by the Allied guns directed at adjacent peaks, notably Point 575, about 1km. distant, failed to clear the top of Snakeshead Ridge, and landed amongst the leading companies, Battalion headquarters and the reserve company of the 1st Royal Sussex as they formed up to commence the attack, causing several casualties. But the attack proceeded as planned, B Company together with a platoon of A Company moving on Point 593 from the left, and the remainder of A Company creating a diversionary attack on the right. It was the intention that following the success of B Company in taking Point 593 from the Germans, D Company would then relieve B Company on Point 593 and make ready to deal with the inevitable German counter attack. Those who remained of C Company, depleted in the attack of the previous night, were held in reserve.

As on the previous night, only about 50 metres had been covered when the leading soldiers of the 1st Royal Sussex were again met with intense machine-gun fire and hand grenade attacks. The reinforced B Company succeeded in destroying a number of enemy machine-gun nests and fought their way on to the main part of Point 593, but failed to dislodge the Germans. Meantime, the balance of A Company, who were providing the diversion, found themselves on the edge of an almost vertical 15 metres drop. They then moved round to the left, only to be confronted by a further impassable gully, and had to be content in providing their comrades with covering fire. After some 2 hours of chaotic hand-to-hand fighting the 1st Royal Sussex began to run out of hand grenades, whilst the Germans appeared to have an unlimited supply. In a final attempt to win the day, D Company was sent in to attack but was greeted with the same murderous machine-gun fire and grenade attacks that the reinforced B Company had suffered earlier. It became evident to Lt.-Colonel Glennie that this second attack on Point 593 had failed, the remnants of the four companies of the 1st Royal Sussex being withdrawn before daylight to behind their start line. On this second night 10 out of 12 officers and 130 out of 250 men became casualties, either being wounded, taken prisoner or killed. Thus, in just two nights, a foremost battalion of the British Army, and one which had always fought with success, was virtually decimated. And nothing had been achieved in return for its sacrifice: Point 593 was still firmly in German hands.

Once more, on the night following, an attempt was made to capture Point 593. The 4th/6th Rajputana Rifles of 11th Indian Infantry Brigade passed through the remains of the 1st Royal Sussex, attacking at midnight. In order to ensure that the 4th/6th Rajputana Rifles had a more than adequate supply of ammunition and hand grenades, the 2nd/7th Gurkha Rifles acted as porters to carry these, thus avoiding the shortages suffered by the 1st Royal Sussex. But as with the attacks on Point 593 of the two previous nights, the 4th/6th Rajputana Rifles soon became subject to intense machine-gun fire and hand grenade attacks, and could make no real progress in their attempt to dislodge the Germans.

Some 2 1/4 hours after the 4th/6th Rajputana Rifles began their assault on Point 593, the 1st/9th Gurkha Rifles, about 300 metres to their left, set off in a direct line towards the Monastery, with Point 444 at the end of Snakeshead Ridge nearest the Monastery as their initial objective. Almost as soon as they left their start line they too came under

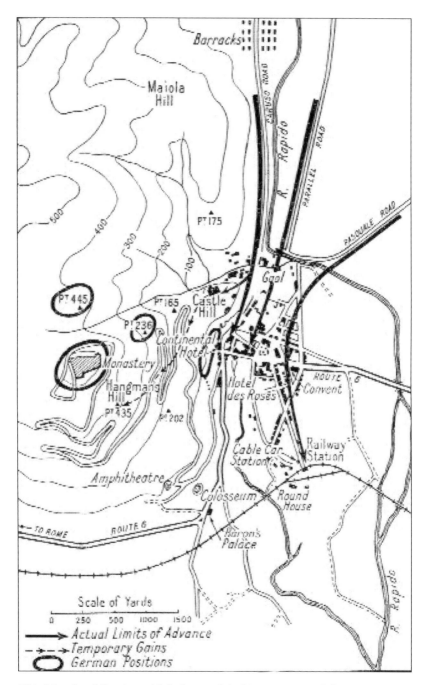

Third Battle of Cassino: 4th Indian and 2nd NZ Divs attack from north. Castle Hill and Station were captured but Hangman's Hill, daringly held for eight days, had eventually to be relinquished.

intense cross-fire from Point 593 and adjacent heights, and could make no further progress.

The second Gurkha unit in action that night, the 1st/2nd Gurkha Rifles, moved off around 02.30 hrs., hoping to approach the Monastery by way of Point 450. Making their way down to the ravine at the base of the north slope of Monastery Hill, they were showered from above by hand grenades. In an attempt to take cover in what appeared to be scrub, the 1st/2nd Gurkha Rifles found themselves in a thicket of breast-high thorn laced with barbed wire and sown with anti-personnel mines activated by interconnected trip wires. Many of the men in the leading platoons were killed by the mines, whilst a great many others were mown down by machine-gun fire directed by the Germans towards the cries of the wounded and the shadowy figures of the Gurkhas lit up by the flashes from the exploding mines.

Ignoring this severe setback, following companies of the 1st/2nd Gurkha Rifles attempted to continue with the attack, but failed to get closer to the Monastery than about 400 metres. As the sky lightened and the dawn of the 18th February approached, the Gurkha units were withdrawn to their start lines having lost 12 officers and 138 men. And yet again, no ground had been conceded by the Germans.

Concurrent with the attacks by the 4th/6th Rajputana Rifles on Point 593, and by the 1st/9th and 1st/2nd Gurkha Rifles on Monastery Hill, the 28th (Maori) Infantry Battalion of New Zealand 2nd Infantry Division attacked from behind Mt Trocchio towards Cassino station along the causeway carrying the Naples–Rome main railway line. Their advance started at 21.30 hrs., the Maoris moving cautiously but surely through barbed wire entanglements and minefields, constantly subjected to intense machine-gun and mortar fire, until they reached and took Cassino railway station at around midnight.

Following the Maori infantry came the sappers who worked ceaselessly throughout the night under heavy fire to remove mines and obstructions placed by the Germans, and to erect two Bailey bridges, one over the River Rapido and the other over a canal, so as to provide a route to accommodate the passage of tanks, guns and trucks from behind Mt Trocchio to Cassino railway station in order to exploit the success of the Maoris. But despite their stupendous efforts, the sappers just failed to complete the necessary work prior to daybreak on the 18th February. Thus, the Maoris who held Cassino station had to continue to do so throughout the daylight period without the support of tanks and anti-tank artillery.

After going forward to visit the Maoris, General Kippenberger decided to screen the view of the railway station from Monastery Hill by smoke fired from artillery shells, thus enabling the sappers to continue and complete their work. Few smoke shells were available in the vicinity, but in a relatively short time the Royal Army Service Corps (R.A.S.C.) had fetched 30,000 such shells from Naples, some 100km. distant, enabling the gunners to maintain the smoke screen.

It was realised that this smoke screen might also be advantageous to the enemy; and so it turned out. Late in the afternoon of the 18th February German infantry and tanks moved forward through the smoke screen to attack the railway station complex and in a sharp engagement retook the position, the Maoris retiring back along the causeway. Casualties amongst the New Zealanders, including sappers, totalled around 160 officers and men, the only gain being a Bailey bridge over the River Rapido.

By the evening of the 18th February, the second battle of Cassino was at an end. For the Allies the gains were minimal and the casualties disproportionate. Victory again went to the Germans whose confidence in the defences of the Gustav Line was recon-firmed, although the temporary loss of Cassino railway station had caused them more than a little concern. There was a need on the part of the Allies to re-evaluate the means to be employed to break through the German defences at Cassino and enter the Liri Valley, and additionally to take full cognisance of the significance of Point 593 in any attack directed at the Monastery itself.

The Third Battle of Cassino

Following the failure by the Allies to make any significant progress in the second bat-tle for Cassino and its subsequent termination, consideration was given as to how the third battle could best be undertaken. Within 4 days of the end of the second battle, by the 22nd February, all was planned and prepared for the third battle to commence on the 24th February. In essence, the plan comprised an initial saturation bombing of Cassino town, followed by attacks from a northerly direction in an attempt to capture the town itself and the railway station beyond, together with an attack directed against the Monastery via Castle Hill. But the weather deteriorated, rain falling continuously for 3 weeks and giving rise to a day-by-day postponement of the attacks, as well as causing a deal of stress and heightened apprehension amongst the soldiers waiting to go into ac-tion. By the 13th March the weather began to improve and the ground to dry out, re-sulting in the date for the attacks being set for the 15th March.

Commencing at 08.30 hrs. on that day some 500 bombers dropped in excess of 1,000 tons of bombs on the approximately one kilometre square of Cassino town, reducing it to rubble. Immediately following the bombing 600 or so guns opened up their bombardment of the town, and the soldiers of 25th New Zealand Infantry Battalion, preceded by tanks, started to move southwards along Caruso Road in the direction of Cassino town. Other tanks moved in concert down Parallel Road some 100 metres away on the remote side of the River Rapido. On reaching the nearest point to Castle Hill, D Company, whose task it was to take this feature, moved off towards it. Climbing an almost vertical rock face and fighting on until the late afternoon they captured both Castle Hill and Point 165, the lower hairpin bend in the road up to the Monastery, at a cost of 6 soldiers killed and 15 wounded. The New Zealanders also took 44 prisoners. The remaining three companies of 25th New Zealand Infantry Battalion entered the town of Cassino, making their way through the ruins towards the Convent on Route 6, and meeting with increasing opposition from the defending Germans.

It soon became obvious that the bombing and shelling had made many large craters, and these were proving a major obstacle to progress by the tanks. In many instances tank crews had to use picks and shovels to fill in craters or move mounds of rubble so as to permit their tanks to advance. Notwithstanding the hold up of the tanks, the 25th New Zealand Infantry Battalion had by early afternoon occupied a major part of Cassino town. It was, therefore, an opportune time for the 26th New Zealand Infantry Battalion to move down Pasquale Road on the left of their sister unit, into the town, and through it to Cassino railway station. But dusk had fallen before the 26th New Zealand Infantry Battalion was ordered to advance, the onset of darkness bringing with it heavy downpours of rain. It was 21.00 hrs. before the rain-soaked New Zealanders reached Route 6 in the centre of Cassino town. With no hope whatsoever of reaching the railway station that evening, they consolidated in the vicinity of Route 6 until dawn on 16th March.

The heavy rain itself caused enough misery to the New Zealand soldiers. It also turned the rubble and building dust into an unpleasant and greasy mud, and the craters into lagoons of unknown depth. Moreover, the rain clouds blotted out the moonlight on which the sappers had been relying in order to enable them to see whilst clearing mines and making safe routes through the debris. It has to be said that the craters in themselves were no surprise to either the Air Force or the sappers, both of whom had rightly predicted that these could well hamper the movement of tanks early in the battle. But with the advent of heavy rain the crater problem became insoluble. To crown all their other difficulties the New Zealanders, now in Cassino town and its environs, were bereft of radio communication, their radio sets proving unable to withstand the ingress of water. At half an hour before midnight on the 15th March the 1st/4th Essex began, as scheduled, to take over Castle Hill and Point 165 from the 25th New Zealand Infantry Battalion. The 1st/4th Essex were followed by the 1st/6th Rajputana Rifles whose two rear companies suffered heavy casualties from enemy shelling as they made their way along Caruso Road. But their two leading companies, who escaped the shelling, continued on to Castle Hill from which it was intended they should mount an attack on Point 236, the hairpin bend immediately above Point 165 on the road up to the Monastery. In the wake of the 1st/6th Rajputana Rifles came the 1st/9th Gurkha Rifles, who, in the early hours of the 16th March, when the Rajputana Rifles were clear of Castle Hill, were themselves to pass through this feature and make for Point 435, known as Hangman's Hill, some 250 metres short of and just below the elevation of the Monastery. Hangman's Hill was so called because on it were the damaged remains of a pylon which at one time supported part of a cableway between Cassino town and the Monastery, the pylon having some resemblance to a gibbet.

Receiving no message from the 1st/6th Rajputana Rifles as to the progress or otherwise of their attack on Point 236, Lt.-Colonel Nangle, commanding the 1st/9th Gurkha Rifles, decided to continue on to Hangman's Hill by way of the northern end of Cassino town and Castle Hill, with C and D Companies leading, and the remainder of the battalion following. The prescribed track up through Castle Hill was untenable, being under continuous German fire, so the lead companies were directed to an alternative route which itself then split into two, both ways appearing to go in the required general direction. D Company soon ran into strong enemy opposition which they could not overcome, but C Company, taking the other path, avoided such problems and disappeared into the darkness of Monastery Hill. Just after first light on the 16th March the Germans in the Monastery spotted the Gurkhas of C Company approaching the top of Hangman's Hill. The Gurkhas were subjected to sustained machine-gun fire and forced to take cover, but the Germans failed to dislodge them. Later that morning a New Zealand artillery spotter noticed movement on Hangman's Hill, and in the early afternoon a radio message was received from C Company that they had taken this feature from the Germans during a brisk encounter, after making their way between the battles for Point 236 and the Continental Hotel on the southern side of Cassino town. As soon as darkness fell on the 16th March, Lt.-Colonel Nangle started to move the remainder of his battalion up Monastery Hill to join C Company on Hangman's Hill. Coincident with further attacks by the 1st/6th Rajputana Rifles on Point 236 and the New Zealanders against the Continental Hotel, the A, B and D Companies of the 1st/9th Gurkha Rifles moved off, working their way up Monastery Hill, so that by dawn on the 17th March all four companies of the battalion occupied Hangman's Hill.

The attack on Point 236 by the 1st/6th Rajputana Rifles, mentioned above, was successful, but around dawn on the 17th March this hairpin bend was again lost to the Germans in a counter attack.

One other significant gain was, however, made on the 17th March, when the 26th New Zealand Infantry Battalion, supported by tanks, moved along Pasquale Road and through the eastern side of Cassino town to recapture Cassino railway station.

In an attempt to overcome the strongly-held German positions along the eastern base of Monte Cassino, the New Zealanders sought to capture the Continental Hotel from the rear. On the night of the 17th March they moved via Castle Hill and Point 165 to Point 202, another hairpin bend on the Via Serpentina, the road up to the Monastery from Cassino town. Until this time Point 202, some 900 metres almost due south of Point 165 and directly below Hangman's Hill had experienced none of the fighting on the mountainside. From Point 202 the New Zealanders swept down the hillside to attack at the rear of the Continental Hotel, only to find it very strongly defended by the Germans who inflicted numerous casualties on the New Zealanders, the latter ultimately retiring to Point 202 and remaining isolated there until the end of the third battle. Because of their isolation, both the New Zealanders on Point 202 and the Gurkhas on Hangman's Hill were supplied by means of air drops, rather than by troops acting as porters. Many of the supply canisters dropped from aircraft failed to reach their intended recipients, any attempt to retrieve such canisters by the troops for whom they were meant invariably resulted in a burst of machine-gun fire from the ever-vigilant Germans, and certain casualties. Inevitably too, many of these supplies fell into German hands.

A unique feature of the third battle was the tank attack on the 19th March along the track known as Cavendish Road. During the course of the second battle, in mid-February, Indian Engineers worked hard to make a track commencing at Caira village and passing to the west of Snakeshead Ridge that was suitable for use by jeeps. This was done in order to compensate for the lack of mules required to supply the 7th Indian Infantry Brigade then occupying Snakeshead Ridge and other nearby features. Between the 1st and 11th March, Engineers of the 12th and 21st Indian Field Companies, together with a section of the 6th New Zealand Engineering Field Company, worked continuously at widening, strengthening and extending this track so as to make it suitable for use by tanks. Much of this work was carried out behind a previously erected camouflage screen in order to conceal both the Engineers involved and the completed sections of the track from detection by distant but overlooking enemy observation posts. On completion, the track, now called Cavendish Road by the Allies, led from Caira village, passing on the north side of Colle Maiola, south between Phantom Ridge and Snakeshead Ridge, just east of the German strongpoint of Albaneta Farm, then turning south-east below Point 593 and around Point 569 to end some 1,000 metres short of and to the rear of the Monastery.

Prior to Cavendish Road featuring in the battle, the combined 1st/6th and 4th/6th Rajputana Rifles began the relief of the 1st/4th Essex on Castle Hill and the lower hairpin bend, Point 165, early on the morning of the 19th March. Initially the changeover went well, with the two leading companies of the 1st/4th Essex moving off to join the 1st/9th Gurkha Rifles on Hangman's Hill, having handed over their positions to the Rajputana Rifles.

The 1st/9th Gurkhas were anxiously awaiting the arrival of the 1st/4th Essex in order that together they could begin their attack on the Monastery from Hangman's Hill. Coincidentally, the artillery were poised to bombard every German strong point that was a safe distance in front of the advancing Allied troops, with tanks of the 20th New Zealand Armoured Division, the 7th Indian Infantry Brigade and the United States 760th Tank Battalion ready to move along Cavendish Road. Ready too was the fresh 28th (Maori) Infantry Battalion to attack and hopefully take the Continental Hotel.

But as dawn broke on the 19th March the Germans launched a strong and determined attack against Castle Hill. The attack was made at battalion strength by the 4th Parachute Regiment, and was preceded by a heavy concentration of machine-gun and mortar fire. Racing from the Monastery down the mountainside the Germans passed through Point 236, overran the mixed force of Rajputana Rifles and 1st/4th Essex at Point 165 and reached the walls of the Castle.

The Castle itself contained a mixed garrison of about 150 men comprising sappers, gunners and two companies each of Rajputana Rifles and 1st/4th Essex. Using hand grenades and rifle butts, the garrison repulsed the German parachutists who were attempting to scale the Castle walls. But the Germans persisted with their attacks, with additional forces coming down the mountainside in support of those already engaged. After recovering from the shock of the initial onslaught, machine-gun and mortar crews of the 1st/4th Essex adjacent to the nearby Point 175 attacked the German flank, eventually forcing the Germans to retire to the cover of Point 165. Twice more on the morning of the 19th March men of the German 4th Parachute Regiment attacked the Castle. On each occasion they were repulsed, the Castle remaining in Allied hands.

During the second of the German attacks on the Castle part of its west wall collapsed, burying a dozen or so of its defenders. It was thought initially that this collapse resulted from the wall being hit by a tank shell. Later it became obvious that this breach in the outer west Castle wall was caused by explosive charges laid by the Pioneer Battalion of the German 1st Parachute Division. However, despite this breach, the Castle garrison held firm.

At the same time as the Germans were making their series of determined attacks to take the Castle, 28th (Maori) Infantry Battalion began their onslaught against the Continental Hotel. Because of the piles of masonry and deep craters the tanks of New Zealand 19th Armoured Regiment were unable to give the necessary support to the Maoris who, although they took around 100 German prisoners, found it impossible to neutralise the main centre of enemy resistance at the base of Monastery Hill in the southern part of Cassino town.

Again, on the 19th March the combined New Zealand, Indian and American tank force set off towards the rear of the Monastery along Cavendish Road. It is difficult to comprehend why this tank attack was timed for 06.00 hrs. when it was known that the main attack against the Monastery from Point 435 by the 1st/9th Gurkha Rifles and the 1st/4th Essex had been postponed to 14.00 hrs. that day. However, it went ahead as scheduled, but without any infantry support, this being due to the heavy losses previously sustained by the 7th Indian Infantry Brigade. Although some of the tanks shed their tracks due to the poor surface of Cavendish Road, the leading tanks had, by 09.00 hrs., reached Albaneta Farm. Some of the tanks then made their way around the southern end of Snakeshead Ridge, close to Point 569, whilst three others moved towards the Monastery, now in full view and only about 1,000 metres distant. The arrival of the tanks in the vicinity of Albaneta Farm came as a complete surprise to the Germans.

Leut. Eckel of the German 2nd Battalion, 1st Parachute Regiment's anti-tank company was detailed to investigate, and observed the three tanks moving in the direction of the Monastery. The route for these tanks lay along a steep sided hill path sloping up to the Monastery and of insufficient width to allow the tanks any room to manoeuvre. Leut. Eckel's platoon, quite by chance, found three German T mines nearby. Overtaking the tanks on their flanks, the platoon got sufficiently far ahead of the tanks to place the T mines on the path without being detected. This ploy was successful, the tracks of the leading tank being blown off by one of the mines, rendering the tank immobile and blocking the path forward for the two accompanying tanks. Leut. Eckel then hurried back to his battalion headquarters to pick up a number of additional T mines, along with detonators and a length of fuse. Hastening back to the tanks, Leut. Eckel stealthily approached the damaged tank, climbed on to it, opened its turret hatch and dropped in a primed T mine. Within seconds the mine exploded completely wrecking the tank, although two of its crew members got out in time to avoid being killed. German paratroopers watching the exploits of Leut. Eckel and his platoon from the slopes of Points 593 and 569 descended from their positions to adopt similar tactics, destroying a further four tanks. Without infantry support the tank attack was doomed to failure, and at 17.30 hrs. the order was given for those tanks that were able to do so to withdraw. By the end of the encounter six tanks had been destroyed and 16 others damaged, of which 11 were later recovered. More seriously, the New Zealanders had suffered 14 casualties.

During the night of the 19th March the 6th Royal West Kents from British 78th Infantry Division which, on the 17th February had been transferred over to Cassino from the Adriatic front, moved into the Castle to relieve the survivors of the 1st/4th Essex and the two companies of Rajputana Rifles. The importance of the Castle was well recognised by both sides in the conflict, and it was with this in mind that the fresh troops took possession.

Elsewhere it was appreciated that new gains were out of the question, the order of the day being to make secure such gains as had already been made in the battle. During the next 3 days various operations took place to effect the required degree of security. On the night of the 20th/21st March a company from the 2nd/7th Gurhka Rifles was ordered to take Point 445 so as to prevent the Germans from infiltrating further reinforcements down the ravine between Castle Hill and Point 175. Despite their best efforts the Gurkhas failed to take their objective. The 6th Royal West Kents now occupying the Castle were given orders to attack and take the lower hairpin bend, Point 165, through which German paratroopers were moving down to the south of Castle Hill. As soon as they moved off, the leading soldiers found themselves in a newly-planted minefield, the explosions from the detonating mines alerting the Germans who brought fire on to the Royal West Kents, causing them to abandon their attack. In Cassino town the New Zealanders attempted to move up Monastery Hill to join up with their detachments on Points 146 and 202. Again, little progress was made, the attacks by the New Zealanders foundering on the defences of and around the Continental Hotel that continued to be strongly held and defended by the Germans.

At a conference of senior Allied commanders held on the 23rd March the decision was taken to bring the third battle to an end. This decision was reached mainly in the light of the fact that the Indian 4th Infantry Division and the New Zealand 2nd Infantry Division comprising New Zealand 2 Corps were exhausted after almost 6 weeks of exposure to the most atrocious weather conditions and the rigours of combat against a skilful and determined enemy. Most significant amongst the remaining problems were the withdrawals of the 1st/9th Gurhka Rifles from Hangman's Hill and the New Zealand detachment from Point 202. However, both these isolated groups were successfully withdrawn without suffering further casualties after dark on the 25th March. German sources state that 185 dead Gurkha soldiers were later found on and around Hangman's Hill, a heavy price to pay for the 9 days of occupation. Moreover, the 1st/9th Gurkha Rifles expressed deep disappointment at having to abandon Hangman's Hill without being relieved by other Allied soldiers.

The soldiers of 7th and 11th Indian Infantry Brigades on Snakeshead Ridge and in the near vicinity of Point 593 were also relieved by units of British 78th Infantry Division, the Indians having been exposed for 6 weeks to the most severe elements, some suffering from frostbite as a result, and constant harassment by the Germans. After being relieved many of the men were physically and mentally unfit for anything. They had to be subjected to persuasion, bullying and in some cases physical violence in order to get them to complete the 8km. or so from their forward positions to the transport that was to take them for a period of rest and rehabilitation, before again entering the fray.

On the 18th March my own unit, British 13 C.T.W., left Atessa on the Adriatic front and moved via Vinchiaturo to Pietravairano, to support and come under the command of New Zealand 2 Corps during the closing phases of the third battle. By the 26th March the third battle had ended. On so doing New Zealand 2 Corps headquarters was disbanded and its functions taken over by British 13 Corps, with my own unit once again coming under the command of its parent Corps.

As with the first battle, the third battle almost succeeded in breaking the German Gustav Line at Cassino. Significant gains were made, including the capture of the major part of Cassino town and Cassino railway station, while the tank attack along Cavendish Road caused the Germans considerable disquiet. But as with the two previous battles, and despite their heavy losses, the third battle ended in a further victory for the Germans.

The military significance of the third battle for Cassino was to divert German attention and efforts away from Anzio. In the event, the effects of the third battle on the happenings at Anzio were minimal. The decision to persist in attacking the formidable defence system at Cassino arose mainly as a result of governmental pressure on General Alexander to continue to engage the Germans by all possible means in the Italian theatre until the cross-Channel invasion was launched.

It is easy with hindsight to criticise some aspects of how the third battle was conducted by the Allies. The initial heavy bombing and subsequent artillery bombardment of Cassino town did not achieve what was expected: the German defenders were not annihilated, the bombs and shells making craters that prevented the easy deployment of tanks. Although remote from control by the Allies, the weather gave rise to many difficulties, notably the heavy rain which fell during the night of the 15th/16th March. As well as making life quite unbearable for the advancing New Zealand infantry, the rain filled the bomb and shell craters turning them into lagoons, giving rise to untold problems in clearing routes both for infantry and tanks.

Criticism has also been directed at the delay in sending the 26th New Zealand Infantry Battalion into action along Pasquale Road towards Cassino railway station, and in limiting the infantry initially deployed to two battalions. The view has been expressed that additional infantry in Cassino town in the first days of the battle, with such forces advancing on an alternative axis might just have won the day.

Lastly, it is beyond comprehension that the tank attack along Cavendish Road towards the rear of the Monastery and the attack by the Gurkhas on the Monastery from Hangman's Hill were not timed to coincide. Moreover, the tank attack was rendered less effective by the absence of infantry support. Whether or not a combined assault would have captured the Monastery is open to doubt, but the attack times being 8 hours apart led to almost certain failure.

In the event, the conclusion must be drawn that bombing and shelling, no matter how heavy, will not dislodge and defeat highly disciplined, skilled and determined troops such as the German paratroopers, that any bombardment must be immediately exploited before those soldiers on the receiving end have any opportunity to recover, and a sufficient superiority in infantry numbers must be employed.

10
The Fourth and Final Battle of Cassino

It is quite by chance that the day on which I began to write this particular chapter is the 53rd anniversary of the start of the fourth and final battle for Cassino: the 11th May.

Since the ending of the third battle on the 26th March, preparations had proceeded apace for what was to be the last battle at Cassino and final victory there for the Allied forces.

The strategic purpose of the Italian Campaign had been clarified by General Alexander as forcing the Germans into committing as large a number as possible of their divisions in Italy coincidental with the cross-Channel invasion. To achieve this aim necessitated drawing the German forces into a major battle and subjecting them to a decisive defeat.

What differed in the plan for the fourth battle compared with the three previous battles was that the United States 5th Army and the British 8th Army would attack side by side, with the Americans on the left and the British on the right. The combined front would stretch from just north of Cassino south to the sea at the Gulf of Gaeta. Having broken through the Gustav Line, and with the Germans in retreat, the Allied forces at Anzio, now with a strength of 6 divisions, would break out of the beachhead to cut off the Germans in the vicinity of Valmontone. If all went as planned, not only would the Cassino defences be overrun, but large numbers of Germans would be taken prisoner.

Much movement of forces across from the Adriatic front to Cassino, regrouping and the employment of elaborate deception plans took place in the 6 to 7 weeks between the end of the third battle and the beginning of the fourth. In the deception arena, the objective was to have the Germans believe that the Allies considered the penetration of the Gustav Line at Cassino to be impossible.

Moreover, any summer offensive by the Allies would be in the form of a further seaborne landing on the Tyrrhenian coast north of Rome, perhaps at or near Civitavecchia. With this ruse successful, German mobile forces would have to be kept well north of Rome and consequently remote from the real point of attack. To sow the seeds of this deception, the United States 36th (Texas) Division were involved in extensive seaborne training exercises in the coastal area south of Naples. Here, embarkation areas were identified as for a real operation, and roads in the zone were overtly marked with the insignia of the Canadian 1 Corps. In addition, a great deal of signal traffic was generated in the vicinity and as part of the exercises in order to persuade the Germans that it would be the United States 36th (Texas) Division and two divisions of the Canadian 1 Corps who would be carrying out the assault. All the above was complemented by Royal Navy activity associated with seaborne assault landings in and around Naples, while Allied aircraft made numerous reconnaissance sweeps across the Civitavecchia beaches.

Regrouping of the Allied forces was carried out in great secrecy and under cover of darkness. In the sector north of Cassino and to the rear of the Monastery the Polish 2 Corps took over from the British 78th Infantry Division. So that the use of the Polish language would not betray their presence, Polish wireless traffic was strictly curtailed or carried out by an attachment from the Royal Corps of Signals. On the left of the Polish 2 Corps was British 13 Corps comprising the British 4th Infantry Division and the Indian 8th Infantry Division, with the Canadian 1 Corps in reserve. The task of British 13 Corps was to break through the German defences to take Cassino town and to advance into the entrance of the all important Liri Valley.

My own unit, 13 C.T.W., which had already moved across to Pietravairano behind the Cassino front in mid March to support the now defunct New Zealand 2 Corps, and then went on to Presenzano in early April, again moved forward in the early hours of the 11th May. After being served with a mug of hot tea at 00.45 hrs., the unit moved off in convoy at 01.25 hrs. Our journey took us the 5½km. from Presenzano on to Route 6, and then along Route 6 for a further 13km. in the direction of Cassino to San Cataldo. Here we turned back sharp right, and then in ½km., which included a steep hill, took a track along the hillside in the direction of San Vittore del Lazio and Cassino into the new location for the workshops which was already partly occupied by the unit's Gun Shop. For this journey I drove a 15cwt. Dodge truck and carried two passengers. During the first 9½km. along Route 6 every fourth vehicle was permitted to use its sidelights, while every vehicle switched on its convoy light – a low wattage lamp under the rear of the vehicle that shone on to the white painted differential casing of its rear axle – for the benefit of the vehicle following immediately behind. But after the 9½km. point, identified as 'Horse Shoe Bend', no lights whatsoever were allowed, since the road was under enemy observation. It was around 02.30 hrs. when we

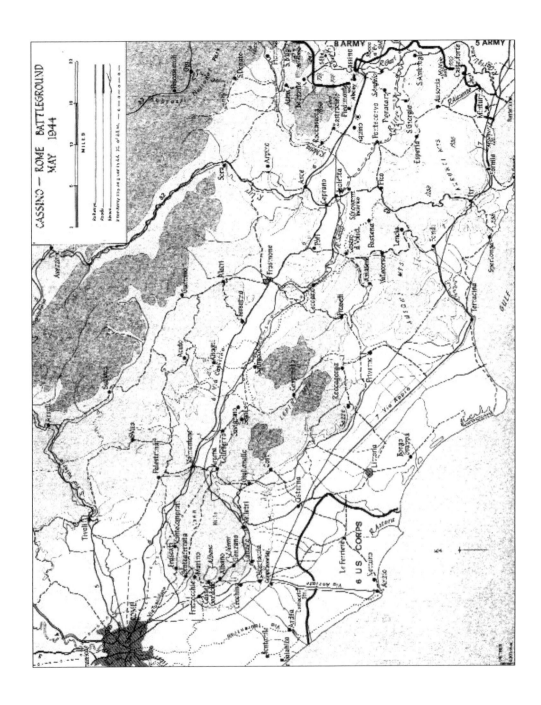

arrived at our new location, many difficulties being encountered in manoeuvring heavy machinery lorries into their required positions and camouflaging them, all without the aid of lights. Moreover, it was not particularly reassuring to learn that the site was under observation from heights held by the Germans, and consequently liable to come under occasional shell fire.

During the daylight hours of the 11th May work continued with setting up the workshops, my own section being concerned with getting electrical power firstly to all the machinery and workshop lorries and then to stores and administration vehicles. Because of the possibility of enemy shelling I put my bed in a hole dug, I suspect, by the Germans during their defence of San Pietro Infine earlier in the year. With the exception of a small space for access, I covered the hole with some supporting timber and a sheet of corrugated iron, thus giving me reasonable protection from anything other than a direct hit. Most of my fellow soldiers took similar precautions, with some, I recall, bedding down in nearby caves.

In the early afternoon the soldiers of 13 C.T.W. were assembled in small groups to be given the broad details of the coming fourth battle and its objectives. We were aware that our present location was amongst the artillery lines, with the 25 pounders in the valley just in front of us and the 4.5, 5.5 and 7.2 inch guns behind and firing over us. At these briefings we learned that the battle was due to commence at 23.00 hrs. that evening, and would be opened by an artillery barrage from 1,600 guns. We were also told that if the coming attacks proved to be other than successful, then a retreat southwards was a possibility. Apart from the fact that the last retreat by the British 8th Army had taken place almost two years previously at the end of June 1942 to El Alamein, and to retreat was currently unheard of, many of my comrades and I were left with the uncomfortable feeling that our senior commanders were less than confident that the coming battle would end in an Allied victory.

Exhausted after being active for some 20 hours or so, I took to my bed as soon as darkness fell. After a short sleep I climbed out of my hole. All was very quiet, with none of the usual sporadic artillery fire. I then heard the murmur of voices from some 25 metres distant where a small group of men was standing on the edge of a drop into a cemetery and overlooking the valley along which Route 6 led towards Cassino, and saw too the glow from a lighted cigarette. Going towards this group I saw that it comprised A.S.M. Fred Chaplin, Sgt. George Wright, Staff Sgts. Ron Painton and Jack Richards with one or two other senior N.C.O.s. They greeted me, and I asked if I had missed the

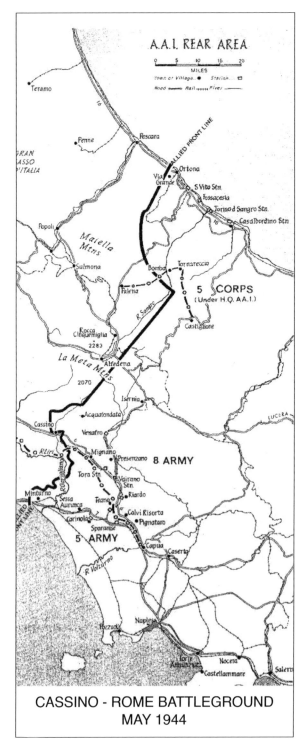

CASSINO - ROME BATTLEGROUND
MAY 1944

fun. One of the group then looked at his watch and said there was about 5 minutes to go to 23.00 hrs. Together with the silence, the night was quite lovely. It was warm, with bright starlight, and all around were clusters of fireflies. Moreover, the moon was due to rise before midnight. No scene could have been more removed from the horrors of what was about to come.

At 23.00 hrs. precisely the bombardment by the Allied guns started. The explosions echoed and reverberated around the hills and moutains, earth and sky alike being illuminated by the flickering light given out from the guns as they were fired. Much more eerie and scaring was the soughing of the shells from the Allied heavy guns as they passed overhead.

As the barrage started the 85th and 88th Divisions of the United States 2 Corps, with the 85th Division nearest the sea, began their attack on the left of the United States 5th Army sector. Then at 20 minutes before midnight the French Expeditionary Corps comprising the 2nd Moroccan Division, the 4th Moroccan Mountain Division, the 3rd Algerian Division and the 1st Motor Infantry Division began their attack into the Aurunci mountains on the right of the Americans.

On the right of the French Expeditionary Corps and on the left flank of the British 8th Army sector, the Indian 8th Infantry Division and the British 4th Infantry Division moved off at 23.45 hrs. to spearhead the British 13 Corps attack across the River Rapido, whilst at 01.00 hrs. on the 12th May the 5th Kresowa and 3rd Carpathian Divisions of the Polish 2 Corps moved forward in the hills north of Cassino towards the Monastery.

Overnight and during the 12th May the two divisions of United States 2 Corps made little or no progress. In contrast, the French Expeditionary Corps, on the right of the Americans, reached their initial objective while it was still dark, and at dawn and thereafter the 1st Motor Infantry Division moved both forward and to the right to suppress German positions on the line between the United States 5th and the British 8th Armies.

On the British 13 Corps front the Germans laid down a heavy smoke screen in the vicinity of the River Rapido, the effect of this smoke being made more acute when supplemented at dawn on the 12th May by a thick river mist. Under cover of this smoke and mist Indian 8th Infantry Division successfully completed its first bridge over the River Rapido allowing a squadron of tanks to cross the river and strengthen the bridgehead. A second bridge across the River Rapido soon followed, positioned by Engineers and tank crews from Canadian 1 Corps, who were in reserve. This was accomplished by a tank carrying a Bailey bridge being driven into the river, with a second tank secured

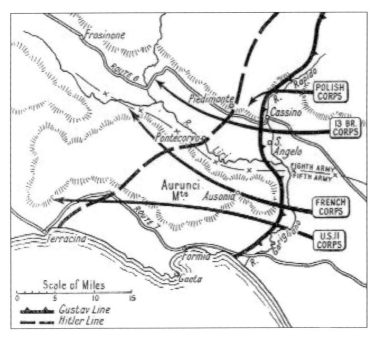

Fourth Battle of Cassino: Fifth and Eighth Armies break through and begin successful advance on Rome.

to the rear end of the bridge in order to keep it reasonably level. As the tank carrying the Bailey bridge reached the middle of the river and submerged, its crew bailed out, while the second tank pushed the bridge across the top of the submerged tank and on to the remote bank of the river. British 4th Infantry Division was less fortunate than their Indian comrades. Although they had successfully made a crossing of the River Rapido, during the night of the 11th May and the whole of the following day they failed to put a bridge across the river, only just managing to hold on to their small bridgehead in the face of determined German counter attacks. A prodigious effort by the Engineers, who suffered many casualties, put Bailey bridges across the River Rapido during the night of the 12th May and the daylight hours of the 13th May, so that by the morning of the 14th May British 4th Infantry Division were across the river in strength and had taken San Angelo.

Concurrent with the fighting at the lower levels, the two Polish divisions began their advance in the heights to the north of Cassino. Like the Americans, Indians and British before them, the Poles made their way to Phantom Ridge and along Snakeshead Ridge towards Point 593. Although both divisions reached their initial objectives, they had suffered severe casualties as a result of sustained machine-gun fire and hand grenade attacks by the Germans. By daylight on the 12th May survivors of the Polish formations exposed on Snakeshead Ridge and the lower slopes of Point 593 began to be elimi-

114

nated by the Germans, but continued to fight on from the minimal cover afforded by the inhospitable landscape. During the afternoon of the 12th May those Polish soldiers who were able were ordered to withdraw, having made no territorial gains. They had, however, inflicted serious damage on the Germans, and by so doing had taken some of the pressure off British 13 Corps in the valley below.

By late on the 12th May, although the Americans near the Tyrrhenian coast and the Poles north of Cassino had made little or no progress, the French Expeditionary Corps was pushing forward into the trackless Aurunci mountains and the two divisions of British 13 Corps were expanding their bridgeheads across the River Rapido and towards the entrance to the Liri valley, the road to Rome.

The next few days were crucial in this fourth battle for Cassino and saw much heavy fighting. The Germans were determined to hold Cassino, while the Allies, with their numerically superior infantry, were equally determined to achieve victory. By the morning of the 13th May the German defences nearest the Tyrrhenian sea began to yield, having been subjected to continuous pressure by the 85th and 88th Divisions of the United States 2 Corps, and pierced by units of the French Expeditionary Corps, who had taken Monte Maio and were poised to move on to Ausonia and enter the Liri valley from the south.

It was against British 13 Corps that the Germans put up the strongest resistance, resulting in the relatively slow advance of their British 4th Infantry and Indian 8th Infantry Divisions. By this time the Germans had come to realise that the fall of Cassino to the Allies was a distinct likelihood, and were attempting to gain as much time as possible to enable them to fall back in an organised manner to their next defence line, the Adolf Hitler Line, by opposing British 13 Corps with every available means. In an attempt to hasten the advance of British 13 Corps, heavy armoured units were deployed in support of the infantry, and the reserve units, Canadian 1 Corps and British 78th Infantry Division, were moved forward to exploit any breakthrough.

Throughout the 14th May the infantry and armoured units of British 13 Corps maintained their pressure on the Germans, while on that day the French Expeditionary Corps captured Ausonia. After its fall, General Juin, commander of the French Expeditionary Corps, ordered his Moroccan goumiers to advance beyond Ausonia into the trackless and desolate Aurunci mountains. The Germans believed that no Allied troops would attempt to move through such an inhospitable area, and as a consequence the goumiers met no opposition and were able to make a rapid advance. Their forward movement outflanked the Germans in the Liri valley to the north of the Aurunci mountains and in the event greatly aided the progress of British 13 Corps subsequent to its breakthrough at Cassino.

In an attempt to achieve the by now urgently required and necessary breakthrough by British 13 Corps, the reserve British 78th Infantry Division, on the 15th May, was ordered to pass through the British 4th Infantry and Indian 8th Infantry Divisions and engage the Germans. This famous division, the 78th, known as the 'Battle Axe' division because of its divisional insignia, entered the battle on the morning of the 16th May with a set piece attack and the support of British 6th Armoured Division. They fought throughout that day and the following night, achieving the isolation of Cassino town and then wheeling northwards to reach Route 6.

In the light of the progress made by British 78th Infantry Division and the French Expeditionary Corps on the left of British 13 Corps, Lt.-General Leese, the British 8th Army commander, concluded that the morning of the 17th May would be the appropriate time for the Polish 2 Corps to renew its attack in the mountains north of Cassino. The attack was preceded by a heavy artillery bombardment of the German positions on Point 593, Snakeshead Ridge and other nearby strongpoints. It was those battalions of the 5th Kresowa and 3rd Carpathian Divisions that had not been deployed in the costly and abortive operation on the 12th May that led the attack on the morning of the 17th May. The plan of attack differed little from that for the earlier one, with the German defenders ready and waiting. But the assault by the Poles was made somewhat easier by the fact that during the previous night a Company of 16 Battalion of the 5th Kresowa Division had taken a number of lightly held German positions on Phantom Ridge. Polish reinforcements were brought forward to strengthen these positions which held against a German counter attack. Thus, on the morning of the 17th May, 17 Battalion of the 5th Kresowa Division was able to quickly clear most of Colle San Angelo, apart from some pill-boxes on the western extremity. The Germans soon counter attacked using artillery, mortars and machine-gun fire, the battle continuing throughout the day. To compensate for the heavy Polish casualties, and to prevent the Germans retaking Colle San Angelo, a force comprising units of both 16 and 18 Battalions of the 5th Kresowa Division reinforced the survivors of 17 Battalion and helped in retaining such gains as had been made.

At the same time as the 5th Kresowa Division was fighting to take and hold Colle San Angelo, the 3rd Carpathian Division, with tanks from Polish 2nd Armoured Brigade in support, began their fresh attempt to take Point 593 and Massa Albaneta. 6 Battalion of the 3rd Carpathian Division cleared the gorge on which the attack of the 12th May had foundered, and advanced on Massa Albaneta, only to be brought to a halt some 200 metres from it by determined German opposition. 4 Battalion then made strenuous efforts against Points 593 and 569. Both Poles and Germans took heavy losses, but by dusk on the 17th May these two salient features, along with Massa Albaneta below, were still held by the Germans. By the end of the 17th May progress by British 13 Corps around the base of Monte Cassino along Route 6 and towards the entrance of the Liri valley, together with that by the French Expeditionary Corps on the left of British 13 Corps, made the position of the Germans in Cassino town, on and around Monte Cassino and in the Monastery itself quite untenable. Thus, during the night of the 17th/18th May the German 2nd Battalion Parachute Regiment withdrew from Cassino town and up the slopes of Monte Cassino to the Monastery. Together with their comrades in the 1st Battalion 3rd Parachute Regiment, who had resolutely defended Point 593, the Monastery and the surrounding heights, they made their way down the track leading from the Monastery past Massa Albaneta and to the German rear.

In the course of the 18th May the Poles mopped up the German rearguard positions and took firm possession of Points 593 and 569, together with Massa Albaneta. And at 10.30 hrs. a patrol of 12 Podolski Lancers entered the ruins of the Monastery to take the surrender of the 30 or so Germans therein, most of whom were suffering from wounds. The Polish flag was then raised and flown over the Monastery. A second ceremony was enacted that morning on Route 6 some 3km. west of Cassino town when 3 corporals of the British 78th Infantry Division, all holders of the Military Medal, met with and conveyed to their Polish comrades the compliments of British 78th Infantry Division.

With the Cassino battles now ended, giving eventual victory to the Allies, the cost in dead, wounded and missing soldiers required assessment. The combined casualties of both sides totalled circa 50,000. The Poles alone lost around 3,500, most of the dead being buried in the Polish Military Cemetery situated between the Monastery and Point 593. On Point 593 itself is a monument bearing the names of the Polish dead, the monument being surmounted by a tall obelisk which carries in a different language on each of its four faces the following inscription:

We Polish soldiers,
For our freedom and yours
Have given our souls to God Our bodies to the soil of Italy
And our hearts to Poland.

A second smaller obelisk overlooks Route 6 from Piedimonte Alta, some 7km. west of Cassino, and bears the names of the Polish soldiers killed in the actions there. In the British Military Cemetery at Cassino there are 4,267 graves, with memorials to a further 4,068 soldiers listed as missing. And at Venafro, in the French Military Cemetery there, lie 3,414 soldiers of the French Expeditionary Corps killed at and around Cassino. No Americans are buried in the vicinity of Cassino, but the German Military Cemetery near Caira village contains over 22,000 graves, although not all the soldiers buried there were killed in the Cassino battles.

During the course of the fourth battle, 13 C.T.W. was busily engaged with its normal tasks of repairing the impedimenta of a Corps in combat with the enemy. The Gun Shop was particularly busy because of the extensive use of artillery, and much work was undertaken by the Recovery Section, some of this in the most hazardous of conditions. At one point a request was received from an American artillery unit to manufacture a particular part for the firing mechanism of their 155mm. guns, 'Long Toms', the part having proved defective when in almost continuous use. Those of us who could operate a lathe, irrespective of trade or rank, were organised to man all the available lathes around the clock for some 48 hours. Using spare and cannibalised vehicle half-shafts as raw material, the required parts were made. Our American friends were delighted, since it enabled their heavy artillery to continue uninterrupted its bombardment of the Germans.

The immediate foregoing brings to mind another incident. When in Sicily 13 C.T.W. collected as booty an ex-Italian army machinery lorry containing a large capacity combined lathe, shaper and milling machine of Czechoslovak manufacture: a potentially most useful item of equipment. It was unfortunate that this machine required a 400 volts, 3 phase, alternating current electricity supply which 13 C.T.W. did not possess, British army equipment utilising direct current electricity at 110 volts. However, when passing through Foggia, I discovered, in a deserted sugar factory, a 25kVA. alternator having a suitable voltage output, together with its control panel, but less a prime mover. By the time 13 C.T.W. reached Cassino, and working on them in such spare time as there was, the alternator and control panel had been overhauled and mounted on a trailer, the alternator being driven by an engine removed from a wrecked lorry. But no matter what was done, the alternator could not be persuaded to produce an output. In desperation, I approached my Officer Commanding, Major Hunter, for technical advice on the problem, knowing him to be a Chartered Electrical Engineer. Who can say, but he was, I believe, only too pleased to indulge in a little hands-on engineering. In the event, he discovered that a small length of cable was missing from the pilot exciter circuit of the alternator. With this cable in place, and to the gratification of all concerned, the alternator voltage rose to 400 and the ex-Italian army machinery lorry was in business. It was operated thereafter by Craftsman Fisk, who produced from it much excellent and valuable work while jealously protecting his new acquisition and lavishing on it a great deal of care and attention.

No account of the final battle at Cassino would be complete without examining its immediate aftermath. On the 18th May, units of British 13 Corps moved from Cassino along Route 6 towards the Adolf Hitler line, which was pivoted on Piedimonte Alta and Piedimonte San Germano. Because the Germans had retreated in good order to this well prepared defence line, and the weight of British 13 Corps attack was currently insufficient to penetrate it, further progress along the Liri valley towards Rome was temporarily halted. As I personally saw, the Adolf Hitler line in the vicinity of the two Piedimontes was strongly fortified in considerable depth with mines, series of both fixed and transportable pill-boxes housing machine-guns, 88mm. gun emplacements having heavy steel protective shelters for the gun crews and buried tank gun turrets.

It took a further 5 days, until the 23rd May, before British 13 Corps and Canadian 1 Corps, operating side by side, attacked the Adolf Hitler Line along the Liri valley. Simultaneously, the Poles attacked along the hills on the north side of the Liri valley from the Monastery towards Piedimonte Alta and Piedimonte San Germano below. The decision was taken by General Alexander that the 6 Allied divisions in the beachhead at Anzio would also break out on the morning of the 23rd May, heading east of the Alban Hills and towards Valmontone. This timing was particularly fortunate for the Allied forces at Anzio, since at that time the Germans were moving their armoured units southwards to oppose the breakthrough at Cassino, which left the German 14th Army at Anzio with only very sparse armoured support. Moreover, the German 26th Panzer Division, which had been held in reserve north of Rome in anticipation of further Allied landings at or near Civitavecchia, moved southwards on the 22nd May to take part in the defence of the Adolf Hitler Line and was, therefore, in transit on the following day, and could not be deployed either at Anzio or in the Liri valley.

By the 24th May armoured units of British 13 Corps and Canadian 1 Corps had penetrated the Adolf Hitler Line in the Liri valley and were moving along Route 6 towards Rome. It was on the following day, the 25th May, that the Poles completed the conquest of the Adolf Hitler Line by taking both Piedimonte Alta and Piedimonte San Germano. Also on the 25th May, units of United States 6 Corps, having broken out of the Anzio beachhead, took the town of Cisterna and joined up there with units of United States 2 Corps that had advanced northwards along Route 7.

At this point in time all the well laid plans of the Allies appeared to be falling into place. Both the Gustav and Adolf Hitler lines had been breached, and the British 8th Army was moving through the Liri valley towards Rome, driving the German 10th Army before it in disarray. Similarly, the United States 5th Army had breached its sector of the Gustav Line, as well as breaking out of Anzio, and was pursuing the German 14th Army across the Italian peninsula. All seemed set for a large part of the German 10th and 14th Armies to be destroyed or captured south of Rome. Indeed, by late on the 25th May spearheads from United States 6 Corps were threatening Valmontone, which lies on Route 6 some 40km. south of Rome, and along which a major part of the German forces from the Adolf Hitler Line were retreating northwards.

But for reasons which have never been properly explained or justified, General Mark Clark, commander of the United States 5th Army, ordered United States 6 Corps to change the axis of its attack from the direction of Valmontone to that of Rome itself. The commander of the United States 6 Corps, General Truscott, attempted to contact General Mark Clark in order to discuss this change of plan, but was unable to do so. Thus, the change in direction of the attack by the United States 6 Corps was put into effect on the 26th May. There can be no doubt that had the original plan of the Allied forces following their break out from Anzio been adhered to, then the greater part of the German 10th Army would have been trapped. In the event, most escaped to fight another day, particularly at the Gothic Line north of Florence. There was, however, some compensation when the United States 36th (Texas) Division ascended Monte Artemisio on the south-east side of the Alban Hills during the night of the 30th/31st May, reaching the road between Velletri and Rome, and cutting off the line of retreat for the German garrison at Velletri. The gap in the German defences thus made was fully exploited, the United States 2 Corps attacking around the northern side of the Alban Hills, taking Valmontone and cutting Route 6 en route. The United States 6 Corps simultaneously attacked around the south-west side of the Alban Hills, while the United States 36th (Texas) Division drove from Monte Artemisio through the Alban Hills towards Frascati. By the 3rd June all the German forces had pulled back to north of Rome leaving the city virtually intact, including the bridges over the River Tiber, since Field Marshal Kesselring, the German commander in Italy, had declared Rome to be an 'open city'. In the evening of the 4th June units of the United States 88th Division entered Rome to be followed on the morning of the next day by General Mark Clark. The conquest of Rome by the Allies was complete.

It is pertinent to comment briefly here on the decision by General Mark Clark to change the direction of attack for the United States 6 Corps from Valmontone to Rome. The change was not justifiable on military grounds, and appears to have been made in the absence of any consultation with General Truscott, the commander of the corps involved. Indeed, General Truscott believed that General Mark Clark did not properly adhere to his instructions received from General Alexander, and as a result the strategic objective of the Anzio operation was not fully realised. Moreover, General Truscott learned from General Mark Clark early in May 1944 that the latter believed the British were planning surreptitiously to be the first to enter Rome. Such suspicions were quite without foundation, since General Alexander had made it clear to all that Rome lay in the United States 5th Army sector, and it was that formation who would take Rome. The British 8th Army were equally clear that at the appropriate time they would by-pass Rome on its eastern side to continue northwards in pursuit of the Germans.

It can be argued that General Alexander ought to have countermanded General Mark Clark's change of plan when it became known. To have done so would have given rise to a direct confrontation between the two men, so characteristically, General Alexander allowed the new plan to proceed in the hope that it would achieve a large measure of the success hoped for in the original plan. In the event, it failed to do so.

It has to be said that General Mark Clark was a somewhat tetchy character. At times he felt inferior to many of his British counterparts who were more experienced in warfare than he was. Moreover, on occasion he made quite hasty and irrational decisions. But despite his faults, General Mark Clark showed great personal courage, always acting with enthusiasm and vigour.

Perhaps Fred Majdalany's words from his book Cassino: Portrait of a Battle are the most appropriate comment on the above episode:

The decision of General Clark to make this change of direction must remain one of the mysteries of the Italian Campaign. There are grounds for believing that it diminished the extent of the defeat which the Allies were able to inflict on the enemy at that time.

11

Journey of British 13 Corps
through Central Italy

A protracted advance by Allied forces from Rome through central Italy began on the 5th June. United States 5th Army and British 8th Army moved forward side by side, with the River Tiber acting as the general boundary between them. As part of British 8th Army, British 13 Corps advanced with South African 6th Armoured Division following Route 3, the Via Flaminia, on the west side of the River Tiber, and British 6th Armoured Division taking Route 4, the Via Salaria, on the east side of the river, with British 4th Infantry Division giving close support to the armoured formations. Until the 17th June the move northwards by units of British 13 Corps was a rapid one, South African 6th Armoured Division taking the city of Orvieto on the 14th June and Allerona three days later. Meanwhile, British 6th Armoured Division reached Todi on the 15th June and Marsciano by the 17th June. But from then on the advance became markedly less rapid due to increasing German resistance. Following some limited regrouping of available divisions, British 10 Corps took up position on the right flank of British 13 Corps, the intention being that the latter would pass around Lake Trasimeno on its west side, with British 10 Corps moving simultaneously around the east side of the lake, both corps then moving forward to capture the key rail and road centre of Arezzo. But by the 20th June British 13 Corps was brought to a standstill at Chiusi, just south-west of Lake Trasimeno and British 10 Corps, with British 6th Armoured Division under its command and having taken Perugia, was also halted on the eastern side of Lake Trasimeno. This situation marked the end of the almost uninterrupted advance by British 8th Army northwards from Rome, since the Germans had now established an effective defence line right across Italy from Civitanova on the Adriatic coast, through Lake Trasimeno, Chiusi and San Quirico to near Castiglione della Pescáia on the Tyrrhenian coast. For ten days from the 20th June the Allies assaulted this defence line, the most difficult and hard fought operations involving British 10 and 13 Corps, who attempted to make their ways forward on either side of Lake Trasimeno. Then, between the 30th June and the 5th July, the Germans withdrew to a further defence line running from south of Ancona in the east to south of Arezzo, through Volterra and on to just north of Cecina on the Ligurian coast. This withdrawal by the Germans allowed units of British 13 Corps to occupy Sinalunga by the 2nd July and Cortona on the day following.

With but a brief pause, the advance recommenced northwards through the Val di Chiana towards Arezzo and then along the valley of the Middle Arno. British 13 Corps comprising British 4th Infantry Division, British 6th Armoured Division, South African 6th Armoured Division, Canadian 1st Armoured Brigade and British 6 Army Group Royal Artillery (6 A.G.R.A.), moved forward from Cortona on the 4th July, with New Zealand 2nd Infantry Division joining British 13 Corps on the 7th July. The Val di Chiana ends about 8km. short of Arezzo in a ridge of hills between it and the valley of the Middle Arno. Arezzo itself lies in a flat plain with mountains on three of its sides, the two main roads to it from the Val di Chiana, Routes 71 and 73, passing through a defile in its south-west corner. All the northern end of the Val di Chiana, including Route 71, is dominated from the east by hills topped by Mt Lignano. Understandably, the Germans decided to take full advantage of the ideal defensive locations at the approaches to Arezzo, and as a consequence much heavy fighting took place there. Indeed, British 6th Armoured Division did not commence its final assault on the town until the 15th July, taking it from the Germans on the following day. From Arezzo this division went on to take Laterina on the 19th July, Castiglion Fibocchi by the 21st July, and Faella on the 29th July, reaching both S. Ellero and Reggello by the 5th August. South African 6th Armoured Division, advancing through Rapolano and Castello di Brolio, reached Radda in Chianti by the 18th July and Mercatale on the 26th July. Concurrently, British 4th Infantry Division captured both Civitella in Val di Chiana and Tuori on the 5th July, Montevarchi on the 18th July, Ricasoli on the 21st July and San Giovanni Valdarno on the 23rd July, closing up by the month end to Figline. Finally, New Zealand 2nd Infantry Division, after having made some limited gains in the direction of Arezzo from Cortona, moved over to the left flank of British 13 Corps to take Tavernelle on the 23rd July, and Cerbaia and S. Casciano on the 27th July.

At this point the formations of British 13 Corps were drawn up against yet another German defence line, known as the Paula Line, which lay between Montelupo in the west, at the confluence of the Lower Arno and the River Pesa, and Figline, near the Middle Arno, in the east. Over the 28th and 29th July the Paula Line was breached along the whole of its length by units of New Zealand 2nd Infantry Division, South

African 6th Armoured Division and British 4th Infantry Division, with the Germans retiring to the north side of the River Arno in and around Florence on the 4th August,
having demolished all the bridges across that river with the exception of the Ponte Vecchio. By the 5th August all of Florence was in Allied hands. In the next three weeks the
Allies closed up to and prepared the assault on the Gothic Line, bringing to an end the
journey of British 13 Corps through central Italy.

For British 13 C.T.W. the long haul northwards through central Italy in support of
the fighting formations began on the 27th May when the unit moved from the location
it had occupied throughout the fourth and final Cassino battle. Characteristically, reveille
on that day was at 03.15 hrs., with breakfast an hour later, the lead vehicle in the workshops convoy moving off at 05.00 hrs.

The convoy retraced the short distance back to Route 6, turning right along it in the
direction of Cassino and Rome beyond. It was a bright sunny morning as the vehicles
of the unit passed over a Bailey bridge across the River Rapido to enter what remained
of the lower part of Cassino town, the bridge traffic being controlled by an impeccably
turned out Military Police Corporal. The devastation was total as the convoy turned left
in the town, skirting around the base of Monte Cassino, with the entrance to the Via Serpentina, the road up to the Monastery, on the right hand side. The convoy was urged to
keep on the move because of the large volume of traffic scheduled to use Route 6, but
the writer recalls that during one brief halt all necks and eyes were strained to look up
the steep slope of Monte Cassino to see the red and white Polish flag flying over the
ruins of the Monastery.

As we moved clear of Cassino town along the flat entrance to the valley of the River
Liri, but with the heights of the Abruzzi looming on the near right, the devastation less-
ened somewhat, but reappeared, although to a reduced extent, as the convoy approached
Piedimonte San Germano, some 7km. from Cassino. The extensive German defences
at and around Piedimonte San Germano, which was the hinge of the Adolf Hitler Line,
have been described in an earlier chapter. On our arrival these remained just as the
Germans had left them. The workshops convoy turned right off Route 6 at Piedimonte
San Germano in the direction of Piedimonte Alta, and in a few hundred metres occupied the new location in a vineyard alongside the narrow road. One vehicle, a Scammell
heavy tractor, used extensively in recovery work, had a front wheel blown off by a mine
as it entered the new location. By good fortune no one was injured, since the floor of
the vehicle's driving cab had been sandbagged in anticipation of such an occurrence.

It was still early morning as we set about establishing the workshops and getting into operation, for there was much work to do. By noon that day a great deal of order had been achieved and we enjoyed a short break for tiffin.

All the soldiers of British 13 C.T.W. had been warned not to wander far afield since the surrounding area was still being checked for the presence of mines and booby traps. We were aware that the Poles had taken Piedimonte Alta from the Germans only some thirty-six hours earlier, and believed that Monte Cairo, a peak of 1,670 metres that over-looked the Liri valley and our new location, had also been cleared of the enemy on the 25th of May. Such was not, in fact, the case. Early on that Saturday afternoon the sough-ing of heavy artillery shells was heard, fired from German guns on Monte Cairo, these shells landing not too far distant. A battery of British 5.5 inch guns, which was occu-pying part of the same vineyard as British 13 C.T.W., soon opened up in reply. There was an energetic exchange of shell fire for ten minutes or so during which we all sought cover, the writer sharing the space beneath a machinery lorry with two other soldiers. In the event, it appeared that the German guns had been successfully silenced, since sometime later that afternoon the British gun battery moved on.

During the ten days that British 13 C.T.W. was at Piedimonte San Germano I made two trips on foot up to Piedimonte Alta. Almost every building in this latter village had suffered damage, mainly from shell fire, but despite this, some of the inhabitants had already returned. The church, although exhibiting hits by artillery shells and small arms fire, was not severely damaged. On entering, it was immediately evident that the dust and rubble from fallen masonry had all been cleared away: it was indeed an oasis of cleanliness and peace in a desert of destruction. The slopes leading up to Piedimonte Alta were littered with the graves of young German soldiers, all of whom had been buried temporarily where they had fallen, and who would find their final resting places in the German Military Cemetery later to be built near the village of Caira. It was at this time and on one of the days that Piedimonte Alta was visited that I reached my 21st birthday.

The evening of the 7th June saw British 13 C.T.W. packed and ready to move for-ward. At 23.15 hrs. the head of the convoy set off, returning the short distance to Route 6 and going towards Rome. But after travelling a short way along Route 6 the unit was halted and ordered to return to Piedimonte San Germano, since the next location, near Valmontone, had yet to be secured. The manoeuvre to reverse the direction of the con-voy in the dark gave rise to numerous difficulties, but eventually British 13 C.T.W. arrived back in its Piedimonte San Germano location by dawn on the 8th June. Only the cookhouse and Orderly Room were reactivated, the remainder of the unit remaining packed and ready to move after a 24 hours delay. Moving off again at 23.15 hrs. on the 8th June, and travelling through the night along Route 6 through Arce, Ceprano and Frosinone, the workshops convoy covered the 100km. to Valmontone, arriving there around daybreak on the 9th June. The remainder of that day was spent setting up the workshops and getting into operation.

But the stay at Valmontone was brief. During the afternoon of the 11th June we were again packing up to move forward. It was at 23.40 hrs. on the 11th June that we departed Valmontone bound for Faleria, some 50km. north of Rome. The short hours of the 12th June had arrived when our convoy entered the Eternal City by way of the Via Casilina. Keeping to the east of the River Tiber, we picked up the Via Flaminia, eventually crossing the river by the Ponte Milvio on the northern outskirts of Rome and pushing northwards on Route 3, the Via Flaminia. Rome itself was quiet, peaceful and dimly lit, with all evidence of the German occupation, as far as one could see, being removed. Two particular memories remain of that night time journey through Rome: the engine noise of the machinery lorry in which I was travelling being reflected with varying intensities from the walls of the buildings in front of which we passed, and the much more gentle reflection of lights seen in the waters of the River Tiber when crossing over the Ponte Milvio.

Continuing northwards up Route 3, Rome was soon left behind, and on reaching Rignano Faminio the workshops convoy turned left on to a minor road leading directly to Faleria. We reached the new location by daybreak on the 12th June, after another journey of some 100km. As was usual, there soon began the job of unpacking and establishing the workshops as an operational unit, for much work was waiting to be done as a result of the long distances travelled and the engagements fought by the formations serviced by British 13 C.T.W. The soldiers of the unit were more than thankful when midday arrived, bringing a break from their labours, some food, and a brew of tea.

The eight days at Faleria were arduous and in the main uneventful. But there was an interesting if brief interlude when a small group from British 13 C.T.W., including the writer, visited Monte Soratte, the then recently vacated headquarters of Field Marshal Kesselring. This facility was cut into a rock face, its upper accommodation overhanging and sheltering the access and loading area, with both lifts and stairs between the levels. The natural rock apart, the structure was of precast concrete, with a barriered

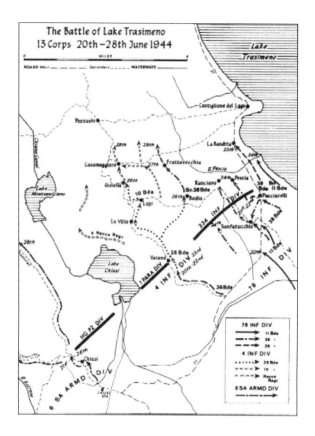

concrete access road, the whole giving an appearance of quality and permanence, this being accentuated by the provision of neat curbing and drainage downspouts. Little or no trace of the Germans remained, and surprisingly, the facility had been left virtually intact.

It was through the early hours of the 19th June when British 13 C.T.W. moved forward from Faleria to just north of Orvieto, a distance of some 80km. The unit arrived at the new location at about 08.00 hrs., immediately setting up the workshops near to the River Paglia. Again, our stay was to last only eight days, but much work required to be done over this period on guns, trucks and other equipment. A further move was due to take place on the 26th June to a location just south of Lake Trasimeno. But this new location had not been properly secured in time to allow the move to proceed as scheduled, this then being postponed for 24 hours. As with previous delays, only the Orderly Room and cookhouse were put back into service, with those troops who wished being given the opportunity to visit the lovely Etruscan hill city of Orvieto. This con-

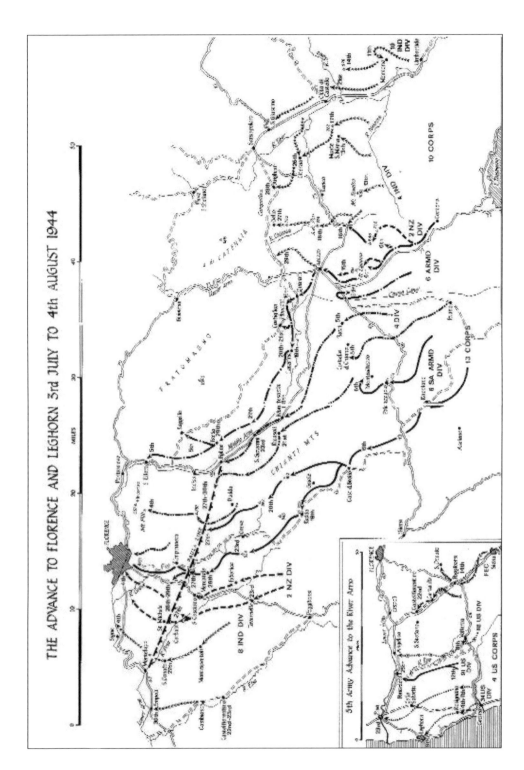

THE ADVANCE TO FLORENCE AND LEGHORN 3rd JULY TO 4th AUGUST 1944

cession was ill advised, since many during the visit over-imbibed of the local wines, and as a result made nuisances of themselves. One group of men shouted abuse at the then Workshops Officer and future Officer Commanding British 13 C.T.W., who himself was visiting Orvieto. It has to be said that the officer concerned was not a particularly likeable or popular man, but most found such conduct quite inexcusable. And later in the day a soldier of British 13 C.T.W. drowned in the River Paglia when he was attempting to swim whilst drunk. For myself that day, the morning was spent washing denim overalls first in petrol and then in the river, with the afternoon taking in a trip up to Orvieto. The highlight of the afternoon was a discovery in a garage of a wonderfully preserved Isotta-Fraschini motor car having a V-16 cylinder engine.

When British 13 C.T.W. moved on the 27th June, the unit travelled overnight from Orvieto north up Route 71 to Città della Pieve, and then via Panicale to the south side of Lake Trasimeno, near Cascina. There was much heavy fighting around the south and west sides of the lake, with the area in the vicinity of Sanfatucchio not being consolidated until the 23rd June by British 78th Infantry Division. The stay in this location extended to around three weeks, any further move northwards being prevented by determined German resistance on the western side of Lake Trasimeno. Work apart, the area in which British 13 C.T.W. was located was paid a number of night time visits by German aircraft that dropped canisters containing anti-personnel bombs which, on being discharged from their canister, floated down to earth like the seed pod from a sycamore tree. These small devices could not be easily detected, and if touched would instantly detonate, causing either maiming or death.

The unit was also visited by a detachment from the Royal Army Medical Corps (R.A.M.C.), whose job it was to ensure that every member of British 13 C.T.W. was up to date with regard to vaccination and inoculations. It was the rule that inoculations should be given every twelve months. However, if it was six months plus a day or more since a soldier had received a particular inoculation when a check was made, then a renewal inoculation was given. In common with many fellow soldiers of British 13 C.T.W., the writer's Soldier's Service and Pay Book, in which such inoculations are recorded, shows that a cocktail of anti-typhus, tetanus-toxin and typhoid-paratyphoid A and B inoculations was given on the 6th July. It was said that our R.A.M.C. colleagues poured the three inocula into an old jam jar, stirring the mixture with a spoon, and then charging their hypodermic syringes in preparation for administering the concoction. That such was not, in fact, the procedure followed is reasonably certain. However, on the morning of the 7th July, those who had been given the inoculation cocktail were physically incapable of moving from where they lay, as well as feeling decidedly ill. All were carried away from the workshops and tent area and put down in the shade of trees along a hedgerow. A Lt.-Col. of the R.A.M.C. was called as a matter of urgency to investigate the occurrence and examine those affected. To the writer this officer appeared genuinely concerned and worried, but unsure of what action to take. As is prudent in such circumstances, he did nothing.

No doubt the Lt.-Col. was greatly relieved when by early afternoon the effects of the multiple inoculation began to wear off, and in a little over twenty-four hours had almost disappeared, leaving only a residue of slight unsteadiness. The relief of the R.A.M.C. officer was surpassed only by that of those who had been afflicted.

Leaving the vicinity of Lake Trasimeno on a mid July morning, British 13 C.T.W. travelled via Castiglione del Lago into the beautiful Val di Chiana, and thence through Foiano della Chiana to near Mugliano, a journey of some 90km. Arriving at the new location around mid morning, having departed from the old at 05.00 hrs., the usual routine of setting up the workshops began immediately, and soon the customary work pattern was in progress. While the unit was located near to Mugliano, King George VI visited the forward areas, normal workshop operations being suspended for a day when the majority of the unit's personnel were engaged on Royal protection duties. These included confining all Italians in the area under supervision to their local church or community centre, with those failing to comply running the risk of being shot. Ironically, it was at Mugliano that rumours were first heard of Italian civilians being massacred by the Germans at nearby Civitella in Val di Chiana and San Pancrazio as reprisals for Partisan activities.

The next move by British 13 C.T.W. that took it to Santa Barbara in the Valdarno and brought the writer into close contact with the massacres by the Germans in the Comune di Cavriglia in July 1944 is covered in the chapter headed 'From Chiana to Chianti'.

12
The Italian Partisans

To trace the evolution, period of peak activity and subsequent demise of the Partisan movement in Italy during the two years between Mussolini's fall from power in July 1943 through to mid 1945 it is necessary to have some understanding of the indigenous and international political and military circumstances within which it occurred.

The political and military influence/time profiles of the Partisan movement differed widely. From unco-ordinated and scattered beginnings the political influence of the movement soon became significant with the establishment of the Milan Committee in January, 1944. By the end of the Italian Campaign the movement's political authority showed a high degree of responsibility and wisdom, being of great help to the Allies in their efforts to re-establish in Italy democratic peacetime government. In contrast, military activity by the Partisans did not become organised and significant until a little before Rome fell to the Allies in early June, 1944, peaking to its maximum effect in the summer months of that year. Following a lull in the winter months of 1944/45, the Partisans again became militarily active in the spring of 1945 in support of the renewed and final offensive by the Allies in Italy. This military activity spilled over for more than a month beyond the end of the Italian Campaign, extending into retribution attacks against and the execution of Fascists in northern Italy. Although quelling this spate of summary violence and obtaining the agreement of the Partisans to disarm was eventually achieved with the aid of the Special Assize Courts set up by the Allied Military Government, the period presented the Allies with many difficult problems.

What follows is an attempt, not exhaustive in its scope, and to an extent simplified, to provide an explanation for the life cycle of the Italian Partisan movement in the context of both Italian and wider and more powerful influences.

Following the vote on the 25th July, 1943, by the Fascist Grand Council to remove Mussolini from office and his arrest later that day after an audience with the King, Marshal Badoglio was installed as the new Prime Minister of Italy.

The Badoglio Government held power in Rome for the forty-five days between the 25th July and the 8th September. In this period it would not permit the re-establishment and overt activity of any of the political parties suppressed under Mussolini's rule after he became Prime Minister of Italy on the 29th October, 1922. Notwithstanding this ban, the various political parties met initially in Florence and subsequently in Milan with the aims of being involved in the Italian Government and also setting up an organisation, including civilians, to take part in military activities against the Germans. Of those who met, the Communist and Socialist parties signed an agreement on the 4th August to also act jointly against the Fascists

The demise of Mussolini and the establishment of the Badoglio Government in Rome came as a surprise to the Allies. As a consequence, the opportunity to make an unopposed landing on the Italian mainland was lost, since at that point in time there was but a single and only partly equipped German division, together with several small paratroop units in central Italy. Moreover, as at the 25th July, the Germans had only two divisions in southern Italy, with a further four divisions engaged against the Allies in Sicily. Joint action at the time by Allied and Italian army and naval forces could have prevented the Germans withdrawing from Sicily across the Straits of Messina to the Italian mainland, as they did with relative ease on the 17th August, and led to their capture. But by the end of August, 1943, the Germans had seven fully equipped divisions in Italy totalling some 100,000 men, and had taken control of all the principal Italian airfields.

On the 3rd September the military terms of the Short Armistice between Italy and the Allies were signed at Cassibile in south-east Sicily by General Castellano on behalf of the Badoglio Government and U.S. General Bedell Smith, representing General Eisenhower, the supreme Allied Commander. Later that day British forces landed near to Reggio di Calabria in southern Italy, thus opening the Italian Campaign and commencing the liberation of Italy.

During the evening of the 8th September Badoglio, despite his fear of the Germans and the likelihood of his own arrest, reluctantly, and under severe pressure from the Allies, announced the terms of the armistice to the Italian people, the Allies having made a similar announcement about an hour earlier. Immediately following the armistice announcement, U.S. and British forces landed in the vicinity of Salerno during the night of the 8th–9th September, where they were subjected to strong and sustained counterattacks by the Germans. At one stage of the assault the Allied forces were almost driven back to the sea, but by the 16th September the Salerno bridgehead had been secured.

At around the same time that the Allied landings were being made at Salerno,

Badoglio received news that Rome had been surrounded by German forces. Although such was not, in fact, yet the case, Badoglio and the Royal Family barricaded themselves in the building of the Ministry of War. Learning that an exit route out of Rome through one of its eastern gates was still open, Badoglio urged King Victor Emanuele, the Queen and Crown Prince Umberto, together with various Ministers of his Government and their principal officers to leave Rome without delay. This they did in the early hours of the 9th September, travelling by road to Pescara where they embarked on two Italian naval corvettes. Reaching Brindisi on the morning of the following day the party disembarked and made immediate efforts to re-establish the essential offices of an anti-Fascist Government. But the authorities at Brindisi had little or no influence in that part of Italy not occupied by the Allies because of the prompt and decisive action by the Germans in taking over some 80% of the country and disarming almost all of the Italian army, this latter process being aided by an instruction from the Italian War Office in Rome to the Italian army on the 9th September not to take any initiative in attacking the Germans. It was not until the 11th September that the Italian War Office at Brindisi ordered that the Germans be treated as enemies, although it was to be the 13th October before Italy declared war on Germany.

Arising from the departure of Badoglio and his Government, a vacuum of indecision obtained in Rome. This was only partly filled by the arrival of the veteran Marshal Caviglia who, on his own authority, negotiated with the Germans encircling the capital city, which terminated with a truce being signed on the 11 September, thus giving the Germans free access to and through Rome.

When Milan came under German control the leaders of the Socialist, Communist, Liberal, Christian Democrat and Action parties in northern Italy combined in the Comitato di Liberazione Nazionale (C.L.N.) under the leadership of Bonomi, a pre-Mussolini Liberal Prime Minister. In the south of Italy the five parties comprising the C.L.N. were joined by the Bonomi-Ruini Labour Democrat party.

These disparate political parties were mistrustful of one another and possessed insufficient common ground to make firm and incisive decisions. Some wished to co-operate with the Badoglio Government, some wanted the King to abdicate and an emergency Government to be set up, and others, while also wanting the King to abdicate, wished to retain a Regency in the person of Crown Prince Umberto. But despite their differences, all the parties were united in their resolve to liberate Italy both from the Germans and the Fascists.

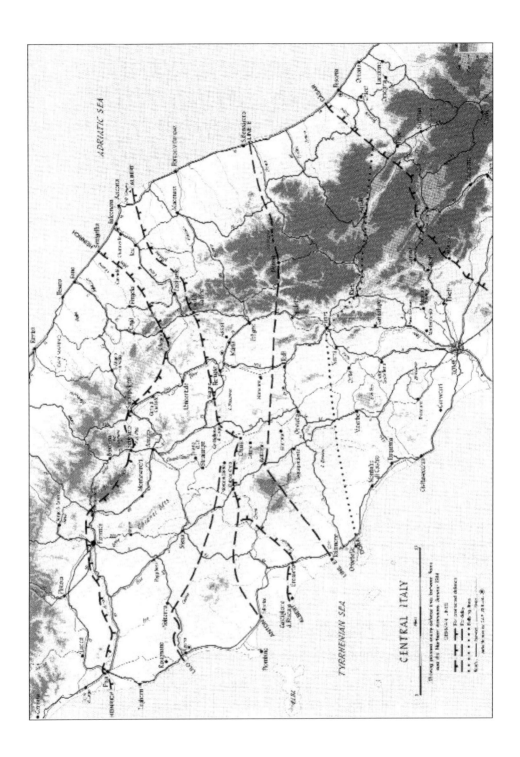

The Italian Partisans

Limited and unco-ordinated resistance to the Germans began immediately after Mussolini was deposed, the Italian Fascist Government fell, and the invasion of Italy by the Allies appeared to be a certainty. Networks of spies and armed guerrilla groups were formed early in September 1943, these consisting mainly of escaped or released Allied prisoners of war and Italian soldiers who had deserted or whose units had been disbanded. Many of these groups attempted to fight their way south through the German 10th Army to reach the Allied lines. Despite their general dislike and suspicion of irregular forces the Allied Military Command in Italy acknowledged the success of these guerrilla bands in providing valuable intelligence regarding the disposition and movement of the German forces in Italy, together with the assistance given to escaping British prisoners of war endeavouring to reach Switzerland.

Many of the most active Partisans were also Communists, and by the end of November 1943 much bitter rivalry had arisen between them and the non-Communist groups. However, negotiations involving all the underground political parties resulted in the establishment in Milan of the Comitato di Liberazione Nazionale per l'Alta Italia (C.L.N.A.I.), known as the Milan Committee, in January 1944. The Milan Committee comprised five political parties and became the most influential organisation in German occupied Italy. It proclaimed itself as the provisional Government of Northern Italy, retaining this status until the Italian Campaign ended in May 1945.

During the winter months of 1943/44 the political and resistance situations in the north and south of Italy were markedly different. The south of the country was occupied by the Allies and under the control of the Allied Military Government of Occupied Territories (A.M.G.O.T.). But once the Long Armistice between Italy and the Allies was signed in Malta on the 29th September, 1943, and Italy was recognised as a co-belligerent, A.M.G.O.T. became much less authoritative. On the 18th October it restyled itself Allied Military Government (A.M.G.), its authority reducing to a mere formality. But in the north of Italy the C.L.N.A.I. was increasing in influence and authority, and military activity by Partisan groups was beginning to become more widespread, with their spontaneous and unco-ordinated actions against the Germans being consolidated. Co-operation between the underground politicians in German occupied Italy and those politicians in Allied occupied Italy who were outside the Badoglio Government became strongly apparent. The C.L.N., which was opposed to both the monarchy and the Badoglio Government had, because of its base in Milan, much the greater influence over Partisan activities.

Two non-Communist Partisan leaders, Alfredo Pizzoni and Ferruccio Parri travelled to Switzerland, and on the 3rd November met with John McCaffery, the head of the British Special Operations Executive (S.O.E.) at Lugano. The meeting was held in an agreeable atmosphere, the two Italians expressing in forthright terms their hostility to the Badoglio Government. As a result of the meeting the Partisans were promised material support by the British. When McCaffery told his American counterpart, Allen Dulles, who headed the U.S. Office of Strategic Services (O.S.S.) of the talks with Pizzoni and Parri, agreement was reached that both the S.O.E. and O.S.S. would send money and arms to the Partisans, as well as providing liaison officers. Pizzoni and Parri made it clear to both S.O.E. and O.S.S. representatives that the C.L.N. wished to have political authority over large areas of German occupied Italy, and to be considered as the rightful Government over these areas as opposed to the Badoglio Government and the monarchy.

The S.O.E. head informed the British Foreign Office of the difficulties vis-à-vis the Communists and non-Communists within the C.L.N., including their differing military and political views and aims. This scenario failed to gain for the C.L.N. the approval and support of the British Foreign Office, and as a result supplies and liaison officers sent to the Partisans in the winter of 1943/44 were strictly limited.

Moreover, on the 22nd February, 1944, Winston Churchill, the British Prime Minister, in a speech to the House of Commons, applauded the Badoglio Government and made disparaging comments about the C.L.N. The speech gave no succour to the Partisans and their cause. But undeterred, Parri wrote to the S.O.E. head some four weeks later asking that the Allies give official recognition to the C.L.N. who were then proposing to move from guerrilla to organised and formal military activity against the Germans.

In March 1944 the U.S.S.R. officially recognised the Badoglio Government, both Governments involved agreeing that diplomatic relations would be established between them. At the same period of time the Italian Communist leader Togliatti returned to southern Italy from the U.S.S.R. and agreed to become a member of the Badoglio Government until such time as the Germans had been expelled from Italian soil. With Togliatti in the Badoglio Government the C.L.N. found itself able to recognise the authority of that Government, and this, in turn, allowed Badoglio to invite politicians from most of the other political parties to become members of his Government. Resulting from the foregoing, there was a significant improvement in relationships between the Allies and the Badoglio Government which, amongst other benefits, gave rise to a marked increase in arms and supplies to the Partisans, as well as the provision of additional liaison officers.

The British Prime Minister wanted the King and Badoglio to govern Italy until the end of the war and beyond. But the two latter had lost much of their support and credibility by leaving Rome immediately following the announcement of the armistice between Italy and the Allies, and on the 16th March the King made public the fact that he would abdicate, handing over his powers to his son Crown Prince Umberto who would become Lieutenant-Governor of Italy. A royal decree to this effect was signed on the 12th April which was to come into force as soon as Rome was liberated by the Allies.

Badoglio's second and broadly based Government, with the Ministries being equally distributed between the six parties of the C.L.N., officially took office on the 24th April, 1944. On the 27th April this National Government said that it intended to pursue all-out prosecution of the war against Germany, the purging of all undesirable elements from within Italy, and the creation, in collaboration with the C.L.N., of a Consultative Council. Thus, the first National Government, which would last for but less than fifty days, was established in southern Italy on both firm and sustainable principles.

This political activity in the south of Italy prompted Bonomi to withdraw from his stated intention to resign as leader of the C.L.N., and as a consequence the C.L.N. continued to be strongly influential in German occupied territory in Italy.

When Rome fell to the Allies on the 4th June, Badoglio resigned as Prime Minister. With the C.L.N. being more than capable of forming a new Government, six days later, on the 10th June, Bonomi formed his first post Fascist Government in which the leaders of the six parties comprising the C.L.N. were nominated as 'Ministers without Portfolio'. Concurrently, King Victor Emanuele III abdicated, his son becoming Lieutenant-General rather than Lieutenant-Governor of Italy, thereby safeguarding the Crown by the King investing his powers in the heir apparent to the throne.

The spring of 1944 saw the expansion of the Partisan movement in the regions of Lazio and Umbria. Development of the movement also accelerated in Tuscany where it reached a peak of activity in the summer of 1944. At the core of the Partisan movement were the veteran anti-Fascists, mostly all of whom were Communists, many having fought in the Spanish Civil War.

At this point in time the C.L.N.A.I. recognised the need for a rationalisation of Partisan military forces. These forces were rapidly re-organised, taking on the form they

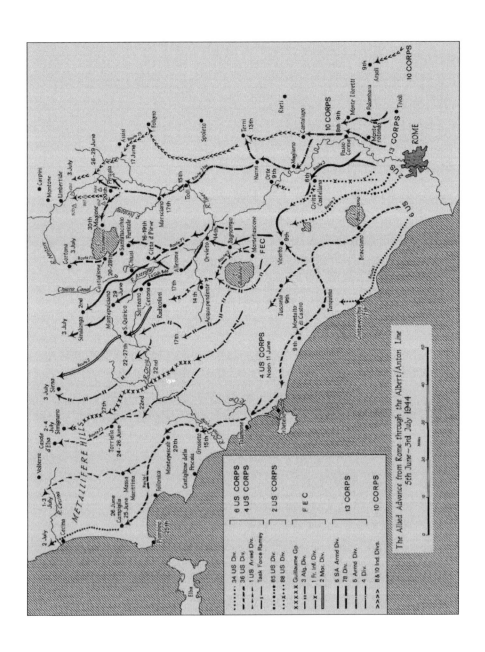

The Allied Advance from Rome through the Albert/Anton Line
5th June–3rd July 1944

were to retain with great effect until the end of the Italian Campaign. In this re-organisation the original and often isolated bands and groups of Partisans were combined into the brigades and battalions of army formations proper under the unified command of the Corpo Volontari della Libertà (C.V.L.) which was established on the 9th June. Responsibility for the effective functioning of the C.V.L. was borne by the non-Communist leader and post-war Italian Prime Minister Parri, together with Luigi Longo, the Communist leader of the Partisans in Milan.

Following the fall of Rome to the Allies, Partisan activity became much more widespread and aggressive. In part, the Germans believed this increase in Partisan activity to be provoked by the broadcasts to the Italian people by General Alexander and Marshal Badoglio.

For the Allies the Italian Resistance was a very powerful liberation movement. It was politically significant in that it became a symbol of Italian national unity, bringing together both politicians in the towns and cities and bands of men in the countryside to oppose not only the occupying Germans but the Republican-Fascist Government, the Salò Republic, established by Mussolini and supported by the Germans, and thus constituting the nucleus of a possible future provisional Italian Government. The ordinary Italian Partisan, however, displayed a minimum of interest in politics, although the Partisan leaders gave allegiance to one of the many political parties in the area in which they were active and on whom they depended at least in part for supplies, information and financial support.

Shortly after the C.V.L. came into being the Allied Military Command, with the support and agreement of the Bonomi Government, appointed Italian Major-General Cadorna, the ex-commander of the Ariete Armoured Division, to act as military adviser to the Milan Committee. He was parachuted into northern Italy on the 12th August to fulfil this role. The initial reaction of the Milan Committee to Cadorna's arrival was one of enthusiasm, but this was not sustained since the philosophical outlooks of the professional soldier and the political leaders of groups of insurgents were much at variance. Moreover, those who led the C.V.L. were Communists, having the strongest and best organised Partisan forces under their control, and wanting to maintain their political identities. In contrast, the Allied Military Command wanted Cadorna to control all Partisan activities, and to limit these to sabotage, intelligence gathering and helping escaped prisoners of war.

The liaison and command structure of the Allied Military Command for dealing with the Partisans was together complex and cumbersome. But on the operational level both the British and the Americans had liaison officers working closely and to good effect with the Partisan formations.

With one notable exception, dealt with below in detail, there was little really effective military activity by the Partisans until early June 1944, some halfway into the Italian Campaign. Then, after a period of intense and invaluable activity by the Partisans between early June and October 1944, with brutal and sadistic countermeasures by the Germans, it was clear that by November 1944 the Partisans could at that time make little significant contribution to the progress of the Italian Campaign. Although the Allied forces had breached the Gothic Line (the formidable German defence line from Pesaro on the Adriatic coast through Belforte, the Mandrioli, Muraglione, Il Giogo and Futa Passes in the Northern Apennines, to some 6km. north of Pistoia and west to the Ligurian coast between Carrara and Massa) by the end of September 1944, they had failed to reach both Bologna and the Via Emilia. As a consequence General Alexander advised the Partisans to go on the defensive and conserve their supplies until the renewed Allied offensive in the spring of 1945, this advice being proffered in the absence of any consultation with the S.O.E. and O.S.S. or the Partisans themselves.

By December 1944 Major-General Cadorna was in difficulties with the C.L.N.A.I., resulting from its dominance by the Communists. Cadorna's problems were exacerbated by his lack of radio sets with which to communicate with the Partisan leaders, the initial batch of equipment destined for this purpose having been destroyed in a plane crash. In contrast, the Communists possessed a most effective radio communications system.

With a view to strengthening the influence of the democratic political parties and curbing that of the Communists, members of the Allied hierarchy met with Parri and the Communist deputy Pajetta at Allied Forces Headquarters (A.F.H.Q.) at Caserta. The meeting resulted in a bipartite military agreement between the Allies and the C.L.N.A.I., signed on the 7th December. This agreement committed the C.L.N.A.I. to recognising the Bonomi Government set up in Rome on the immediately previous 10th June and to handing over authority to A.M.G. as soon as Italy was cleared of Germans. Moreover, the C.L.N.A.I. undertook to disarm and disband the various Partisan formations once the fighting in Italy had ceased. Included also in the agreement was the payment of some £1.5 million each month by the Allies to the Bonomi Government, this payment being made at the discretion of Field Marshal Alexander. (The announcement of Alexander's promotion to Field Marshal was made on the 25th November, but was back-dated to the fall of Rome to the Allies, i.e., 4th June, 1944.) The discretion to make payments to the Bonomi Government was exercised on Alexander's behalf by Cadorna, which gave the latter a much increased influence with the C.L.N.A.I.

A new Bonomi Government was formed in December 1944, and was comprised initially only from representatives of the Liberal, Christian Democrat and Communist parties. As soon as this new Government came into power, the previous Bonomi Government having resigned, it made a formal agreement with the C.L.N.A.I. in which the new Government recognised the C.L.N.A.I. as the official organ of the anti-Fascist parties in German occupied Italy. In this agreement the new Bonomi Government delegated the C.L.N.A.I. to represent it in the struggle against the Fascists and the Germans in that part of Italy still occupied by the Germans, authorising the C.L.N.A.I. to act on behalf of the Government, as well as being recognised by the Allies as the only legitimate government in such parts of Italy as had been or would be returned to the Italian Government of the day by A.M.G.

On their return to Milan from Caserta, Parri and Pajetta informed both Cadorna and the C.L.N.A.I. in Milan of the agreement reached and signed with the Allies. Arising from this agreement the Communist elements of the C.L.N.A.I. in Milan would not agree to Cadorna becoming commander of all the Partisan forces as the Allies wished. In January 1945, following a disagreement between Cadorna and the C.L.N.A.I. with regard to Partisan units in north-east Italy passing to Yugoslav command, Cadorna threatened to resign if not appointed as Commanding Officer of all Partisan forces. A compromise was eventually worked out with Cadorna being appointed as Partisan General Officer Commanding, and having two second-in-commands and three political advisers. Cadorna then left Milan for Berne, Lyons, back again to Berne, and thence to Caserta, not returning to Milan until the 18th April. But on his return he was able to act with great effectiveness in his true capacity.

Following his return, Cadorna discovered that the Piedmont command of the C.L.N.A.I. had ordered the summary execution of all senior Fascist officials, together with all members of the Fascist armed forces to be carried out immediately after the departure of the Germans, an order which Cadorna speedily and firmly countermanded. The Piedmont C.L.N.A.I. order would, if carried out, have resulted in the deaths of many thousands, some of the victims being guilty of only the most minor offences. As the Allies pushed northwards, the Partisans, under Cadorna's influence, gradually gave up their arms, and the Communists were persuaded to allow the A.M.G. to function as both intended and required. Cadorna also attempted to establish a police force from Partisan members to assist the carabinieri in maintaining order. Although several thousand men from southern Italy joined this force, it was impotent when opposed by tens of thousands of rioting anti-Fascists, many of whom had only elected to become Partisans as the Germans and Fascists disappeared.

When U.S. forces entered Milan on the 30th April they found Cadorna was in firm control of the military situation, all the public services were operating, and the Germans had either been prevented or deterred from carrying out any demolitions. It was also on the 30th April when U.S. forces entered Turin. Liberation of the city commenced on the 18th April with a series of strikes in which the workers barricaded themselves in the factories, and the Partisans began to enter the city from the surrounding countryside. As a result the Germans and Fascists lost control of Turin, the C.L.N.A.I. taking over its administration including the preservation of public order and services. In Venice too the Partisans fought a number of skirmishes with the Fascists, the C.L.N. taking control of the city on the 28th April. Although the Germans threatened to shell Venice, this was avoided through an agreement engineered by the British in which the Partisans undertook not to continue to attack the Germans in the vicinity of Venice provided the latter withdrew without bombarding the city.

During and immediately after the final phase of the Italian Campaign mass executions by anti-Fascists began. Partisan groups established ad hoc tribunals to try Fascists, and many thousands were summarily executed. As Allied troops arrived in number in northern Italy, and effective co-operation between the C.L.N.A.I. and A.M.G. developed, these extreme activities began to subside. Most towns were under Partisan control when they were first entered by Allied forces, the Fascist officials having been dismissed. But many prospective administration problems were avoided through A.M.G. accepting the choice of replacement officials made by the C.L.N.A.I.

It was within the broad and somewhat simplified framework described above that the significant and effective military activity by the Partisans took place. However, with one notable exception, this military activity did not properly commence until early June 1944.

Via Rasella Attack and Ardeatine Caves Massacre

The exception, which was to shock and horrify all the Western World, was initiated during the afternoon of Thursday the 23rd March, 1944 when a column of one hundred and fifty-six men belonging to the 11th Company, 3rd Battalion of the S.S. Polizeiregiment Bozen was attacked by a group of sixteen Partisans in the Via Rasella in central Rome. The men of the German unit attacked belonged to the Südtiroler Ordnungsdienst, who were voluntary militia from the Alto Adige region undertaking military police duties.

The Partisan group was led by Carlo Salinari, who later became a professor of Italian literature at the University of Rome. The attack was made through the medium of an explosive device being placed in a street cleaning cart left outside No. 156 Via Rasella, at the entrance to Palazzo Tittoni, and which was detonated as the police column marched past. Subsequent to the attack all sixteen Partisans escaped from the immediate area and none were ever arrested by the Germans.

It was possible to arrange the attack, including the siting of the street cleaning cart with its explosive charge, since it was common knowledge that a detachment of the S.S. Polizeiregiment Bozen, in a show of force, marched along the Via Rasella at around 14.00 hrs. each day. Much to the consternation of Salinari and his Partisan group the column failed to appear at its usual time on the 23rd March. It was, in fact, some one and three quarter hours late, the time at which the bomb was detonated being 15.45 hrs. In the initial blast twenty-six Germans were killed outright with a further sixty being wounded. Ultimately thirty-three Germans would die as a result of the explosion.

At the time of the bombing Field Marshal Kesselring was absent from his headquarters visiting front line troops. He returned to his headquarters at Monte Soratte around 19.00 hrs., to learn of the incident and to be informed that General von Mackensen, commander of the German 14th Army, had provisionally set a death rate in which ten Italians would be executed for every German soldier killed by the explosion in the Via Rasella. But when Hitler learned of the Via Rasella attack he initially gave orders that fifty Italians be executed for every German killed, but was eventually persuaded to reduce his figure of fifty to von Mackenson's ten.

Field Marshall Kesselring issued orders to this effect during the evening of the 23rd March, these being passed down via General von Mackensen and General Mälzer, German Commandant of Rome, to S.S. Obersturmbannführer Kappler, who, it will be recalled from an earlier chapter of the book, was Head of the Sicherheitsdienst (S.D.) in Rome. Late on the 23rd March Kappler received confirmation that ten Italians were to be put to death for every German killed in the Via Rasella attack, and that the executions were to be carried out within the next twenty-four hours.

By midnight on the 23rd March, thirty-two Germans had died as a result of the bombing, and Kappler realised that he would have to work through the night in order to finalise a list of those to be executed. Initially Kappler could only find the names of three persons who had actually been condemned to death. But by dawn on the 24th March, and drawing on lists of Italians under arrest by the German authorities, Kappler's list had reached two hundred and seventy. At this point Kappler turned for assistance to Caruso, the Fascist Chief of Police in Rome, asking him to produce a further fifty names of persons for execution. Under direction from the Italian Minister of the Interior, Buffarini-Guidi, Caruso produced the requisite fifty names, including those of several Jews, thus enabling Kappler to achieve his total of three hundred and twenty. Early in the afternoon of the 24th March Kappler informed General Mälzer that by 13.00 hrs. on that day a list of three hundred and twenty persons for execution would be available.

On receipt of this information from Kappler, General Mälzer then told Major Dobbrick, commander of the 3rd Battalion of the S.S. Polizeiregiment Bozen, that he should now avenge the deaths of his men and arrange to carry out the executions. But Dobbrick prevaricated, whilst Col. Hauser at 14th Army headquarters refused to detail troops to perform the shootings. In order to meet the time scale laid down by Field Marshal Kesselring, General Mälzer, with a degree of desperation, ordered Kappler that he and the men under his immediate command were to be the executioners.

By this time the Ardeatine Caves, some 3 km. south from the centre of Rome, and close to the catacombs of S. Callisto, had been identified as the place of execution. German engineers sealed off all the entrances but one of a particular section of the caves, the intention being to seal this final entrance with those executed inside.

In the early afternoon of the 24th March a further German died as a result of wounds sustained in the Via Rasella attack, making the total of dead thirty-three. Without reference to higher authority Kappler added to his death list the names of ten Jews who had been arrested by the German authorities only that morning.

The men to be executed were not informed as to their fate, but had their hands tied behind their backs before leaving the Regina Coeli prison for the Ardeatine Caves, escorted by their executioners. At 14.00 hrs. on the afternoon of the 24th March the first batch of men due to be executed left the Regina Coeli prison in the backs of sealed trucks normally used by the Germans for transporting meat, bound directly for the Ardeatine Caves, where the executions commenced at 15.30 hrs. There, in groups of five, the prisoners were led into the caves, made to kneel, and were then shot at short range in the back of the head. On Kappler's instructions those about to be killed were offered no religious rites, since dispensing these would have made unacceptable inroads into the twenty-four hours time constraint for completing the executions. The shootings were all carried out by the S.S. officers and other ranks under Kappler's command, with Kappler himself participating. One of his officers, S.S. Hauptsturmführer Wetjen was most reluctant to be involved in the killings, but he was escorted by Kappler into the caves who then 'in comradely fashion' (Kappler's words) shot a victim alongside and at the same time as Wetjen. In the event, three hundred and thirty- five Italian males were massacred, their known ages being between fifteen and seventy-four years. The explanation given to Kappler by S.S. Hauptsturmführer Priebke, who was in charge of arranging the numbers to be killed, for the shooting of five additional men, was that this arose out of an error in counting, but since the five men were already at the place of execution, they were killed anyway.

Two days after the massacre a fetid odour began to issue from the caves, this becoming more acute as each day passed. Don Valentini and Don Giorgi, two local priests, entered the caves on the 30th March through a small hole left unsealed and found the piles of corpses then in an advanced state of decay. When the Germans learned of this breach their engineers ensured that this and no other entrance to the caves remained open.

Soon after Rome fell to the Allies on the 4th June, that part of the Ardeatine Caves which contained those massacred was opened up, and Dr Attilio Ascarelli, a forensic medicine specialist from the University of Rome, began work there. After much painstaking effort he was eventually able to positively identify three hundred and twenty-four out of the three hundred and thirty-five corpses. In his book Death in Rome, Robert Katz lists the names of three hundred and thirty-two men who are known to have been killed by the Germans on the 24th March. The names of the remaining three have never been discovered. But one man thought to have been a victim, a Russian, Alexy Kubjsckin, somehow escaped, and returned to live in his native land.

After Dr Ascarelli had completed his work the remains of the victims were put into three hundred and thirty-five sarcophagi, these in turn being placed in a mausoleum located within the Ardeatine Caves at the site of the killings. On the 24th March, 1949, the fifth anniversary of the massacre, the Ardeatine Caves were consecrated as a national monument.

Commencing just prior to Easter (Easter Day was on the 9th April) and through into May of 1944, as a final demonstration of their brutality and callousness, the Germans sent out notifications to the families of the victims. These were entirely in German and identical, except for the name of the victim, stating that the person named had died on the 24th March, 1944. It continued, saying 'Personal belongings, if any, may be recovered at the office of the German Sicherheitspolizei in Via Tasso, 155, where they are being held'.

As indicated earlier, military activity by the Partisans began to increase significantly from around mid May and into early June 1944, following the fall of Rome to the Allies.

In an attempt to counteract this activity, Field Marshall Kesselring prepared an order dated the 19th May which was issued on the 17 June. In part, this order read:

New Measures in Connection with Operations against Partisans

1. The partisan situation in the Italian theatre, particularly in Central Italy, has recently deteriorated to such an extent that it constitutes a serious danger to the fighting troops and their supply lines as well as to the war industry and economic potential.

The fight against the partisans must be carried on with all means at our disposal and with the utmost severity. I will protect any commander who exceeds our usual restraint in the choice and severity of the methods he adopts against partisans. In this connection the old principle holds good, that a mistake in the choice of methods in executing one's orders, is better than failure or neglect to act ... All civilians implicated in anti-partisan operations who are apprehended in the course of reprisals, are to be brought up to the Assembly Camps which are being erected for this purpose ... for ultimate despatch to the Reich as workers.

2. Active operations will be conducted especially in partisan- overrun districts where it is vital to maintain the life-line of the Armed Forces. These partisans will have to be attacked and wiped out. Propaganda amongst partisans (as well as use of agents) is of utmost importance.

Three days after the issue of the foregoing, on the 20th June, Kesselring prepared a related combat order. This was issued on the 1st July, its complete text being as follows:

The Italian Partisans

Anti Partisan Measures

In my appeal to the Italians I announced that severe measures are to be taken against the partisans. This announcement must not represent an empty threat. It is the duty of all troops and police in my command to adopt the severest measures. Every act of violence committed by partisans must be punished immediately. Reports submitted must also give details of counter measures taken. Wherever there is evidence of considerable numbers of partisan groups, a proportion of the male population of the area will be arrested and in the event of an act of violence being committed, these men will be shot. The population must be informed of this. Should troops, etc., be fired at from any village, the village will be burnt down. Perpetrators or the ring leaders will be hanged in public. Nearby villages to be held responsible for any sabotage to cables and damage inflicted to tyres. The most effective counter measure is to recruit local patrols. Members of the Fascist party will not be included in any of these reprisals. Suspects will be handed over to the prefects and a report sent to me. Every soldier will protect himself outside villages by carrying a fire arm. District Commanders will decide in which towns it will also be necessary to carry fire arms. Every type of plunder is forbidden and will be punished severely. All countermeasures must be hard but just. The dignity of the German soldier demands it.

Concurrent with Kesselring's orders, instructions were issued to the Partisans in the Adriatic zone and the Marches on the 19th and 20th June from General Alexander's headquarters and broadcast by the Italia Combatte programme over the Bari-Naples-Rome radio network. These instructions, in part, said:

Listen attentively to the following: Kill all enemy soldiers who are left in the rear in order to carry out demolitions. Prevent them from carrying out any demolitions whatsoever. Act so that the bridges remain intact, in the same way as the patriots of Teramo acted ...

Again on the 27th June further instructions were issued to the Partisans from General Alexander's headquarters in the Italia Combatte programme over the Bari-Naples-

Rome radio network, these being relayed by United Nations Radio on the 29 June and by the B.B.C. on the 30th June and 1st July. The broadcasts said:

> We will now read the latest instructions issued from General Alexander's headquarters and by the Italian High Command: Patriots of Siena, here are special instructions for you ... Considerable enemy forces stand between you and our advancing armies. We ask you to undertake a difficult and most valuable task: to attack the enemy from the rear while we attack him from the front and from the air. We ask you to use the following methods: obstruct roads to stop enemy transport and give us targets for our aircraft and your snipers. Let your activities be such as to make travelling by road in cars or on motor cycles mean death for the enemy ...

At the peak of the Partisan military activity in the late spring and summer months of 1944 the Germans estimated the total Partisan strength to be of the order of 100,000. Allied estimates put the figure around 145,000, with some 85,000 operating in the countryside and a further 60,000 in and near the towns and cities. After assuming operational control over their activities in July 1944, General Alexander sought to deploy the Partisans over a wide area so as to cause maximum disruption to German communications and supply lines, thereby forcing the Germans to use a large proportion of their forces to deal with internal security.

Much Partisan activity took place in the vicinity of Grosseto and Orbetello such that by the 13th June, due to blown bridges and blocked roads, no essential supplies could be brought by the Germans to Grosseto from Siena. In view of this, General Lemelsen, commanding the German 14th Army, requested and was granted the necessary authority by Field Marshal Kesselring to shoot up to ten Italian males of military age for every German soldier killed by Partisans or for proven acts of military sabotage.

In the advance northwards from Rome and the battles for Trasimeno, Arezzo and Florence over the two months between the 4th June and 4th August, British 13 Corps gave generous recognition to the support and many acts of assistance they received from the local Partisan forces.

When in the latter months of 1943 and the first half of 1944 the Comune di Cavriglia, which is situated on the slopes of the Monti del Chianti some 34 km. south-east of Florence, was occupied by German forces, the wooded and mountainous areas of the region, particularly in the vicinities of Castelnuovo dei Sabbioni and Cavriglia, provided shelter for the various Partisan groups that were formed, flourished and began operating against the Germans. The 3rd Company 'Chiatti' was commanded by Nello Vannini, and had its principal base at Casalmonte, some 3 km. south-west of Castelnuovo dei Sabbioni. However, this Company frequently moved along the crest of the Monti del Chianti and the Valdarni and Chiantigian slopes of the mountain itself. On the 8th July, 1944, when the Germans, guided by Ivario Viligiardi commenced their round-up of Partisans, the 3rd Company 'Chiatti' was at Casalmonte, the path to it from Poggio alle Valli going via Casa Corneto.

The 4th Company 'Castellani' was commanded by Guelfo Billi, and had its principal base at Casa Monte Domenichi, some 3 km. west by north-west of Castelnuovo dei Sabbioni. This unit operated mainly in the area of Meleto–San Cipriano, moving there by way of C. Piari di Teri, San Martino, Pianfranzesi and Bomba.

A possible explanation for the omission in the British S.I.B. reports of any mention of the 4th Company 'Castellani' Partisan formation was due to the fact that when the front line between the Allies and the Germans passed north beyond the Comune di Cavriglia, the 3rd Company 'Chiatti' and the 4th Company 'Castellani' amalgamated into a single unit, taking the title 'Chiatti' Company.

In his statement to the British S.I.B. on the 5th December, 1944, Nello Vannini, who commanded the 3rd Company 'Chiatti' Partisans, says that amongst other activities, his formation, on the 23rd May, 1944, destroyed six road bridges in the vicinity of San Cipriano. Some doubt has been cast upon this as within a radius of 5 km. around San Cipriano there did not exist six road bridges, and they could not, therefore, have been destroyed in that number. The possible reasons for this discrepancy are copious, and the events so far in the distant past that they deny certain resolution.

Boris Gatteschi states that the bridge at San Cipriano was blown up in order to impede the transportation of machinery away from the mining complex by the Germans, and that it was he who transported the Partisans with their explosives to the bridge, but this was circa the 10th June, 1944.

During the period from the 23rd May to the 25th June, 1944 Vannini and his 3rd Company of Chiatti claimed to have carried out six separate actions against the German forces in the Comune di Cavriglia, causing them many difficulties and the deaths of ten German military personnel. Details of these actions are as follows:

23rd May. Destroyed six road bridges in the vicinity of San Cipriano, some 2 km.

from Castelnuovo dei Sabbioni, seriously hindering the transportation of lignite fuel from the nearby mining complex.

25th May. Attacked a group of German soldiers again near San Cipriano, killing three of them. The bodies of the dead soldiers were taken off by their comrades.

30th May. Attacked a German military motor vehicle carrying two soldiers at Castelnuovo dei Sabbioni. One of the soldiers was killed and subsequently interred by the Partisans in the local cemetery. The other soldier was wounded but escaped. The vehicle was retained and used by the Partisans.

4th/5th June. Two Luftwaffe servicemen who became lost whilst making their way to a German military hospital which had recently been moved to nearby, decided to spend the night in their vehicle under a road bridge at Castelnuovo dei Sabbioni. The presence of the two Germans was made known to the local Partisans who killed them both, burying their bodies in woodland near Berci, some 8km. from Castelnuovo dei Sabbioni. Again, the vehicle was retained and used by the Partisans.

12th June. Disarmed the Italian Military Police at Castelnuovo dei Sabbioni who were working in support of the Germans.

12th June. Attacked three German military motor vehicles carrying German soldiers at Radda in Chianti, some 12km. south-west of Castelnuovo dei Sabbioni. Three German soldiers were killed, their bodies being taken off by their comrades.

Thus, the die was cast for the many massacres that were perpetrated by the Germans principally in the months of June, July and August 1944, including those at Civitella in Val di Chiana, a hill village about 15km. south-west of Arezzo on the 29th June; Castelnuovo dei Sabbioni, San Martino, Meleto and Massa dei Sabbioni, all in the Comune di Cavriglia, and on the 4th July; Le Matole, a district of Castelnuovo dei Sabbioni on the 11th July, and at the Fucecchio Marshes some 40km. west of Florence on the 6th July and the 24th August.

13

Castelnuovo dei Sabbioni and its environs prior to July 1944

There has been a village at Castelnuovo dei Sabbioni for many centuries, the earliest recorded dates of its existence being AD 1120, 1190 and 1192 in L. Pagliai's Il regesto di Coltibuono, 'Regesta Chartarum Italiae', published in Rome in 1909. The first citation relative to the church of Castelnuovo is also confirmed as AD 1260 (although the church is believed to date much earlier), and appears in the 'Libro di Monteperti'.

Prior to and as at July 1944 the old village was situated some 30km. south-east of Florence at an elevation of about 300 metres, and on the eastern slopes of the Monti del Chianti. In mid 1944 the population of Castelnuovo dei Sabbioni was around 1,500, with a further 130 or so souls inhabiting the adjacent district of Le Matole.

From earliest times the area around Castelnuovo dei Sabbioni has possessed an economic significance because of its lignite deposits, these being one of the few indigenous fuel sources in the whole of Italy. Mention is made of the modest use of lignite as a fuel as far back as 1574. However, the main lignite mine workings were commenced and developed near to Castelnuovo dei Sabbioni, and in the latter half of the 19th century a concentrated exploitation of the lignite deposits in the Valdarno took place.

The early recovery of lignite was carried out manually and with minimum difficulty from the deposits just below the overlaying soil strata on the slopes of the Monti del Chianti. When these initial deposits were exhausted and recovery operations moved into the valley below the Monti del Chianti, the strata of soil covering the lower lignite deposits was found to be much greater than that at the higher elevation, thus making the manual recovery process more arduous. In view of this, in 1875, soon after the ironworks was built at San Giovanni Valdarno, the work of lignite recovery using underground tunnels began, although the earlier surface method continued to be used where this was practicable. The recovery of lignite by underground tunnelling continued until mid 1944 and several years beyond, with the Santa Barbara mine being extensively upgraded in the early 1940s, including the installation of a conveyor belt system which carried the

The main shaft of the mine Le Bicchieraie.

Mine of Santa Barbara.

lignite directly from the mine workings to the screening plant and silos.

Initially, and prior to the construction in the near vicinity of a main railway line, the lignite was only used in the arca close to the mine workings, being transported in animal drawn carts. It was utilised both as a domestic heating fuel and in the boilers of small industries, but its principal use was to fire the furnaces of the local brick works.

Extraction chamber in a mine of the Mining Company of Valdarno in 1938.

In 1866, following the completion of the main railway line between Florence and Arezzo, the extraction of lignite from the area was significantly increased. Almost all the output from the mines in the Comune di Cavriglia was transported to the rail head at San Giovanni Valdarno, which was on the main line from Florence to Arezzo, for distribution over the rail network for use in many diverse industries, some of which were hundreds of kilometres distant, the railway locomotives themselves also utilising the lignite for steam raising.

The Italian Society for Ironworks was established in 1872, with an ironworks being constructed at San Giovanni Valdarno, some 6km. north-east of Castelnuovo dei Sabbioni. This ironworks consumed in its furnaces large quantities of lignite which initially was transported from the mines to the ironworks in horse drawn drays. Then, in 1874, a narrow gauge rail track was laid from the mining area to the railway station and the newly built ironworks at San Giovanni Valdarno, the wagons running on it and carrying the lignite still being horse drawn. But within a few years this rail track was changed from narrow to standard gauge, the lignite wagons then being hauled by steam locomotive.

During the latter years of the 19th century and the beginning of the 20th, concurrent with the expansion of the lignite mining complex, the local rail transportation system was developed such that there were some 40km. of standard gauge track on which operated four steam locomotives hauling between them a total of seventy-five lignite wagons. For the movement of lignite from the galleries in the various parts of the mining complex to the stock yards, some 130km. of narrow gauge rail tracks were laid. Operating over this narrow gauge network were many small steam and diesel locomotives, together with over 1,700 saloons and decauville trucks. But in the mine galleries themselves, and in the open mine yards, horse drawn trucks continued to be used.

Overhead cableways were also employed to transport lignite from some of the smaller and more remote workings to the main mine with its railway connection, as well as to deliver lignite direct to various large industrial users in the vicinity. Where neither rail nor cableway systems were installed the lignite was usually transported by lorry.

Just after the turn of the century a thermo-electric power station was built at Castelnuovo dei Sabbioni, this being commissioned in 1907. For steam raising in its boilers the power station consumed considerable quantities of waste and unsaleable lignite that had accumulated over the years in the stockyards of the mines. The initial capacity of the power station was a modest 1,800kVA, most of the electricity it generated being consumed locally. Its electrical system was, however, connected by overhead lines to those of the nearby cities of Siena and Florence. Transportation of lignite to the power station from the mining complex was effected by wagons on a narrow gauge rail track drawn by a steam locomotive. In 1928 a modernisation of the power station was completed, including the installation of two Ljungström turbo-alternator sets (very quiet machines, capable of accepting electrical load changes with great rapidity), which increased its capacity three-fold to 5,400kVA, the output terminals of the station then being connected to the national electricity network. This capacity increase brought with it a corresponding increase in the requirement for lignite, and to handle this increase the earlier narrow gauge railway between the mining complex and the power station was replaced by a standard gauge rail link over which lignite wagons were hauled by steam locomotive. The power station continued to operate without further major modifications until its destruction by the Germans on the 7th July, 1944.

Many of the workers at the lignite mining complex lived either at Castelnuovo dei Sabbioni or at one of the other nearby villages, making their own ways to and from their homes and place of work. However, at shift change times, two carriages were attached to the wagons of the lignite transporting trains travelling between the mining complex and San Giovanni Valdarno so as to carry those mineworkers who were coming from or returning to their homes in the adjacent Comunes of Figline, San Giovanni Valdarno and Montevarchi. As with the power station, this transportation system, with only minor running modifications, continued to operate until mid 1944.

At the beginning of World War II there was a dramatic increase in the demand for lignite in order to supply both the existing and additional industries engaged in the production of war material. This, in turn, led to the need for a considerable increase in the number of operatives to work at the mine, which figure peaked in the first half of 1944 to a little less than 4,000. In the first instance, these new workers who lived a significant distance from Castelnuovo dei Sabbioni, and could not, therefore, travel to and from work on a daily basis, took up lodgings in or around Castelnuovo dei Sabbioni where these were available, either for themselves alone or for themselves and their families. Then, in October 1939, with financial assistance from central Government, the Mining Association of Valdarno commenced the construction of a group of a dozen or so apartment blocks near to the village of San Cipriano some 3 1⁄2 km. north-east of Castelnuovo dei Sabbioni, in order to provide permanent accommodation for many of its additional workers with their families. The shops and wine cellars of the new development were provided by the Valdarno Agricultural Society, which had for many years been the proprietor of a large number of farms nearby, where grapes were grown and processed, the locality being known as 'La Tinaia', i.e., 'a cellar where there are vats'. However, the new village was officially named Santa Barbara after the Patron Saint of Miners. With construction completed in August 1941, the first residents then began to take up occupancy in the new village, including some families from the nearby district of San Martino which was in danger of collapsing due to excavations for lignite at the Allori mine. Furthermore, in 1942, the Mining Association of Valdarno provided dormitories and a dining hall for those miners without families who came from locations well remote from Castelnuovo dei Sabbioni.

It has been suggested that the motives of the Mining Association of Valdarno for building the village of Santa Barbara were other than altruistic. It is said that substantial tax reliefs were granted to the Mining Association of Valdarno for carrying out and part funding the construction of Santa Barbara. Moreover, this funding was an investment for the considerable sums of money the company had made from the sale of lignite, the latter having substantially increased both in quantity and unit value since the outbreak of World War II.

Until mid 1943, and although Italy was at war, life in and around Castelnuovo dei Sabbioni continued much as previously, with the economic prosperity of the area being sustained by the unrelenting requirement for lignite. The maximum production from the main mining complex was achieved over the twelve months of 1940 when 950,024 tonnes were extracted. Although many much smaller lignite mines were concurrently being worked in the vicinity of the main complex, their combined maximum output was estimated not to exceed 20% of that of the main complex.

But following the demise of Mussolini in July 1943, the signing of the Short Armistice between Italy and the Allies on the 3rd September, 1943, and the resultant oc-cupation by the Germans of almost the whole of Italy, life in the Comune di Cavriglia, including Castelnuovo dei Sabbioni, and indeed, in all of Italy, took on a quite differ-ent and more menacing aspect. For the lignite mining industry, the twelve months of 1943 saw the output from the Castelnuovo dei Sabbioni complex fall to 685,186 tonnes. A further fall in output from the complex occurred in the first half of 1944, with the major proportion of the production during this period going to the ironworks at San Giovanni Valdarno, and the balance being consumed in the furnaces of other local in-dustries. For this local use, transportation of the lignite reverted to animal drawn drays and carts. During the whole of 1944 the mining complex at Castelnuovo dei Sabbioni produced only 174,471 tonnes of lignite, less than 20% of the maximum figure reached in 1940.

Some of this significant loss in output during 1944 can be attributed to the damage caused to mining equipment together with the total destruction of the nearby power sta-tion by the Germans in early July 1944. Moreover, the battle zone moved north through the area between the 18th July, when Montevarchi was taken by units of British 13 Corps, and the fall of Florence on the 5th August. The main reason for the reduction in output was, however, the inability to transport the lignite away from the mining area ei-ther by rail, due to the damage caused to the rail network by Allied bombing, or by road, because of bridges again damaged by Allied bombing or Partisan activity, and a dearth of lorries, since increasing numbers of these were requisitioned by the German forces.

As a result of this reduction in output from the lignite mining complex at Casteln-uovo dei Sabbioni, a progressive reduction in the mining workforce commenced in May 1944. A number of those dismissed sought new employment with the German Todt Organisation, [1] which had a recruiting agency at Montevarchi, some 14km. east of Castelnuovo dei Sabbioni. Those ex-mineworkers who were taken on by the Todt Or-ganisation were engaged on carrying out repairs to railways, rail and road bridges in the area that had suffered damage either as a result of Allied bombing or action by Parti-sans. But some of the younger ex-mineworkers, who lost their exemption from military service on being dismissed from essential employment at the lignite mining complex, and who, at best, might well have been conscripted to work in Germany, joined the ranks of one of the local Partisan formations. Thus was the situation in and around Castelnuovo dei Sabbioni as at the end of June/early July 1944. As such, what obtained at Castelnuovo dei Sabbioni and its environs at this time was not unique, but was generally in common with the situation in a zone across Italy immediately north of an approximate line from Cecina in the west, through Perugia to Ancona on the Adriatic coast. In this zone, which was under strict German domination, the movement of people and goods was both difficult and hazardous because of damage caused to roads and railways by Allied bombing, Partisan activity and frequent air raids by Allied planes. The few trains that did manage to operate were used mainly to transport German troops and war material. Moreover, food was in short supply, employment prospects were diminishing and the battle zone was approaching from the south.

And then, during the week between the 25th June and the 2nd July, additional German forces moved into the Comune di Cavriglia in the vicinity of Castelnuovo dei Sabbioni, the dreadful purpose behind their so doing soon to become painfully evident to the unsuspecting civilian population.

1 The German Todt Organisation was named after Dr Todt who was appointed German Minister of Armaments and Munitions in 1940. But his activities extended far beyond those indicated by his official title, since he was, in fact, in charge of the entire German construction industry, both within Germany itself and in those countries that were under German control. Todt was killed in a flying accident on the 8th February, 1942 at Rastenburg airfield when the Heinkel III in which he was a passenger crashed just after taking off for Munich. Immediately following Todt's death, Speer was appointed by Hitler to take over and continue as previously with all of Todt's duties as Minister of Armaments and Munitions, including the German construction industry.

At that time the Todt Organisation was responsible for all road building operations, navigable waterways and their improvements, and all electric power generating plants. As part of the Four Year Plan, originated in September 1936, with Goering as its Commissioner, the Todt Organisation had under construction the West Wall, U-boat shelters along the Atlantic coast and new roads in all the occupied territories. It also worked alongside German Army Engineers in the construction of the major defence systems such as those at Monte Cassino during 1943/44 and the Futa Pass in the Gothic Line in 1944, as well as working to repair the damage caused by Allied bombing to railways, roads, canals, bridges and airfields. Although all the technical expertise of the Todt Organisation and the supervision of its operatives were in the hands of German Engineers, the major part of the work force for any particular project was obtained from the local population. In Italy, many of the work forces were so obtained or provided by the Italian Army.

14

Massacres of Italian civilians carried out by German forces in the Comune de Cavriglia during early July 1944

As a result of Partisan activity in the Comune di Cavriglia, which has been described at the end of chapter 12, the German military, acting under the authority of the Order issued by Field Marshal Kesselring on the 20th June, 1944, began on the 25th June to move a number of additional units into the area. The purpose behind this concentration of forces was not immediately evident to the civilian population of the Comune di Cavriglia, but became disastrously so when the Germans began, on the 4th July, to carry out a series of massacres resulting in the deaths of 187 innocent Italian male civilians.

The German units concerned, together with their initial locations in the area, included the following:

A 70 strong motorised anti-Partisan unit under the command of Leut. Wolf which set up its headquarters on the 25th June at Via Vittorio Veneto, 1 in Terranuova. This house was owned by Dr Luigi Corsi, but he and his family had evacuated from the area leaving the property in the care of Nella Terni, a young local girl who was the family servant. Whilst some of Leut. Wolf's men were billeted at the headquarters, the majority moved into the Scuola di Musica, Via Verdi, 33, Terranuova, Wolf himself taking up residence in the house of Vittorugo Lavacchi, Secretary of the Comune di Terranuova, at Via Vittorio Veneto, 7, Terranuova.

On the following day, the 26th June, a section of German Feldgendarmerie, under the command of a Warrant Officer, arrived at San Cipriano, taking up residence in the then unoccupied house next door in the case delle 'Carpinete', San Cipriano, to the home of Osvaldo Amidei.

Three days later, Ober-Leut. Danisch, Commander (Guard) Company, 76 Panzer Corps (FPN Dienststelle 05009W) and his driver/batman Casuski arrived at San Cipriano. Danisch forthwith set up a headquarters in San Cipriano 297, the house of Fanny Ficai, who was ordered to vacate her residence and take with her such personal effects as she had, since the Germans required the property as a billet. San Cipriano 297 was close to the house occupied by the section of German Feldgendarmerie. Accompanying Ober-Leut. Danisch was a Warrant Officer, a Sergeant Tries, and about 30 other ranks, some of whom were Italians wearing German uniforms. Also with this unit were two Italian females, one known as Trieste and believed to come from Velletri, the other called Maria. The other ranks were billeted at San Cipriano 15, the house of Diva Sbardellati, who was forced to leave her residence, which was situated about 50 metres from Danisch's headquarters. For transport the unit had at its disposal a Fiat 1100 car and two Fiat trucks each carrying a rear mounted machine-gun.

Also on the 29th June a German field officer of 76 Panzer Corps and believed to be of Major rank, together with 5 junior officers and some 30 other ranks established another headquarters at the residence of Nicomede Cliceri, an agricultural agent of the Santa Maria estate, near San Giovanni Valdarno, and some 4 km. from San Cipriano. With this contingent were three Italian females, two of whom came from Littoria. For transport the unit possessed 5 military trucks.

A detachment of 11 Hermann Goering Panzer Grenadier Regiment arrived at Cavriglia on the 29th June and set up a headquarters there. On or about the same date a German officer, Leut. Kronowetter, called at the Villa Bonarotti, a large building on the fringe of Cavriglia standing in its own grounds. The officer asked Maria Allegri, who resided at the Villa Bonarotti, if she would be prepared to billet his Oberst who commanded the detachment of 11 Hermann Goering Panzer Grenadier Regiment, to which she agreed. It was on the 2nd July when Leut. Kronowetter returned with his Oberst, accompanied by a batman, a driver and an Italian female.

A further Herman Goering unit, some 100 soldiers strong, and thought to belong to a 'Flak' Regiment, descended upon the village of Montegonzi, about 5 km. south of Castelnuovo dei Sabbioni, on the 1st July. This unit, which was under the command of Major Seiler, possessed about a dozen military trucks. The Major, together with his two junior officers and 6 Warrant Officers, took up billets in the Castello di Montegonzi, the home of Anna Viligiardi, the other ranks of the unit being billeted in the village school and nearby private houses.

The 1st July also saw Leut.-General Richard Heidrich, the commander of the German 1st Parachute Infantry Division, together with his staff, arrive at the Villa Renacci, San Giovanni Valdarno, establishing his headquarters there. Villa Renacci is on the Estate Renacci and situated about 4 km. from San Cipriano and 2 km. from the Santa Maria Estate.

Finally, on the 2nd July, a second German General and his staff, one of whom was believed to be Hauptmann Forster, Commandant, 1st Panzer Regiment 4, 76 Panzer Corps, established his headquarters in the Villa Cetinale, San Cipriano, a few hundred metres distant from the headquarters of Ober-Leut. Danisch. The residents of Villa Cetinale, Giuseppe and Maria Corsi, were evicted from their home by the Germans, then taking up temporary residence on a farm at Caiano, some 9 km. from Castelnuovo dei Sabbioni.

Thus, by the 2nd July all the German units were assembled to wreak the most dreadful reprisals upon the population of Castelnuovo dei Sabbioni and the surrounding villages as a punishment for the recent Partisan activities, and in retribution for the death of 10 German service men.

Prior to the atrocities carried out by the Germans that commenced on the 4th July, a number of preliminary and associated events took place. The first of these involved the arrest during the early afternoon of the 29th June of Ivario Viligiardi, a 24 years old resident of Castelnuovo dei Sabbioni and a worker at the nearby lignite mine. He was arrested by the Germans near Cavriglia on suspicion of being a Partisan and for having in his possession an Italian hand-grenade. Viligiardi was not a member of the local 3rd Company of Chiatti Partisan group, but was on close and familiar terms with its commander, Nello Vannini, and the men under his control. A spare time hairdresser, Viligiardi paid frequent visits to the headquarters of Vannini's Partisan group near San Martino, a small village about 2½ km. from Castelnuovo dei Sabbioni, in order to cut the hair of the members of the group. Following his arrest near Cavriglia, Viligiardi was taken by the Germans to a house in Montevarchi, a fairly large town some 8 km. east of Cavriglia.

For the purpose of describing what then happened to him and justifying his actions, Viligiardi made three separate statements to the British Special Investigation Branch between the 20th December, 1944 and the 27th June, 1945. All three statements differ materially from each other in some of their essential aspects, but what follows is as near to the truth as it is likely to get, and can be substantiated by the statements of various witnesses. At Montevarchi, Viligiardi spent the night following his arrest in the

lavatory of a house. On the following morning he was taken in a German military vehicle from Montevarchi to Terranuova, a distance of about 3 km., there being detained
under guard in the garden of the Scuola di Musica. Here he was questioned by Rudi
Groner, a member of Leut. Wolf's anti-Partisan unit. Groner, who had a fair command
of the Italian language, asked Viligiardi to give his home address. This Viligiardi did.
Groner then accused Viligiardi of being a Partisan, asking him to provide the name of
the Partisan leader in the area and where the headquarters of this Partisan group was located. At first Viligiardi said that he possessed no knowledge as to who led the local Partisans or where their headquarters was situated. However, following threats to carry out
reprisals against his family, Viligiardi disclosed to Groner that the leader of the Partisans in the Comune di Cavriglia was called Nello Vannini, and members of his group
could be found in the vicinity of Poggio alle Valli. Groner then left Viligiardi still under
guard.[1]

About half an hour later Groner rejoined Viligiardi, this time accompanied by a
young Italian male civilian. The young Italian, Pericle Sorbi, was but 18 years of age,
and a language student who spoke fluent German. Sorbi had met Groner quite by chance
at the home of Signorina Teresa Francini in Terranuova during the evening of the day
on which Viligiardi was arrested, when Groner and Sorbi had casually conversed in
German. During the early afternoon of the 30th June Sorbi was accosted in the Corso
(main street of) Terranuova by Groner, the latter insisting that Sorbi accompany him to
the Scuola di Musica where Groner required his assistance. What Groner, in fact, required, was that Sorbi act as an interpreter whilst he, Groner, subjected Viligiardi to a
prolonged and forceful interrogation.

On entering the garden of the Scuola di Musica, Viligiardi was seen sitting on the

---

1 There is some confusion here in the mind of the writer regarding the location of
the 3rd Company of Chiatti Partisan group led by Nello Vannini. Ivario Viligiardi
states quite clearly that the headquarters of this Partisan group was (in the hills)
above San Martino, but then goes on to say that members of this same Partisan
group were to be found in the vicinity of Poggio alle Valli. Now Poggio alle Valli is
4½ km. from San Martino as the crow flies, and more like 8½ km. distant by road,
hence the confusion.
Poggio alle Valli is much more isolated than San Martino, so it is possible that
while the 3rd Company of Chiatti Partisan group had its headquarters at San Martino, many of the group, which grew to be over 70 strong, had their hideout near
Poggio alle Valli.

steps of a hut. As Sorbi and Groner approached Viligiardi, Groner told Sorbi that the man before them was a Partisan, and that he, Sorbi, was required to explain quite precisely several important matters to Viligiardi. Sorbi protested that it was somewhat distasteful for him to take part in the interrogation of a fellow countryman. To this Groner replied, 'It is the war'. Sorbi then cautioned Viligiardi not to say too much, but was immediately warned by Groner that he, Sorbi, was not to speak to or with Viligiardi until instructed to do so. During the interrogation Viligiardi wrote down on a piece of paper the names and addresses of three men who were said to be Partisans. Precise details of what Viligiardi wrote are not known, but it is thought that the addresses of two of these men were at Castelnuovo dei Sabbioni, with the address of the third man being at Meleto. It is also believed that Viligiardi confirmed Nello Vannini to be the local Partisan leader and a native of the Le Matole district of Castelnuovo dei Sabbioni. Under threat of death by hanging that day if he failed to reveal all he knew regarding the local Partisans, Viligiardi asserted that he had told everything. Groner then said that Poggio alle Valli, the location from which the Partisans were said to be operating, could not be found on the map. To this Viligiardi replied that if such was the case then he would guide the Germans there. Groner, in conclusion, then asked Viligiardi to provide detailed particulars of his family, warning him that if the Germans were led into a trap at Poggio alle Valli then all the members of the Viligiardi family would be killed. With the interrogation at an end Pericle Sorbi left the garden of the Scuola di Musica and went to the home of Signorina Teresa Francini. Shortly afterwards Sorbi, accompanied by his mother, left Terranuova to live in the countryside, not returning to Terranuova until the Germans had departed.

For the nights of the 30th June and 1st July Viligiardi slept among German soldiers in a room of the Scuola di Musica at Terranuova, spending the intervening daylight hours under guard in its garden. Then, on the evening of the 2nd July, Viligiardi was taken by German military transport to the German occupied Villa Silvano at Bagno a Ripoli on the south-east fringe of Florence. He was escorted on this journey by Groner, and on arrival was locked under guard in the garage of the Villa.

Around noon on the 3rd July Viligiardi was taken from the garage into the Villa Silvano itself for interrogation by a German officer of Captain rank, with Groner acting as interpreter. The Captain again questioned Viligiardi regarding the latter's knowledge of the Partisans in the vicinity of Castelnuovo dei Sabbioni. In reply Viligiardi gave the same information he had given under interrogation at Terranuova. According to Viligiardi the Captain then wrote on a sheet of paper the name of the leader of the Partisans operating locally to Castelnuovo dei Sabbioni, Nello Vannini, underlining the same and showing it to Viligiardi. It is unclear as to Viligiardi's response, although he says that the sheet of paper had several other names written on it, none of which he saw very clearly or subsequently remembered. Following this interrogation Viligiardi was returned to the garage where he remained until some 24 hours later. At that time he was again taken into a room in the Villa and subjected to a virtually identical interrogation which had the same outcome. However, at the end of the proceedings the Captain told Viligiardi that he, Viligiardi, would have to accompany the Captain to Poggio alle Valli. Later that day, in order to apply further pressure on Viligiardi he was visited in the garage, to which he had been returned, by Groner. The latter informed Viligiardi that it was quite useless for him to tell his German interrogators half-truths and lies because he, Groner, had been to Castelnuovo dei Sabbioni and had found out all about Viligiardi and his family. Viligiardi says he did not respond, remaining under guard in the garage of the Villa Silvano until the evening of the 7th July.

There can be no doubt that the intelligence provided by Viligiardi to the Germans proved invaluable to them in the planning and execution of the massacres in Castelnuovo dei Sabbioni and surrounding villages on the 4th July and thereafter.

A second preliminary event concerned the unit commanded by Major Seiler that established itself in the village of Montegonzi on the 1st July. Shortly after arriving at Montegonzi, Major Seiler summoned the local Priest, Don Grifoni, to the Castello di Montegonzi. Seiler told the priest that he was in command of the German troops who had come that day to Montegonzi, and asked if there were any Partisans in the near vicinity. Seiler went on to say that Don Grifoni should be aware that any attacks by Partisans on the soldiers of his unit would result in reprisals being carried out as had been done under his command at Civitella in Val di Chiana. (There, on the 29th June the Germans had massacred a total of 212 men, women and children.) The priest gave Major Seiler his assurance that there were no Partisans operating in the area, and that the population of Montegonzi was peaceful. Major Seiler appeared to be satisfied and allowed Don Grifoni to leave.

A further event took place during the evening of the 2nd July when a party of German soldiers led by a Warrant Officer from the unit commanded by Ober-Leut. Danisch entered Meleto, a village 2 km. from Santa Barbara and 4 km. from Castelnuovo dei Sabbioni. The Germans arrived at the village in one of their Fiat trucks with its rear mounted machine-gun. Three villagers, all men less than 40 years of age were arrested by the Germans and held as hostages against any further attacks by the local Partisans against the German troops in the area. The three men arrested, Lorenzo Fabbrini, Livio Lombardini and Omero Quartucci were then taken to San Cipriano in the Fiat truck, to the headquarters of Danisch's unit, to be detained there overnight, their arrival being seen by Diva Sbardellati.

Around mid-morning of the following day Livio Lombardini was interrogated by Ober-Leut. Danisch through an interpreter. Specifically, Danisch asked Lombardini for information regarding those Partisans who had destroyed the 6 road bridges near San Cipriano on the 23rd May. Also, under threat of being shot if he failed to comply, Lombardini was asked to lead the Germans to the location where the local Partisans had their headquarters and hideout. Lombardini convinced Danisch that he knew nothing of the events of the 23rd May or of the headquarters and hideout of the local Partisans, subsequently being returned to the room of the building where he had been detained overnight. There, in addition to Fabbrini and Quartucci, he was later joined by a further two Italian male civilians. One of these he recognised as Paolo Verzetti who lived at nearby Santa Barbara, but the other man was not known either to Verzetti or any of the three men arrested at Meleto. After all five men were again detained overnight, they were put to work on the morning of the 4th July camouflaging German military vehicles. Whilst so engaged the Fiat truck in which they had been transported to San Cipriano arrived carrying some 20 Italian male civilians, including Dr Giuseppe Bruno and Isaia (Giuseppe) Innocenti, both of whom were known by Fabbrini, and who had been arrested at San Martino to be held as hostages against attacks on German troops by the local Partisans.

During the 3rd July the German troops began to take up their final dispositions for carrying out the series of massacres scheduled for the following day. The anti-Partisan unit commanded by Leut. Wolf left Terranuova for an unknown destination. In the event, it can be deduced that this unit moved to Santa Barbara, staying there the night, before proceeding the next morning to Castelnuovo dei Sabbioni where it carried out the brutal massacre of 74 Italian male civilians. This is confirmed by the remarks made late on the 4th July to Teresa Francini by Groner of Leut. Wolf's anti-Partisan unit, with whom he had established a relationship, that he and his unit had just returned to Terranuova from Castelnuovo dei Sabbioni where they had killed about 80 Partisans. Groner added that the Partisans had been betrayed by one of their own number, by which he was presumably referring to Ivario Viligiardi who he had first interrogated on the 30th June.

Also during the evening of the 3rd July, three military trucks belonging to the unit commanded by Major Seiler, all containing armed soldiers, left Montegonzi, returning at about 20.00 hrs. in the evening of the following day. The departure of these vehicles was observed by the local priest, Don Grifoni. It is uncertain as to the whereabouts and activities of this detachment during its absence from Montegonzi, but it can be reasonably assumed without significant doubt that it also travelled to Santa Barbara where it stayed overnight before taking part in some or all of the massacres at Meleto, Massa dei Sabbioni and San Martino. The trucks from Major Seiler's unit could well have been part of the dozen or so such vehicles, each full of German soldiers, seen by Bruno Sabelli to enter the village of Santa Barbara around 19.30 hrs. in the evening of the 3rd July. The German vehicles stopped close by blocks of apartments at Santa Barbara, almost all of which at that time were unoccupied, since the tenants had been evacuated from the war zone. The soldiers split into various small groups to occupy the empty apartments as billets, one of the ground-floor residences being used as an Orderly Room. A Warrant Officer Fräulein of the 4th Hermann Goering Engineering Battalion, together with three Sergeants took over another apartment as a shared billet.

Clearly, Santa Barbara, just 500 metres from San Cipriano, was to be the assembly and starting out point for the German forces involved in the massacres.

A final preliminary event then occurred involving Bruno Sabelli, mentioned above. He was a surveyor employed at the nearby lignite mine who, with his wife, still occupied an apartment in one of the blocks at Santa Barbara, this being directly opposite to that taken over by Warrant Officer Fräulein and his senior N.C.O.s. Fräulein questioned Sabelli as to why he remained in the building when all the other occupants had left. Sabelli, in fear of the Germans, told Fräulein, quite untruthfully, that he was the caretaker of the property.

Before 06.00 hrs. on the fateful morning of the 4th July, Sabelli was seen in the hallway of the apartment block by another German Warrant Officer and taken into the ground-floor apartment being used by the Germans as an Orderly Room. In one of the rooms of this apartment a German soldier experienced in dealing with maps and plans was studying a map of the area. The Warrant Officer told Sabelli to look at the map, Sabelli observing that it was of Italian origin, drawn to the fairly large scale of 1:100,000 (1 cm. = 1 km.) and showing the villages of Castelnuovo dei Sabbioni, Meleto, Massa dei Sabbioni and San Martino. The map had Meleto at its extreme right hand edge and showed the village to consist of only two or three houses. This paucity of houses was causing the German soldier with the map some concern, and he asked Sabelli how many houses there were, in fact, at Meleto. Sabelli answered to the best of his knowledge, totally unaware of the use to which this information would be put.

In retrospect, the concern of the German soldier studying the map of the area, and who questioned Sabelli appears odd, since the party from Ober-Leut. Danisch's unit had entered Meleto and taken three hostages from there less than 48 hours previously, and would therefore have gained some idea of the size of the village. Moreover, the headquarters of the unit commanded by Ober-Leut. Danisch was only a few hundred metres away from the apartment blocks at Santa Barbara. It is just possible that men from Danisch's unit did not join the assembly of troops at Santa Barbara and subsequently take a direct part in the massacres.

Following the receipt of the information from Sabelli regarding the size of Meleto, the German soldier concerned then made a number of rough copies of the 1:100,000 Italian map of the area, giving these to the attendant Warrant Officer. He, in turn, left the Orderly Room and went outside the apartment block, followed by Sabelli, and gave a copy of the map to the Warrant Officer or senior N.C.O. in charge of each of the four trucks drawn up there, full of German troops, and ready to move off. Sabelli recognised Warrant Officer Fräulein as being in charge of one of these trucks.

Between 06.00 and 06.30 hrs. the four trucks left Santa Barbara going in the direction of Meleto, San Martino, Castelnuovo dei Sabbioni and Massa dei Sabbioni.

Massacre at Meleto
A little after 06.30 hrs. on the morning of the 4th July armed German soldiers of a Hermann Goering unit under the command of one or perhaps two officers entered the village of Meleto, some being in a truck with a rear mounted machine-gun, a small number on motor cycles and the remainder on foot. The arrival of these soldiers was witnessed by at least half a dozen of the inhabitants of Meleto, which at this time totalled around 600, including a number of evacuees. The Germans then surrounded the village, sealing off all means of entrance to and exit from it with armed guards, allowing women and children only to leave. The balance of the soldiers then split up into small groups, scouring the village and rounding up without discrimination all civilian males.

One group of German soldiers went to the Morelli farm situated about 500 metres from the centre of the village, seizing there in the farmyard the farmer's two sons, Mario and Giovan Battista Morelli, together with an evacuee, Giuseppe Simonti. This was seen by Erminia Simonti (not related to Giuseppe) from her home in the farm buildings. At about the same time a fourth man, Agostino Mariottini, was walking along the road towards his home and some 100 metres distant from some German soldiers. He was fired at by the Germans and wounded in his right arm, back and abdomen, dying at his home during the evening of the same day in the presence of his wife Gesuina. The two Morelli brothers and Simonti were also shot by German soldiers, their bodies being placed close to a hayrick which the soldiers then ignited. The burning hayrick did not fall as intended on to the three corpses, and as a consequence they avoided complete incineration. Following the shooting at the farm, the barn of the Morelli farm was torched by the Germans.

Just prior to the shooting, Erminia Simonti, in fear, after having been threatened by a German soldier, fled from the Morelli farm with her two children, eventually reaching her mother's home. In the mid-afternoon of the 4th July she made a cautious return to the farm to discover and identify the three partly burnt corpses of Mario and Giovan Battista Morelli and Giuseppe Simonti. Unaided, Erminia Simonti pulled the three bodies from the ashes and deposited them in the stable of the farm, taking them the following day to Meleto cemetery where they were interred.

Elsewhere in Meleto the women and children were ordered by the Germans, through

*Meleto Valdarno. Monument to the Fallen of World War I in the Square
where those massacred on 4th July, 1944 were gathered by the
Germans on the morning of that day.*

the medium of a German speaking evacuee, to leave the village, being told that all the houses comprising the village were to be burned down.

In due course 55 Italian male civilians were rounded up, assembled in the War Memorial Square of the village and guarded by German soldiers armed with machine-guns. Those who carried identity documents had these inspected by a German officer, which resulted in the release of one man, Ido Matassini, who was in possession of a German Work Permit. Matassini was, however, still held by the Germans under guard in a nearby farmyard. A second man, Arturo Panichi, who, because of his infirmity, was permitted to sit on the low wall around the square, counted those under arrest, making the total as indicated above. He too was released to be held under guard along with the man possessing the German Work Permit.

Don Giovanni Fondelli, the local priest, was one of those detained in the War Memorial Square. Anticipating what was about to take place, he gave absolution to all those around him. Those who were about to be massacred were then divided by the Germans into four separate groups, two such groups being taken under armed escort to two farms at the south-western end of the village, while the other two groups were taken to two other farms at the north-eastern end.

Of these four groups, one of 17 men was taken to the Pasquini farm. Although no one witnessed exactly what took place, it appears that all were shot, with the exception of three who managed to escape. Those shot were put close to a hayrick which was then ignited, in turn incinerating their corpses.

Another group of around 27 men was escorted to the Benini farm. Again, no one witnessed exactly what occurred, but the men were killed by machine-gun fire and put in a barn which was then put to the torch, the subsequent fire consuming their corpses.

A similar barbarous event took place at the Melani farm where some 22 men were slaughtered by machine-gun fire. As at the Benini farm the dead men were placed in a barn which was then set on fire in order to incinerate the corpses. But in this case, after the Germans had departed, some of the local inhabitants were successful in extinguishing the burning barn, recovering 22 charred and almost unrecognisable bodies from the debris.

At the Rossini farm much of what took place was witnessed by Ugo Mulinacci, aged 24 years, who was then living in Meleto, but was born at San Donato in Avane in the Comune di Figline Valdarno. When the Germans first entered Meleto early on the morning of the 4th July, Mulinacci, along with Luigi Bindelli, attempted to escape from the village. They had been fired at by the Germans while so doing, Bindelli being killed. Mulinacci who avoided being hit, then concealed himself under a layer of ashes in the bakehouse of the Rossini farm.

The 23 men about to be killed at this location were detained in an outbuilding at the farm, used as an oil presser. The first 5 of this group were taken outside the building and presumably shot, since the men failed to return, and machine-gun fire was heard by Augusto Sottani, one of the intended victims held in the presser room who managed to survive.

In fear of what was likely to happen to them, Sottani and another man, Ivan Pastorini, climbed through a small opening between the presser building and the adjacent oil storage room, Pastorini concealing himself behind an oil vat. Sottani climbed inside another oil vat pulling down the lid, but leaving a small gap through which he could see into the oil storage room and through it to the outside yard. Sottani heard several further bursts of machine-gun fire as small groups of men were taken from the presser building by the Germans and shot. A German soldier carrying out a perfunctory search of the oil storage room discovered Pastorini behind the oil vat and immediately shot him dead. Sottani, however, was not seen by the soldier who, soon after shooting Pastorini, fetched two bales of straw, placing one on top of Pastorini's corpse and the other on top of the oil vat in which Sottani was hiding and igniting them. From inside the oil vat Sottini witnessed the shooting of Pastorini and the igniting of the bales of straw. Although almost overcome by the heat and fumes from the burning straw on the top of the oil vat in which he was hiding, Sottani remained therein, witnessing the Germans heaping the bodies of their victims together in the yard outside, covering them with flammable material and igniting the same. Eventually Sottani could no longer withstand the heat within the oil vat and had to leave his refuge. On so doing he saw the straw on Pastorini's body still burning, but that he was beyond help. Fortunately, by this time, the Germans had left the Rossini farm, thus allowing Sottani to escape and hide in the nearby countryside. Mulinacci too saw the Germans piling and burning the bodies of those massacred, having crawled out from beneath the ashes in the bakehouse. Awaiting his opportunity when the soldiers had their backs turned towards him, he too escaped into the nearby countryside where he remained for some 10 days. In describing his occupation to his interrogators after his capture, Mulinacci said he was employed in the fabrication of 'mattonelli' (bricks of lignite), which were known locally as 'brichette' (briquettes), a term which was misconstrued as bricklayer.

After the shootings and burnings the Germans then looted and put to the torch many houses in Meleto, finally departing at about 15.00 hrs. and taking both Panichi and Matassini with them to Poggio Avane, about 1 km. from Meleto on the road to Santa Barbara. During the evening of the 4th July a German officer attempted to persuade Matassini to work for the Germans in Florence, but Matassini said that his mother was ill and he could not leave her. In the event, the officer extracted a promise from Matassini that as soon as his mother was well, he would report for work to the Germans in San Cipriano. Both Panichi and Matassini were then released and made their way back to Meleto.

A total of 93 Italian male civilians, residents of Meleto, were massacred by the Germans on the 4th July. Some of the women from Meleto and male survivors clearly identified the insignia on the uniforms of those carrying out the killings as being that of the Hermann Goering Division. The ages of those who died ranged from 15 to 80 years, and amongst them was the local priest, Don Giovanni Fondelli. His niece, Loretta Benini, became concerned at her uncle's absence, going to San Cipriano to enquire of the Germans there as to his whereabouts. They told her, 'All the men at Meleto were Partisans and have been killed'.

On the following day Don Giovacchino Meacci, the priest of San Cipriano, on hearing of the Meleto massacre, and that Don Fondelli was one of the victims, went to Meleto to visit the scenes of the massacres. He advised the women of the village to carry the remains of the victims to the new cemetery on the outskirts of Meleto, where burial services were arranged. Families who were able to identify their relatives had them interred in private graves, the unidentified remains being buried in ten communal graves. Particulars of those killed who had been identified and those presumed dead but unidentifiable were furnished to Don Meacci who entered such particulars in the Official Death Register of the Parish of Meleto.

Massacre at Castelnuovo dei Sabbioni

At about 07.00 hrs. on the morning of the 4th July the folk of Castelnuovo dei Sabbioni, at that time numbering about 1,500, were commencing what they thought would be another relatively peaceful, uneventful and pleasant early summer day. Their routine activities were suddenly disrupted by German soldiers from various locations under the command of an officer, most likely Leut. Wolf, who entered the village on foot. The transport used to convey the soldiers from Santa Barbara had been left concealed at the outskirts of the village so as to avoid giving any advance warning of their approach to the unsuspecting victims. Some testimonies confirm that a large squad of German soldiers reached Castelnuovo dei Sabbioni on foot along the road leading from Cavriglia. As at Meleto, all means of entrance to and exit from the village were sealed off by armed guards, while the main body of German troops broke up into small groups and commenced a house-to-house search of the village for its male civilians.

The men of Castelnuovo dei Sabbioni, many of whom were middle-aged or elderly, were seized by the Germans and taken to the Piazza IV Novembre, the main square of the village. Here they were herded together under armed guards commanded by the previously mentioned German officer. Coincidentally, the women of the village, along with their children, were ordered by the Germans to leave the confines of Castelnuovo dei Sabbioni without delay, and to seek refuge in the surrounding countryside.

Agostino Foggi, the local hairdresser, watched the men being assembled in the Piazza IV Novembre from the window of his house which overlooked the scene. He estimated the total number of male civilians under guard to be of the order of 60, of whom he recognised some three-quarters. These included the local priest, Don Ferrante Bagiardi. It is hardly surprising that Foggi himself escaped seizure by the Germans. The rooms of the houses around the Piazza IV Novembre formed real labyrinths where it was possible to hide. Moreover, the searches of the houses by the Germans were not particularly thorough, since they were certain that, in due time, they would capture the number of men they required. The Germans, in fact, seized more men than they thought necessary: subsequent to the massacre releasing some 40 or so men they had captured at the welfare centre. Not knowing the intentions of the Germans, many men, ironically, gave themselves voluntarily into the hands of the Germans, believing this to be less dangerous than to be found in hiding. Aldo Dini did so, although he subsequently escaped when it became clear that he was to be shot. Alas! Giuseppe Polverini, father of historian Emilio Polverini and Professor Leandro Polverini, also gave himself up to the Germans, losing his life as a consequence.

Although those under guard in the Piazza IV Novembre generally had not the slightest inkling as to their fate, Don Bagiardi appears to have soon realised what was about to happen, asking his fellow captives if they wished to take Communion. Most were surprised by Don Bagiardi's question, one man asking, 'But why Signor Priore must we die, what is it we have done?' To this the priest replied, 'Well, we do not know our fate.' Don Bagiardi then approached the German officer who was standing remote from the

Castelnuovo dei Sabbioni, Piazza IV Novembre. The time of the massacre.

Castelnuovo dei Sabbioni, Piazza IV Novembre.Site of the massacre. (September 1944).

Castelnuovo dei Sabbioni, Piazza IV Novembre. The Zannuccoli Palace (September 1944). (Aldo Dini escaped through its door to avoid being massacred.)

captives and their German guards, pleading with him to let the men go free since they were innocent of any wrongdoing. The officer rejected Don Bagiardi's pleading, adopting a cold and arrogant attitude, but acceding to the priest's request to give Communion to all the men held under guard. After so agreeing the officer was then heard to say, 'And then everyone against the wall', the wall indicated being that at the foot of the buttress of the road leading up to the entrance of the village church of San Donato a Castelnuovo, which overlooks the Piazza IV Novembre. A sister of the church was then permitted to fetch from the church and bring into the piazza the sacred container holding the species, which she handed to the priest. In due course Don Bagiardi began to administer Communion to the 60 or so men who were about to die, thus enabling them to comprehend what was about to take place and accept their fate in a calm and resolute fashion.

Some 10–15 minutes prior to the massacre the men held by the Germans were still not all lined up against the retaining wall which supported the buttress of the church. Many were in the shadow of the trees on the left side of the piazza, some standing, and some sitting on the wall which acted as the parapet of the ravine below. Most, if not all, were still unaware of the intentions of the Germans.

In the mêlée Piero Galante bumped against the closed door of the Zannuccoli Palace with his back. The door opened and Galante passed through it without being seen by the Germans, and hid behind the shutters of the half-open door. Shortly after, Estevan Nannoni and Nello Donati also attempted to escape, but were seen by the Germans who shot and killed them. As Don Bagiardi administered Communion to the men herded in the piazza, Dario Ussi threw himself backwards off the wall on which he was sitting, falling some 4 metres below to hide in a tunnel in the base of the wall. There he remained, accompanied by Orlando Goli, who had either just followed or preceded him, until the Germans had departed. Following Communion, the rest of the men were ordered to line up against the retaining wall beneath the church, and while being pushed into line by the Germans, Aldo Dini and Mario Berretti slipped through the half-open door of the Zannuccoli Palace, fleeing to its rear and plunging headlong down the slope to the wall of the dam below. Dini then swam across the stretch of water retained by the dam wall, while Berretti, who was unable to swim, descended along the dam wall to the bed of the underlying stream. Dini and Berretti remained so hidden until the Germans had left the immediate vicinity. Meanwhile, Piero Galante hid in a cellar of the Zannuccoli Palace itself, equally avoiding detection.

The Germans, meanwhile, lined up the rest of the men under guard in the Piazza IV Novembre with their backs to the wall beneath the church, setting up a machine-gun some 20 metres in front of them. Without enquiry, hearing or trial the officer then gave the order for the machine-gunner to open fire on the group of men. The gunner fired several bursts at the men, continuing until all appeared to be dead. The time was between 09.30 hrs. and 10.00 hrs. Subsequent to this major shooting, several small groups of Italian male civilians were brought into the Piazza IV Novembre by German soldiers who had been continuing with the house-to-house search. These small groups of men were also machine-gunned down as was the larger assembly previously.

When the shooting was at last over, the German soldiers were ordered by their officer to heap the bodies of the dead against the wall in front of which they had been shot. Furniture was then taken from nearby houses and placed on and around the corpses, the whole being saturated with petrol and ignited. The funeral pyre, which was lit around 16.00 hrs., burned fiercely for about an hour, continuing to burn intermittently throughout the following night.

All the dreadful events that took place in the Piazza IV Novembre were witnessed by the village hairdresser, Agostino Foggi, from the window of his house. Although petrified by what he had seen he, no doubt, gave heartfelt thanks to his maker that he had not been discovered and then shot by the Germans. Two other inhabitants of Castel-

Cemetery of Castelnuovo dei Sabbioni: Communal tomb for the victims of the massacres of 4th and 11th July, 1944. (1st November, 1944.).

nuovo dei Sabbioni witnessed in part the shootings. The first, Signora Ernesta Borchi, was in the Via Camonti and about 15 metres to the rear of the machine-gun when her husband, Zanobi, aged 65 years, was shot down. The other was Signorina Pia Bonci who, from the garden of her house overlooking the Piazza IV Novembre, saw the massacre of the large group of men which included her father Adolfo, aged 67 years, and her 34 years old brother Fortunato. During the next morning Signorina Bonci went into the Piazza IV Novembre and amongst the corpses identified the body of her father by means of an unburnt leg of the trousers she knew him to be wearing when he was shot, similarly identifying her brother from his unburnt boots.

Not satisfied with the shootings in the Piazza IV Novembre, the Germans in their house-to-house search came across Roberto Filandi. He was 74 years of age and bedridden through being paralysed. His wife left him alive and in his bed around 07.00 hrs. When she returned about three hours later she found him dead on the bedroom floor, having been killed by a bullet in the left side of his neck. It appeared that a German soldier had dragged Filandi from his bed with the intention of taking him to the Piazza IV Novembre, but on discovering that Filandi was paralysed shot him there and then. Another male civilian, Remigio Neri, aged 66 years, was shot in the head and killed that day. He was alive at 08.00 hrs. when his wife, Anita, left their house to go into the nearby countryside with the other women of the village, Remigio saying he would hide from the Germans in the grotto at the rear of their house. The Germans found him there and shot him, his body being discovered by his wife at around 20.00 hrs. when she returned.

The exact time at which the Germans left Castelnuovo dei Sabbioni has not been determined, but can be put at around 17.00 hrs. By this time most of the corpses had been burnt beyond recognition, although a few, as with Adolfo and Fortunato Bonci, were identified from unburnt fragments of their clothing. The funeral pyre was left undisturbed until the 11th July when the remains were conveyed to the local cemetery for interment in a communal grave. Although many women were in attendance, the operation itself was carried out by some thirty men, all volunteers, who had been recruited by Don Aldo Cuccoli from San Pancrazio and Ugo Mercante of S.M.V. The work commenced around 05.00 hrs., with some of the men digging the communal grave in the cemetery, and the others removing the remains of the bodies from the piazza. Some of the cadavers were wrapped in bed sheets provided by the local women, and all were conveyed to the cemetery in horse drawn carts furnished by Mario Biagioni.

*Castelnuovo dei Sab-
bioni, Piazza IV
Novembre.
Bishop of Fiesole,
Mons. Giovanni
Giorgis inaugurates
the Chapel in
memory of the fallen
on the 2nd
Anniversary of the
Massacre.
(4th July, 1946.)*

*Cemetery of
Castelnuovo dei
Sabbioni: defini-
tive arrange-
ment of the
communal tomb
of those massa-
cred 4th and 11th
July, 1944.*

*Cemetery of Castelnuovo dei Sabbioni: Photographs of the
victims of the massacres placed on the communal tomb.
(August 1975.)*

Massacre at San Martino

The small village of San Martino no longer exists, having been swallowed up in the expansion of the nearby opencast lignite mining operation. But in 1944 it lay on a side road about 2½ km. distant from Castelnuovo dei Sabbioni. Its population in early July 1944 amounted to about 100 souls, including a small number of evacuees. At about 05.30 hrs. on the morning of the 4th July two German military vehicles entered the village from the direction of Santa Barbara. One of these vehicles was a Fiat truck having a rear mounted machine- gun and carrying German soldiers armed with sub-machine-guns, the other being a small Fiat car with Ober-Leut. Danisch and his driver, Casuski, as occupants. The arrival of the Germans at San Martino was observed by a farmworker, Renato Cappelli, and the local Priest, Don Giuseppe Cicali.

The Germans posted guards in order to prevent any entrance to or escape from the village, then splitting up into small groups to carry out a house-to-house search. In due course they rounded up and assembled by the village church 14 Italian male civilians, including Don Cicali. Up to this point in time the Germans had provided no explanation for their activities. With the 14 men under guard by 4 soldiers and Ober-Leut. Danisch in attendance, the two German military vehicles were drawn up in the Neri farmyard opposite the church. Through his binoculars Danisch observed some movement in nearby woodland and ordered the soldier manning the machine-gun in the Fiat truck to fire several bursts into the woodland where it was suspected local Partisans were hiding.

Historian Emilio Polverini puts forward the following hypothesis in explanation of the above events. He believes that it was quite unusual for a German officer of Ober-Leut. Danisch's rank to go to such a small place as San Martino. He also takes the view that the Fiat truck with its machine-gun and the 14 captives were deliberately displayed in full view so as to be seen by the Partisans hiding in the overlooking woodland. All this was an attempt by Danisch to obtain the release of a German colonel captured by the formidable 'Castellani' Partisan formation whose base was near San Martino.

It was at about this time that the 14 men seized by the Germans were informed that if they were Partisans they would be shot, but if not, then they would be released.

Around 09.00 hrs. Ober-Leut. Danisch left San Martino in his car, driven by Ca-suski. An hour or so later the car returned to San Martino, again driven by Casuski, but with a German soldier interpreter rather than Danisch as the passenger. Following a brief interrogation, 4 out of the 14 men detained were told by Casuski that they would be held as hostages against Partisan attack and ordered to get into the Fiat truck. The 4 hostages, Giuseppe Bruno, Giorgio Capitani, Isaia Innocenti and Derlindo Bucchi were then driven away under guard in the direction of San Cipriano, the other 10 men who had been detained by the Germans apparently being released. The relatives of the 4 men taken hostage were told by the German soldier interpreter who accompanied Ca-

San Martino In Pianfranzese: 'Madonnino' in memory of the four victims of 4th July, 1944, erected adjoining the site of the threshing shed in which the men were massacred.

suski, 'If you want to hear news of your relatives come to San Cipriano'. En route to San Cipriano, in the vicinity of Pianfranzese, the Fiat truck carrying the 4 men from San Martino stopped to pick up a further 16 civilian males who had been taken as hostages by the Germans. All 20 men were taken to the headquarters of Ober-Leut. Danisch at San Cipriano where they were detained, their arrival being witnessed by Fabbrini, Lambardini, Quartucci and Verzetti who the reader will recall were already held by the Germans. These latter 4 men also recognised the Warrant Officer in charge of the newly arrived hostages as being the same Warrant Officer who had arrested them.

Still in the vicinity of San Martino, the Germans rounded up a further 6 civilian males at around 11.00 hrs., detaining them in the Bigazzi farmyard in the centre of the village. Of these 5 men, 3 were from the group of 10 which had previously been released by the Germans. In the early afternoon of the same day, 2 of the 5 were put into oxen drawn carts commandeered by the Germans and taken under guard to Poggio Avane where they met up with Panichi and Matassini who had been arrested at Meleto earlier that day. Along with Panichi and Matassini these 2 men were released at Poggio Avane by the Germans during the evening of the 4th July. The 3 remaining local men, Pasquale Borgheresi, aged 58 years, Amedeo Ermini, aged 55 years and Giovan Battista Cappelli, aged 63 years, were then taken by the Germans, together with a fourth man of unknown identity, to the Neri farmyard where they were bayoneted to death. The corpses were then covered with straw which was soaked with petrol and ignited.

Before leaving San Martino in the mid-afternoon the German soldiers set light to several of the properties in the village including the Neri farm and the home of Don Cicali, the local priest. After being released by the Germans, Don Cicali took refuge in the nearby woods and from there saw the fires in the village. Returning to San Martino after the Germans had departed he found his own house on fire and discovered in the Neri farmyard the four corpses still burning, all of whom had extensive bayonet wounds, with Pasquale Borgheresi having had his throat cut from ear to ear. Don Cicali informed the relatives of Borgheresi, Ermini and Cappelli of his discovery, they, in turn, recovering the corpses from the fire and identifying the same. It appears that the four corpses were left in the Neri farmyard until the 12th July, when they were interred in a communal grave in the local cemetery, with Don Cicali conducting the burial service.

The identity of the fourth man put to death remains a mystery. Soon after the massacre he was thought to be Giuseppe Corsi of Villa Cetinale, near San Cipriano, but this was subsequently disproved.

Local legend has it that the unidentified fourth man was a German soldier put to death by his own countrymen for refusing to take part in the massacre at Castelnuovo dei Sabbioni earlier that day. But since this more acceptable although fanciful story cannot be substantiated it has been discounted by historian Emilio Polverini.

The 4 men taken hostage by the Germans at San Martino were individually interrogated at around 14.00 hrs. on the afternoon of the 4th July by Ober-Leut. Danisch, speaking through the German soldier interpreter who had accompanied Casuski at San Martino. All were questioned generally about Partisan activity in the area, with Capitani also being asked if he knew the whereabouts of any German military vehicles captured by Vannini's Partisan group. With Danisch convinced that none of the 4 men had the information he required, Capitani was immediately released, although the other 3 men were taken back to their place of detention. At about 18.00 hrs. the hostage Innocenti was again questioned by Danisch through the medium of the German soldier interpreter. Innocenti was asked if he had reflected on the answers he had given during his earlier interrogation. He insisted that he had answered truthfully and to the best of his knowledge, but was told by Danisch that if it was discovered he had not done so then he would be shot. Following a conversation held in German between Ober-Leut. Danisch and the German soldier interpreter, the latter turned to Innocenti and said 'The Captain is very pleased with the way things have gone at San Martino today, so you can go now'. All the other 18 hostages, which excluded the 3 taken at Meleto, Paolo Verzetti and the man unknown, were also released, one of those arrested at San Martino, Dr Giuseppe Bruno, hearing the German soldier interpreter say, 'You are free to go now, you will be able to see what happened at Meleto'.

Massacre at Massa dei Sabbioni

Massa dei Sabbioni is a small village which in July 1944 had a population of around 100, and is located some 1 1/2 km. from Castelnuovo dei Sabbioni. About noon on the 4th July roughly 20 German soldiers armed with rifles and a machine-gun entered Massa dei Sabbioni from the direction of Castelnuovo dei Sabbioni. It is most likely that these German soldiers were part of the unit which had carried out the massacre at Castelnuovo dei Sabbioni earlier that day.

Signorina Milena Baldi was standing at her garden gate and saw the Germans arrive at Massa dei Sabbioni, halting in the Piazza della Chiesa in front of the village church and directly opposite the Baldi house. Some of the soldiers asked Signorina Baldi for food which she provided when they entered the house. The remainder of the soldiers then split into small groups and began a house-to-house search of the village looking for civilian males.

When the German troops arrived in the village, the civilian population had not yet learned of the massacre at Castelnuovo dei Sabbioni. The absence of a large part of the inhabitants of Massa dei Sabbioni, both male and female, arose because of an exchange of small arms fire between two German soldiers and Partisans in the nearby vicinity of Casa Pianale during the afternoon of the 3rd July. The inhabitants of Massa dei Sabbioni, fearing reprisals by the Germans, took refuge in the nearby woods.

Notwithstanding this major evacuation, the Germans captured some thirteen Italian males, but ten of these managed to escape in the confusion when two allied aircraft flying over Massa dei Sabbioni opened fire on the German troops. Don Morini, the local priest who was known to support the local Partisans, and Dante Pagliazzi, an orphan living locally with relatives, together with Giuseppe Virboni, also a native of the village and a road labourer, were, however, detained by the Germans.

While the Germans were eating in her house Signorina Baldi saw Pagliazzi under guard by other Germans soldiers in the Piazza della Chiesa. As they were leaving the Baldi house one of the soldiers told Signorina Baldi that she must leave the house because it was going to be set on fire. She and her father, the latter not being found by the Germans, then left their house to take refuge in nearby woods.

Another local woman, Signorina Silvana Bianconi, was asked to bring some wine from her house to the German soldiers in the Piazza della Chiesa. This she did and saw Don Morini, Pagliazzi and Virboni there under detention by the Germans. She too was told by the Germans to leave the village as they were going to burn down the houses.

Just after 12.30 hrs. two of the Germans soldiers guarding Don Morini, Pagliazzi and Virboni escorted them to outside the local barber's shop, then unoccupied, at the far end of the main village street, some 20 metres beyond which, on the opposite side of the street was a building known locally as the barn Scala. While outside the barber's shop, Don Morini said to the two Germans, 'I am a Priest and an Apostle. I have done no wrong.' In reply, one of the soldiers told Don Morini, 'It is not important, we are taking you into that barn, but no harm will befall you'. One of the soldiers then took the priest from outside the barber's shop into the barn Scala, the other soldier escorting Pagliazzi and Virboni into the barber's shop. After a short interval of time Virboni went to the open door of the barber's shop, since he had become anxious with regard to the welfare of the priest, and saw the soldier who was with Don Morini in the doorway of the barn Scala stab the latter several times in the throat with a bayonet. The priest was seen by Virboni to fall to the ground mortally wounded.

The soldier escorting the two men in the barber's shop made no attempt to prevent Virboni from going to the door of the shop and seeing Don Morini killed at the barn Scala since the soldier knew that both the men he had under guard were due to suffer a similar fate. At this point Virboni realised that he too was in immediate danger of being killed and shouted for Pagliazzi to come to the door of the barber's shop, which he did, accompanied by the German soldier. Virboni then made a dash for freedom, and although fired at by the soldiers, managed to escape unharmed to hide in the nearby woods. It was this incident that was witnessed by Signorina Baldi and her father as they too left the village to take refuge in the woods.

Pagliazzi was less fortunate than his companion. Although there are no witnesses, it can be properly assumed that he too was taken from the barber's shop to the barn Scala and bayoneted to death. The bodies of Don Morini and Pagliazzi were then placed together in the barn Scala which contained a substantial quantity of straw, the straw being ignited by the German soldiers and the two bodies incinerated. At about 13.00 hrs. Isaia Baldi (not the father of Milena Baldi), who lived in Massa dei Sabbioni and who was hiding from the Germans in some elevated woodland about 1/2 km. from the barn Scala, saw smoke and flames coming from the barn which continued to burn fiercely for about 3 hours.

Massa dei Sabbioni. centre left: Chapel erected on site of Barn Scala where Don Morini and Dante Pagliazzi were killed on 4th July, 1944. Near right is the old Barber's shop, now renovated. (1st July, 1979.)

The precise time of departure from Massa dei Sabbioni by the Germans is not known, but before they departed they put to the torch the house of Signorina Baldi who had first witnessed their arrival at the village.

On the following day, the 5th July, Virboni came across another local man, Giuseppe Tanzi, with whom he was acquainted, also hiding from the Germans in the woods, and told him of the happenings of the previous day in the village. Because of what he had learned from Virboni, Tanzi returned forthwith to Massa dei Sabbioni and visited the barn Scala. Although the door of the barn had been destroyed by the fire and the barn roof had collapsed, Tanzi searched among the debris and discovered the mutilated corpse of Dante Pagliazzi whom he had known well. Further searching revealed the headless and limbless corpse of Don Morini. With the help of Giuliano Pagliazzi, Dante Pagliazzi's cousin, Tanzi, wrapped both remains in a sheet and carried them to the local cemetery.

Because the custodian of the local cemetery and grave digger, Guido Magnelli, was also hiding from the Germans in the woods the two bodies were not buried immediately but left on the ground near to the mortuary of the cemetery. Tanzi and Giuliano Pagliazzi went back from the cemetery to the woods to continue in hiding from the Germans. There they met up with Magnelli and informed him of the two unburied corpses in the cemetery. However, it was not until the 6th/7th July that the gravedigger returned to the village to bury the two bodies in a communal grave, no priest being present at the interment.

It was about three weeks after the massacres at Massa dei Sabbioni that Don Cuccoli, the assistant priest of San Pancrazio and friend of the murdered Don Morini, with the help of Luigi Morini, made a further search of the barn Scala. A knife and a rosary both of which Luigi Morini identified as belonging to his dead brother were found amongst the debris. Also discovered was the remains of a human skull, almost certainly that of Don Morini, which had been severed from the torso in the bayonet attack carried out by the German soldier. The priest's limbs were not found as it appeared that these had been destroyed in the fire when the barn roof collapsed on to them. On the day of its discovery the skull was put into a cardboard box and buried on top of the two corpses in the communal grave of Don Morini and Dante Pagliazzi, with Don Cuccoli and Luigi Morini in attendance.

A number of significant happenings related to the massacres are now recorded.

Disappearance of Giuseppe Corsi

The reader will recall that one of the four men massacred at San Martino, and not positively identified, was initially thought to be Giuseppe Corsi, a landowner, of Villa Cetinale, near San Cipriano. The Villa Cetinale was taken over by a German General and his staff on the 2nd July, 1944, with Corsi and his wife Marie moving to alternative and temporary accommodation at Caiano. On the evening of the 3rd July, Guiseppe Corsi left Caiano to travel the 15 km. or so to the Villa Cetinale in order to collect some medicine he required, but had left there. In the event, Corsi failed to reach the Villa Catinale, having been seized by the Germans at about 08.30 hrs. on the morning of the 4th July on the road between Muccherie di Castelnuovo and Massa dei Sabbioni. He was taken to Castelnuovo dei Sabbioni and shot by the Germans along with many others at around 09.30 hrs. on the morning of that day.

Because of the absence of her husband, Signora Corsi made her way to the Villa Cetinale on the 4th July to enquire there as to his whereabouts. En route she saw the fires started by the Germans burning at Meleto and Castelnuovo dei Sabbioni. On her arrival at the Villa Cetinale Signora Corsi was refused permission to speak with the German General in residence, a Warrant Officer telling her that she should contact Ober-Leut. Danisch at San Cipriano and providing her with a note to give to Danisch. It is unclear where Signora Corsi spent the night, but during the following day she met up with Danisch outside his headquarters, the officer informing her that several prisoners had been shot because they were Partisans, and that he had no one in custody as old as her husband, who was 61. Having got no satisfaction, Signora Corsi returned to her temporary home at Caiano, subsequently learning of her husband's death at Castelnuovo dei Sabbioni.

Release of Hostages held at San Cipriano

Late in the afternoon of the 5th July the three men taken hostage at Meleto three days earlier, together with Paolo Verzetti and the man unknown to the other four, all of whom were still being held in custody by the Germans at San Cipriano, were told by Ober-Leut. Danisch about the massacre of civilians at Meleto on the previous day. In explanation for the killings Danisch said they had been carried out because of the destruction by Partisans of several important road bridges in the area. Danisch went on to say that he was most pleased with some information which he had recently received, and as a consequence all five were free to go. Fabbrini, one of the five hostages, then requested that each be given a certificate signed by Danisch saying that they had been released by him, this being in anticipation of any future arrest by the Germans. Danisch acceded to Fabbrini's request, the men then leaving San Cipriano for their respective homes.

Arrival at Santa Barbara of 4th Hermann Goering Engineering Battalion

Two German officers, one a Hauptmann and the other a Tenente, established themselves in the flat immediately below that of the surveyor, Bruno Sabelli, at Santa Barbara during the 6th July. Both officers belonged to the 4th Hermann Goering Engineering Battalion. In conversation with the Tenente, and in the light of what he had been told by Warrant Officer Fräulein during the evening of the 4th July, subsequent to the massacres, Sabelli asked why the Germans had killed civilians in the villages of Meleto, Castelnuovo dei Sabbioni, San Martino and Massa dei Sabbioni. In reply the Tenente told Sabelli that a few days earlier, when he and the Hauptmann were at the German Command Headquarters at nearby San Giovanni Valdarno, two Italian Fascists had reported to the Commanding Officer that all of the above four villages were full of Partisans. It was for this reason that the massacres of the 4th July had been carried out.

Because these two officers belonged to an Engineering Battalion it is more than likely that they supervised the destruction on the 7th July of Castelnuovo Power Station, and that of the principal items of equipment at the nearby lignite mining complex which was carried out around the same period of time.

Movement of German Troops at Montegonzi

Again it will be recalled that the three trucks of the Hermann Goering 'Flak' Unit, commanded by Major Seiler, left Montegonzi carrying troops on the evening of the 3rd July, returning at around 20.00 hrs. on the following day. Although Don Grifoni, the local priest, saw the trucks carrying soldiers depart on the 3rd July, he only saw the empty trucks on their return. It is, of course, likely that the soldiers had already debussed when he observed the trucks on the evening of the 4th July.

There can be no doubt that during their absence from Montegonzi the Germans took part in some or all of the massacres carried out on the 4th July.

During the next day, the 5th July, Major Seiler's unit left Montegonzi for an unknown destination, being replaced on the evening of the same day by another Hermann Goering Unit of about the same strength, and commanded by Major Graf. This latter unit remained at Montegonzi until the 15th July, and can reasonably be assumed to have played a part in the further killings described immediately below.

Massacres at Poggio alle Valli, San Pancrazio, Corneto and Le Matole

In the wake of the massacres of a total of 173 Italian male civilians at the villages of Meleto, Castelnuovo dei Sabbioni, San Martino and Massa dei Sabbioni on the 4th July, the Germans realised that most of those put to death were too old to have been active Partisans. From this they concluded that those younger Italian males who might well be engaged in Partisan activities against the German forces, and who had so far escaped the recent reprisals, were likely to be hiding in the woods and mountains surrounding the various villages. It will be recalled that Ivario Viligiardi, who had been arrested near Cavriglia by the Germans on the 29th June on suspicion of being a Partisan, disclosed to Rudi Groner, a member of Leut. Wolf's anti-Partisan Unit, when under interrogation at the Scuola di Musica in Terranuova on the 30th June, that the leader of the local Partisans was called Nello Vannini, that he came from Le Matole, and members of his group could be found in the vicinity of Poggio alle Valli.

As a result of the foregoing, the Germans decided to put out a drag-net in an area of about 2 km. diameter with its centre some 3 km. south of Castelnuovo dei Sabbioni. There can be no doubt that the German anti-Partisan Unit commanded by Leut. Wolf carried out this search which resulted in the four further deaths of Italian male civilians by shooting at or near Poggio alle Valli, San Pancrazio and Corneto on the 8th July.

During the preparations for this operation, Ivario Viligiardi, who had been incarcerated in the garage of the Villa Silvano at Bagno a Ripoli, was escorted from the garage and put on board one of two German military vehicles, both loaded with soldiers armed with rifles, during the evening of the 7th July. Present was the German officer who had interrogated Viligiardi three days earlier and Rudi Groner.

Before setting off Groner informed Viligiardi that the force was bound for Poggio alle Valli, and that he, Viligiardi was to guide them there. Moreover, in order to disguise his identity, Viligiardi was made to wear a German steel helmet. The two trucks went south from Bagno a Ripoli, joining Route 69 at Incisa and continuing south to San Giovanni Valdarno, a distance of some 35 km. from their starting point. From San Giovanni Valdarno, a route was taken through San Cipriano, Santa Barbara and Castelnuovo dei Sabbioni to a point about 3 km. from Poggio alle Valli, probably on the southern outskirts of Castelnuovo dei Sabbioni. Here the soldiers dismounted from the trucks and proceeded on foot towards Poggio alle Valli. According to Viligiardi, after travelling for about 1 km. from where the trucks were parked he was ordered to go no further and was left under the guard of a soldier whilst the remainder of the force, including Groner, and under command of the officer, went on towards Poggio alle Valli in the direction indicated by Viligiardi.

Massacre at Poggio alle Valli

Fedora Bandinelli, the daughter of Ugo Bandinelli, who had a farmhouse at Poggio alle Valli, states that three armed Germans soldiers approached and entered the farmhouse demanding food at around 21.00 hrs. on the 7th July. Immediately the soldiers were seen approaching, Ugo Bandinelli left his farmhouse by a rear door to hide from the Germans in the nearby woodland. What happened then is not known in detail, but at some point in time, after darkness had fallen, Fedora Bandinelli is said to have been raped by one or more of the soldiers. Following this incident the remainder of the Bandinelli family, including his sick wife Rosa, joined Ugo in the woods so as to avoid any further confrontation with the Germans.

Around 06.00 hrs. on the morning of the 8th July, Ugo Bandinelli left his family in the woods with the intention of returning to his farm to feed and attend to his animals. While at the farm he was seen and shot dead by a German raiding party comprising some 30 soldiers.

Clearly, this raiding party was that which Viligiardi had directed to Poggio alle Valli. Viligiardi says that about an hour after he had been left under the guard of a soldier during the approach to Poggio alle Valli he heard the sound of rifle fire coming from the direction of that hamlet. It seems most likely that this was the rifle fire which killed Bandinelli.

It was at about 14.30 hrs. on the 8th July when Maria Brocchi, a close neighbour of the Bandinellis, who kept rabbits in a hut in the Bandinelli farmyard, returned to her home from spending a night in the woods and went to feed her rabbits. In the vicinity of her home and the Bandinelli farm she saw the 30 strong German raiding party, one of whom advised her to take refuge in the woods for several days. Acting on this advice Maria Brocchi collected some food from her home and was making her way through the Bandinelli farmyard when she saw the body of Ugo Bandinelli lying face upwards with a bullet wound in his head. Because of the presence of the German soldiers Maria Brocchi did not examine the body closely, but to her Ugo Bandinelli appeared dead, as indeed he was.

Maria Brocchi then continued into the woods, eventually meeting up that day with Rosa Bandinelli and her family. But because Rosa was unwell, Maria Brocchi decided against telling her at that time of the likely death of her husband.

Very early on the morning of the 11th July, after spending four consecutive nights in the woods, Maria Brocchi again approached her home. Since the Germans were no longer present she went initially into her home, then making her way to the hut in the Bandinelli farmyard in order to feed her rabbits. On entering the farmyard she immediately noticed that the body of Ugo Bandinelli was no longer where she had last seen it, and that the nearby barn had been partly destroyed by fire. Because she was allowed by the Bandinellis to keep some of her personal belongings in the barn, Maria Brocchi entered the building to see if these belongings had been damaged by the fire. While looking around for her property she came across the badly burnt but still identifiable body of Ugo Bandinelli. Maria Brocchi at once returned to the hiding place of the Bandinelli family in the woods and told Rosa Bandinelli of what she had seen at the farm. At about 14.00 hrs. that day Rosa Bandinelli, accompanied by Maria Brocchi, returned to the farm to verify that the badly burnt corpse was that of her husband Ugo. Both women then went back to their hiding place in the woods where they remained until British troops arrived in the area on or about the 22nd July.

It is evident that the German soldiers comprising the raiding party dragged the dead body of Ugo Bandinelli into the barn from the place in the farmyard where he had been shot and then set light to the straw contained in the barn, the resulting conflagration badly burning Ugo Bandinelli's corpse, as was intended, as well as virtually gutting the two storey barn building.

Ugo Bandinelli's remains were buried at the cemetery of nearby Montaio on the 23rd July, with the local priest, Don Veneri, officiating.

In the preamble to the massacres at Poggio alle Valli, San Pancrazio, Corneto and Le Matole, it will be recalled that Ivario Viligiardi said that he was kept under guard during the evening of the 7th July at a distance of about 1 km. from where the Germans had parked their trucks, the soldiers then going on to Poggio alle Valli in the direction Viligiardi indicated. In an initial account of his movements Viligiardi said that later the same evening the German raiding party which had been to Poggio alle Valli and shot Ugo Bandinelli picked him up along with his guard on their way back to the trucks, then returning to Bagno a Ripoli. In due course Viligiardi modified his account, saying that he, along with the raiding party, remained in the area just south of Castelnuovo dei Sabbioni for another day or two. In fact, they did not leave the area to return to Bagno a Ripoli until the evening of the 11th July.

Massacre at San Pancrazio

Around mid-morning on the 8th July, three male civilians, inhabitants of San Pancrazio, a small village about 1 km. from Poggio alle Valli, were hiding from the Germans in the woods surrounding their village. These three men, Enrico Sani, Faustino Perini and Ivan Gelli were taken by surprise when a group of about 20 German soldiers armed with rifles approached them from the rear and ordered them to 'Halt!'. Sani immediately dropped to the ground and crawled into some nearby dense foliage. At the same moment the soldiers opened fire, both Perini and Gelli being hit and killed. Although Sani heard a number of rifle bullets strike the ground near to him he was not hit and escaped, returning to San Pancrazio that evening to tell the relatives of Perini and Gelli of the encounter with the Germans earlier that day.

On the morning of the following day, the 9th July, Antinesca, the wife of Faustino Perini, by this time much worried about the protracted absence of her husband, went into the woods to the place where she knew he had been hiding. To her horror she discovered him where he had fallen, with multiple bullet wounds in the head and spine. Some 100 metres from her dead husband, Antinesca also found the corpse of Ivan Gelli, who was her nephew. He had been killed by a bullet wound in the centre of his forehead.

Both corpses were removed from the woods by relatives and interred in a common grave in the cemetery at San Pancrazio on the 10th July, the burial service being conducted by Don Cuccoli.

Massacre at Corneto

Pellegrino Vannini, an 82 years old retired miner, was living at the Fabiani farm at Corneto, another small village also about 1 km. from Poggio alle Valli and some 1 1/2 km. from San Pancrazio. Just before noon on the same day that Faustino Perini and Ivan Gelli were shot dead at San Pancrazio a group of German soldiers all armed with rifles came over the crest of a hill about 300 metres from the Fabiani farmhouse and saw Vannini working in one of the fields. A number of the soldiers raised their rifles and fired at Vannini, killing him instantly. On reaching the body of Vannini and seeing life to be extinct the soldiers left him where he had fallen, continuing on to Monastero.

Signora Gioconda Fabiani witnessed the shooting from the doorway of her farmhouse, and as soon as the German soldiers had disappeared from view she went to Vannini to see that he was indeed dead, the top of his head having been shattered by the rifle bullets fired by the soldiers.

Vannini's body was recovered from the field where he had been killed, and on the following day, the 9th July, he was buried at San Pancrazio cemetery, with Don Cuccoli again conducting the burial service.

Following the further shootings of male civilians by the Germans at Poggio alle Valli, San Pancrazio and Corneto, as described above, Ivario Viligiardi admitted that he was increasingly threatened by Groner, which resulted in him, Viligiardi, disclosing to the Germans that Nello Vannini, the leader of the Partisan group 3rd Company of Chiatti was a native of Le Matole, the district on the fringe of Castelnuovo dei Sabbioni where Vannini's relatives still lived. Moreover, it was generally acknowledged that the inhabitants of Le Matole were strongly pro-Partisan. As a consequence of Viligiardi's disclosures the raiding party from Leut. Wolf's anti-Partisan Unit organised yet a further brutal atrocity.

Massacre at Le Matole

In the late afternoon of the 11th July the German raiding party was directed to Le Matole by Viligiardi who, since he was a native of Castelnuovo dei Sabbioni and, therefore, likely to be recognised, for purposes of disguise was made to wear a German steel helmet and a camouflaged mackintosh.

Between 17.00 and 18.00 hrs. on that day the Germans, proceeding on foot, surrounded the district of Le Matole. A number of male civilians who were working on the construction of an air raid shelter in woodland below and adjacent to Le Matole were seized by the German troops, as were others during a house-to-house search.

A local woman, Signora Libera Benucci, whose husband Nello Benucci, a 31 years old labourer, had been taken prisoner by the Germans, together with his brother Dante Benucci, aged 30 years, pleaded with one of the German soldiers to release those who had been apprehended. The soldier replied in the negative, adding, 'They are all Partisans here'. Signora Benucci then attempted to approach and talk with her husband, but was barred from doing so by a man dressed in German uniform. This man spoke to Signora Benucci in Italian, she then recognising him as Ivario Viligiardi and being aware that he had been arrested by the Germans near Cavriglia almost two weeks previously on suspicion of being a Partisan.

The men arrested were then required to produce their identification documents. As a result, one man, Pellegrino Bartoli, aged 65 years, was released, the Germans saying that he was too old to be a member of a Partisan band. In due course 12 men, aged between 21 and 48 years, were selected from the group under arrest, the remainder being released. The Germans then escorted these 12 men towards the intended place of execution, which at the time was cultivated land. Knowing what had happened at Castelnuovo dei Sabbioni and elsewhere during the previous week, the 12 men sensed the intention of the Germans, one managing to get away from his captors and hide in a bush. As the remaining 11 men approached the selected killing ground they started to flee, separating and running in different directions. The Germans opened fire with a sub-machine-gun at those in flight, immediately hitting and either killing or wounding 9 of the men. Some of the men who had been hit in the initial burst of machine-gun fire, although having fallen to the ground, still showed signs of life. Those that did so were finally dispatched by a German soldier shooting them in the head, using a pistol.

The remaining 2 men, Angiolo Redditi and Osvaldo Innocenti, running down the road towards Cavriglia, were fired at by the Germans, Redditi being hit and wounded, and then holding on to Innocenti for support. In order to avoid being caught and shot by the Germans, Innocenti freed himself from Redditi and continued to run down the road in the direction of Cavriglia, eventually hiding under a bridge to save himself from certain death. What then happened to Redditi is unclear. The historian, Emilio Polverini, who has thoroughly researched the massacre, says that he fell into a ditch at the side of the road, crawling from the ditch into a drainage channel beneath the road to hide. It was here, according to Polverini, that Redditi was found dead by his mother in the early hours of the 12th July. But in her statement of the 30th October, 1944 to the British Special Investigation Branch, Redditi's mother, Amelia Gioli, says that she discovered the body of her son amongst those of the other 9 victims of the shooting during the evening of the 11th July.

Historian Emilio Polverini draws attention to the fact that none of the ten witnesses to the massacre, and who made statements to the British S.I.B. between the 30th October and the 2nd November, 1944, including Amelia Gioli Redditi, mother of Angiolo Redditi, made any mention of the escape of Osvaldo Innocenti and Angiolo Redditi, the wounding by the Germans of Redditi, and his eventual death and discovery by his mother in a drainage channel on the morning of the 12th July, 1944.

Polverini accounts for these omissions as arising from the technique utilised by the S.I.B. for collecting and editing such statements, but acknowledges that the S.I.B. were not concerned with the precise minutiae of the massacre, but only in securing proof of the killings in order that the Germans involved could be accused as war criminals. Moreover, most of the witnesses, and particularly those who had lost relatives in the massacre, were consumed with grief, and perhaps had neither the ability, personality nor interest to insist on the exact detailing by the S.I.B. of what had actually occurred.

It would appear that Emilio Polverini's observations regarding the taking of statements by the S.I.B., and his interpretation of the events surrounding the death of Angiolo Redditi are equally valid. The latter is confirmed by the fact that although Angiolo Redditi's name appears on the main memorial to the 10 men massacred by the Germans at Le Matole, a small and separate memorial to Redditi is located adjacent to the drainage channel in which he was found dead.

This brutal massacre was witnessed by Signora Libera Benucci who was hiding some 30 metres away from the shootings in some brushwood. When she saw the Germans preparing to leave she ran away in the opposite direction to that about to be taken by the Germans, but returned to the scene of the shooting some 20 minutes later. By this time the Germans had departed, leaving the victims where they had fallen. Signora Benucci identified all those killed, including her own husband and brother-in-law, noting in each case that life was extinct and that every corpse had suffered bullet wounds. In addition to Signora Benucci, two other female inhabitants of Le Matole, Signora Iolanda Simonti and Signora Antonietta Beccastrini, witnessed the massacre from the windows of their respective homes.

Both of their husbands, Dino Simonti and Armando Beccastrini, were amongst those put to death by the Germans.

During the evening of the 11th July the corpses of 9 of the men killed were recovered from where they lay by members of their respective families and taken to two houses in Le Matole where they were prepared for burial. Although it is not recorded,

Village of Santa Barbara. (It was at this village that the Germans assembled prior to 4th July, 1944, setting out from there on that date to carry out the massacres in the near vicinity.)

it appears likely that the corpse of Angiolo Redditi was taken to join those of the other 9 men subsequent to its discovery early on the 12th July. On the day following the massacre the 10 bodies were conveyed to the cemetery of Castelnuovo dei Sabbioni and buried there in a communal grave adjacent to that of the victims of the Castelnuovo dei Sabbioni massacre of a week earlier. Unlike the burial on the previous day of those massacred at Castelnuovo dei Sabbioni, when the bodies could not be readily segregated and had been tipped into the grave in random fashion, the bodies of those killed at Le Matole were placed separately and side-by-side in the grave. As on the day before, Don Cuccoli, the assistant priest of San Pancrazio, officiated at the burial service.

When interviewed for the third and final time by the British Special Investigation Branch almost a year after the massacres, Ivario Viligiardi admitted guiding the Germans to Le Matole on the 11th July, but denied that he was present at the massacre there, contending he was held under guard just outside Le Matole. He further admitted to wearing a German steel helmet and a camouflaged mackintosh, and to hearing several bursts of sub-machine-gun fire coming from the direction of Le Matole. However, the evidence of Signora Libera Benucci points to Viligiardi being present, albeit unwillingly, at the scene of the massacre.

After carrying out the killings at Le Matole the anti-Partisan Unit commanded by Leut. Wolf returned to the Villa Silvano at Bagno a Ripoli late on the 11th July. Having exhausted his usefulness to the Germans, Viligiardi, who was taken back with them from Le Matole to the Villa Silvano, was finally released from German custody on or about the 17th July, when he made his way back to Castelnuovo dei Sabbioni.

On returning to his home village Viligiardi was apprehended by ex-Partisans and interrogated on the 22nd July by Leonardo Corti who had been second-in-command to Nello Vannini, leader of the local 3rd Company of Chiatti Partisans. Arising from this interrogation Viligiardi made a written confession to Corti to the effect that he, Viligiardi, had been forced by the Germans to divulge the names of local Partisans together with details of their families, thus assisting the Germans in planning and carrying out the wholesale killings in the area. On the same or the following day Corti handed over Viligiardi with his confession to the British Field Security Section that had recently established itself at Cavriglia, which detained him. Subsequently Viligiardi was moved by the British to various locations in Italy, with him finally reaching Avellino in southern Italy, via Naples, where he was released from custody on condition that he reported daily to the local Carabinieri Station.

During my visit to the Comune di Cavriglia in July 2004 I learned that Ivario Vili-giardi, then some 84 years of age, and the man who, as a result of threats by the Germans, provided the latter with details regarding the whereabouts of the local Parti-sans, guiding them to Poggio alle Valli, and was present with the Germans at the mas-sacre at Le Matole on the 11th July, 1944, was now the proprietor of an upmarket hairdressing salon in Florence.

Having completed their brutal task in the Comune di Cavriglia with the massacre at Le Matole, the various German units involved then began to move out of the area. No doubt there was a sense of urgency brought to bear on this evacuation by the advanc-ing British 13 Corps which took Montevarchi on the 18th July and San Giovanni Val-darno 5 days later.

The 12th July saw the German officers and soldiers vacate the flats they were oc-cupying at Santa Barbara. Also on that day Ober-Leut. Danisch and his unit left nearby San Cipriano for Reggello, a small town some 18 km. by road from and due north of San Giovanni Valdarno.

On the 15th July General Richard Heidrich and his staff left the Villa Renacci near San Giovanni Valdarno, also going to Reggello, as did the detachment of 11th Hermann Goering Panzer Grenadier Regiment from the Villa Bonarotti in Cavriglia.

Again, on the 15th July the Hermann Goering 'Flak' unit commanded by Major Graf departed from Montegonzi for an unknown destination.

Somewhat later than its contemporaries, the unit at the Santa Maria Estate from 76 Panzer Corps also left for an unknown destination, but on the 20th July.

The anti-Partisan Unit under the command of Leut. Wolf, which arrived at Terran-uova from its main headquarters at Bagno a Ripoli on the 25th June, left Terranuova on the 3rd July and did not return. However, the unit could not have moved far since one of its members, Rudi Groner, visited Teresa Francini at Terranuova on the 5th July. This unit had quite likely returned to Santa Barbara, having carried out the massacre at Castelnuovo dei Sabbioni. It then went on to carry out the killings at Poggio alle Valli, San Pancrazio, Corneto and Le Matole before returning to Bagno a Ripoli.

Finally, the date on which the General and his staff of 76 Panzer Corps left the Villa Cetinale, San Cipriano is, like their destination, unknown. Having taken up residence there on the 2nd July, their departure can be put at around the 15th July. This General was at one time thought to have been Field Marshall Kesselring, but the writer believes him to have been General Herr, the Commander of the German 76 Panzer Corps.

The movements of the various German units into and subsequently away from the area in which massacres took place leaves no doubt that they were part of a well prepared and integrated plan to inflict severe reprisals on the civilian population of the Comune di Cavriglia for their having indulged in Partisan activities resulting in the deaths in the vicinity of 10 German service men. Neither of the two units under the respective commands of Ober-Leut. Danisch and Leut. Wolf was large enough in itself to carry out all the planned massacres. Thus, additional German forces such as that commanded by Major Seiler were required to supplement those commanded by Danisch and Wolf, and particularly so on the 4th July at Meleto, San Martino and Massa dei Sabbioni.

That Santa Barbara was the starting-out point for the German forces who carried out the massacres on the 4th July is quite certain. It was also used as the base for those German officers, N.C.O.s and soldiers of the 4th Hermann Goering Engineering Battalion who were responsible for damaging equipment at the nearby lignite mining complex, the total destruction of the electricity generating station at Castelnuovo dei Sabbioni and damage by explosives and fire to property in the vicinity of Castelnuovo dei Sabbioni.

Village of Santa Barbara.

15
Castelnuovo dei Sabbioni and its environs: damage and destruction of property and facilities, 4th to 11th July, 1944

Having failed to quench their desire for vengeance towards the local civilian population by the massacre of 173 innocent Italian men during the 4th July in the adjacent villages of Castelnuovo dei Sabbioni, Meleto, Massa dei Sabbioni and San Martino, the Germans continued to wreak havoc and mayhem on that and subsequent days by damaging and destroying both property and facilities.

In Castelnuovo dei Sabbioni, still during the morning, and following the massacre in the Piazza IV Novembre, furniture from nearby houses was taken and used by the Germans to fuel the funeral pyre of the 74 victims of the massacre carried out there, whilst the house of the Boni family, together with several other houses in Via Vittorio Veneto and Via Camonti were put to the torch.

At Meleto too, following the massacres there, the barn of the Morelli farm was torched by the Germans, as were the barns containing the corpses of those killed at the Benini and Melani farms, along with many houses.

Massa dei Sabbioni also suffered damage at the hands of the Germans during the afternoon of that fateful day. The barn Scala, in which Don Morini and Dante Pagliazzi were murdered, was set on fire in order to incinerate their bodies. A fire was also started by the Germans at the house of Signorina Milena Baldi and her father.

Again, at San Martino, during the early afternoon of the 4th July, after bayoneting to death and incinerating four men in the Neri farmyard, the Germans set light to the Neri farm itself, together with several houses in the village, including that of Don Cicali, the local priest.

Then, in the early hours of the 7th July, the Germans began their destruction of the electricity generating station at Castelnuovo dei Sabbioni. The first explosive charges were detonated between midnight and 03.00 hrs., these destroying or severely damaging beyond repair both of the relatively modern Ljungström turbo-alternator sets, the steam raising plant and much of the electrical control equipment and switchgear. At this time the turbine hall itself was also wrecked, although to do so necessitated two attempts, the second resulting in a substantial part of its roof structure falling on to and covering the turbo-alternator sets. Further systematic destructive operations continued at the electricity generating station in the days following, the facility being ultimately rendered beyond salvage and repair.

Concurrent with their destruction of the electricity generating station, sapper detachments of the German army damaged or destroyed much of the principal equipment installed at the Castelnuovo dei Sabbioni lignite mining complex. The equipment and plants affected included that for fabricating lignite briquettes, the extraction plant and the lignite drying and screeding plant. Also damaged were the workshop facilities and many of the locomotives, both steam and diesel, used to haul the lignite wagons.

Typical of the destruction carried out by the Germans at the lignite mining complex was that dealt to the extraction plant. This relatively modern installation comprised a substantial steel structure carrying a battery of screeds and silos to which the lignite was delivered by conveyor belt systems direct from the galleries of the mine. Beneath this plant was access for both railway wagons and lorries into which the lignite was loaded for despatch. To put this key installation out of use the German sappers detonated

Castelnuovo dei Sabbioni: house of the Boni family, burnt by the Germans on the morning of 4th July, 1944. (August 1944.)

197

Castelnuovo dei Sab-
bioni: the end of Via
Vittorio Veneto immedi-
ately adjacent to the Pi-
azza IV Novembre, the
site of the massacre.
(September 1944.)

explosive charges attached to its supporting steelwork legs, causing the plant to collapse to ground level. Despite its so doing, the equipment comprising the extraction
plant sustained little other serious damage.

Surprisingly, the Germans made only rather tentative attempts at destroying the in-
clined shafts of some of the mines in the zone or damaging the mine workings, and
with minimal results. With regard to the latter, they possibly considered such activities
to be unnecessary since many of the workings had become flooded as a result of the
electricity supply no longer being available to power the water extraction pumps.

However, a group of German soldiers went to the entrance of the 'Bicchieraie' mine,
indicating that they intended to drive into its shaft three wagon-loads of explosives.
Italian men present at the mine entrance warned the German soldiers against such action, saying that many civilians, including women and babies, were hiding in the mine
shaft. As a result the soldiers then limited their actions to driving into the shaft three
empty wagons that caused no harm. The same group of German soldiers went on to the

'Allori' mine, asking the women gathered outside its entrance if anyone was inside the mine. Although the women knew that some people were inside, for the best misguided motives, they told the Germans that no one was inside the mine. As a consequence the Germans pushed a number of wagons full of explosives into the mine, detonating them and killing one man and a horse as well as severely injuring several other men. The mine itself sustained only minor damage.

During the last week of July 1944, some ten days or so after the Germans had departed from the area, I examined several of the conveyor belt systems used to carry the lignite directly from the mine workings to the extraction plant. In all cases the drive system or the conveyor belting or both had been damaged by small locally placed explosive charges. Also seen were two or three electricity sub-stations whose transformers, switchgear, insulators and cabling had been similarly damaged.

Until research for this book was in progress, which led to detailed information being made available to me by those with an intimate knowledge of the activities of the Germans, the Partisans and others at and around the Castelnuovo dei Sabbioni lignite mining complex in early July 1944, I wrongly believed, as I had for in excess of fifty years, that the damage caused to the mining equipment and plants resulted from sabotage by its operatives or local Partisans. The motivation for such sabotage would have been to prevent the lignite being taken for consumption in factories in northern Italy en-

Ruins of the power station at Castelnuovo dei Sabbioni blown up by the Germans on 7th July 1944 and the following days.

gaged in the production of war material for the Germans. In all probability this misconception arose out of the certain knowledge that damage to railway lines, roads, and rail and road bridges in the near vicinity of Castelnuovo dei Sabbioni was carried out by local Partisans in order to make difficult and, if possible, prevent the transportation of lignite away from the mining area.

Any long-lasting effects of the damage to the equipment at the lignite mining complex caused by the Germans were minimised by the foresight and prior activities of loyal and trusted workers under the direction of Engineer Ugo Mercante. Although the Germans were in charge of operations at the mine, Engineer Ugo Mercante and his men, during the silent hours of the months previous to July 1944, when German supervision was minimal, secreted away in the most remote tunnels of the mine items of plant and equipment, essential engineering materials required to carry out repairs, instruments and the like, all of which would have been certainly either destroyed or removed by the Germans.

The philosophy behind the damage and destruction of property and facilities by the Germans in and around Castelnuovo dei Sabbioni seems somewhat obscure. To the German mind the massacres carried out by them in the Comune di Cavriglia were easy to justify: they were intended to administer to the local civilian population retribution for encouraging and permitting the activities of the local Partisans in which between the

Ruins of the power station at Castelnuovo dei Sabbioni blown up by the Germans on 7th July 1944 and the following days.

Castelnuovo dei Sabbioni and its environs: damage and destruction

23rd May and the 25th June, 1944, ten German military personnel were killed. Such retribution was carried out in an organised manner, and in accordance with the orders and
full support of Field Marshal Kesselring, the commander of German armed forces in
Italy. The rationale for the destruction of property and facilities is less clear. It can be
argued that such retribution is not as severe a punishment as killing, since death is always permanent, whereas damaged inanimate objects can either be repaired or replaced,
albeit at a high cost. However, for the Germans, both killing and the destruction of property and facilities went hand in hand.

The destruction of housing is wanton, but it must have been obvious to those ordering it that to do so in the summer months of 1944 in Italy would not expose those
made homeless to any rigours of the climate. In any event, the Italian temperament
would allow those deprived to be taken in, if only on a temporary basis, either by relatives, friends or neighbours. Moreover, at that time, because of the reducing work force
at the lignite mining complex, many of the apartments at the nearby village of Santa Barbara were unoccupied, thus providing a source of alternative accommodation, since this
development was left quite undamaged by the Germans.

Of course, at the time that the Germans were damaging the equipment at the lignite
mine and wrecking the power station at Castelnuovo dei Sabbioni, Allied forces were
only some 25km. south of that area and advancing rapidly towards it. Thus, to leave the

The end of the power station at Castelnuovo dei Sabbioni.
Shown is the wrecked boiler house with
boiler drums and pipework.

The end of the power station at Castelnuovo dei Sabbioni.
In the wrecked turbine hall is a Ljungström Turbo Alternator.

area devoid of an electricity supply or sources of fuel and employment would, no doubt, have seemed to the Germans to present to the Allies a legacy of severe problems when the area came under their control.

In fact, experience indicates that damage to property and facilities such as that suffered at Castelnuovo dei Sabbioni is usually dealt with quite speedily, if only on a temporary and perhaps somewhat less than satisfactory basis. Indeed, in this particular situation, a local although restricted electricity supply was soon made available, enabling the lignite mining complex to return to limited production by mid August 1944.

Nonetheless, to destroy or severely damage housing and essential components of the local infrastructure, including the main source of employment, in the immediate wake of a series of brutal massacres can only be regarded as barbaric. With the local population suffering deep shock and trauma as a result of the deaths of so many at the hands of the occupying Germans, for the latter to add to this the destruction of some of the most important necessities of life is together cruel and unforgivable. And so it remains to this day.

16

Germans involved in authorising and carrying out the massacres in the Comune di Cavriglia in July, 1944: their detention, arraignments and punishments

A War Crime Summary prepared by 78 Section of Special Investigation Branch of the British forces in Italy, which deals specifically with the massacres carried out by the Germans in the Comune di Cavriglia in early July 1944 states, as part of its introductory note, 'This War Crime is the biggest and most brutal yet investigated'.

The investigation into these particular massacres commenced on the 11th September, 1944, only two months after they had been perpetrated, and while the events were still fresh in the memories of the witnesses, extending over a period in excess of six months. The Reports which cover the investigation in detail provide the basis of chapter 14 of this book. The chapter identifies the German formations involved and describes how they were marshalled, then deployed and ultimately dispersed. Although many German officers, N.C.O.s and other ranks who took part in the massacres remained unknown to the British investigators, the following members of the German forces, together with the units to which they belonged, have been identified as being suspects in either directly authorising, planning or carrying out the atrocities:

Leut.-General Heidrich	Commander 1st Parachute Division
Major Seiler	Hermann Goering Division , Flak Regt
Major Graf	H.Q., Hermann Goering Division, 1 Flak Regt
Hauptman Forster	Commander 1 Coy. 4 Panzer Regt
Ober-Leut. Danisch	Commander Guard Coy. 76 Panzer Corps
Leut. Wolf	Hermann Goering Division, Anti- Partisan Unit
Maresciallo Fräulein	4 Hermann Goering Division, Eng. Battn
Maresciallo Groner	Hermann Goering Division, Anti- Partisan Unit
Sergeant 'Tries'	Guard Coy. 76 Panzer Corps

In July 1945, 78 Section of Special Investigation Branch issued a Supplementary Report complementing the Main Report dealing with their investigations into the massacres of Italian civilians in the Comune di Cavriglia some twelve months earlier, and following the interrogation of new witnesses and the re-interrogation of several of the original witnesses. In this Supplementary Report a number of additional members of the German forces involved in the above massacres are identified, the names and formation of four of these men being given below, together with copies of their photographs.

Leut. Baer		4/L.N. Regt.
Ober-Leut. Lawrenz	}	(M.T. AFK).
Ober-Feldwebel Nieggestich		{Ex Luftwaffe}.
Sergeant Weiss		

The difficulties involved in discovering the whereabouts of individuals suspected of being concerned with war crimes following the cessation of hostilities in Europe were of enormous proportions. But these were minimised for the British in Italy through the medium of a letter to the Under Secretary of State at the War Office from Brigadier F. N. Mitchell at G.H.Q., Central Mediterranean Forces, dated the 5th October, 1945, in which it was proposed (and subsequently agreed) that only the trials of senior German officers implicated in the Ardeatine Caves massacre together with those suspected of being responsible for planning and carrying out German Reprisals in Italy be dealt with under British Army Order, the remainder of such cases being handed over to the Italian Government for them to deal with as they considered appropriate. This was a variation to the Declaration on German Atrocities proposed in a letter by Churchill dated the 12th October, 1943, and signed in Moscow during the following month by Stalin, Roosevelt and Churchill. The Declaration provided for German war criminals involved in massacres and other atrocities to be sent back to the countries in which the crimes were perpetrated so they could be judged and punished according to the laws of those liberated countries and their free Governments.

Thus, the German Generals von Mackensen and Mälzer were tried by British Military Court Martial for their parts in the Ardeatine Caves massacre, with Obersturmbannführer Kappler being tried before the Tribunale Militare di Roma for his involvement in the same massacre. It follows that, with the exception of General Heidrich, the suspects listed above would come under the jurisdiction of the Italians. As far as the writer has been able to determine none of these suspects appears to have been traced and detained, let alone arraigned or punished, for their participation in the massacres in the Comune di Cavriglia.

In the event, General Heidrich was apprehended and detained in the London Cage. In a voluntary statement made there on the 29th August, 1946, General Heidrich acknowledged that his battle headquarters had been at the Villa Renacci, near San Giovanni Valdarno for a short time, but could not remember when this was. Neither could he recall ever hearing anything from the Italians employed at the Villa Renacci about any massacres in the Comune di Cavriglia, nor learning while there about guerrilla battles or German counter measures against the Partisans. He did, however, remember being visited by Field Marshal Kesselring while at the Villa Renacci. In conclusion, the

Leutnant Baer.   *Ober-Leutnant Lawranz*

Ober-Feldwebel Werner   *Ober-Feldwebel Werner*
Nieggestich and   *Nieggestich.*
Sgt. Paul Weiss.

statement by General Heidrich said that if the massacres in question did, in fact, take place, then they did so outside his area of influence, and it was improbable (not likely) that troops of the 1st Parachute Division took part.

In a sworn affidavit made eleven months later, on the 28th July, 1947, General Heidrich declared, in part, that ... because of their stringent security arrangements, the 1st Parachute Division did not encounter the larger groups of Partisans in the Italian theatre. ... I have not ordered one single action against Partisans, reprisals arising out of Partisan activity, the taking of hostages or the shooting of Partisans without a verdict being passed to do so by a military court. Further, I have no knowledge of any of my subordinate commanders having ordered or executed similar measures.

It has been firmly established that General Heidrich and his staff were resident at the Villa Renacci between the 1st and 15th July, 1944, and were visited there during that period by Field Marshal Kesselring. Given that the massacres in the Comune di Cavriglia were carried out by German forces between the 4th and 11th July, 1944, and the distance between the Villa Renacci and Santa Barbara is barely 4km. by road, the latter being the assembly point for the troops who subsequently perpetrated the massacres, it is very difficult to avoid reaching the conclusion that General Heidrich and his staff were involved in their planning if not in their execution. But because it was impossible to establish conclusive proof that General Heidrich had a significant role in planning the massacres carried out in the Comune di Cavriglia he was not arraigned for so doing and ultimately released from custody.

From the list of suspects given above it will be seen that several were members of the Hermann Goering Division. Indeed, many of the Italians who were witnesses to the massacres saw that of the German troops involved, a large number carried the insignia of the Hermann Goering Division both on their uniforms and motor vehicles. This being so, it is not unreasonable to ask why members of this division were not detained and made to answer for their parts in the massacres. A possible explanation is given by Giovanni Contini in his book La Memoria Divisa (The Divided Memory). In this he quotes second-in-command Geyer of the Hermann Goering Division, who says that the scarcity of documentation regarding the part played by his division in the massacres at Castelnuovo dei Sabbioni and Meleto arises from the fact that immediately following these events, the division was moved to the eastern (Russian) front. Geyer continues, saying that on the eastern front the division was virtually annihilated, being reduced to a single platoon which was then incorporated into the 4th Panzer Division where it finally lost its identity. In a song about the Hermann Goering Division, Bruce Quarrie of the 1st Parachute Division tells of how only one third of the Hermann Goering Division survived the Russian offensive, and how these survivors went to a Russian prison camp where a lonely few remained until being released to return home to Germany in 1956. But Carlo Gentile, who has studied the German documentation applicable to the massacres in question, believes that not all the Hermann Goering Division was annihilated, and some members of it who were involved in the massacres still survive in Germany today.

Before dealing with the case against Field Marshal Kesselring, further statements by two other senior German officers in Italy are worth examination, since they have a bearing on the German attitude to reprisals for Partisan activity. The first is by General der Waffen S.S., Karl Wolff. In this, in part, General Wolff says,

... As a result of Badoglio's treason (arranging the armistice between Italy and the Allies, followed by Italy joining the Allies as a co- belligerent), the best and most aggressive units of the Italian Army took to the mountains and the woods rather than go into voluntary imprisonment in Germany. Besides these units, other smaller and larger bands soon began to form themselves – bands which were made up by anti-social and partly criminal elements which in their numerous treacherous attacks, and in keeping with their Latin mentality, perpetrated such cruelties, that Partisan warfare on both sides soon degenerated from all known standards. Special bitterness caused on the German side, by incidents, which became increasingly more frequent from summer 1944, in which Partisans, dressed in German uniform and thus contravening international law, stopped vehicles by masquerading as military control posts, and then murdered the crews.

As incidents of this kind at first seriously and then gravely endangered our lines of communication, Field Marshal Kesselring in April 1944 for the first time ordered increased anti-Partisan warfare for the purpose of clearing the Apennines, beginning in the Terni area and ending in the neighbourhood of Florence.

General Wolff's statement continues,

... When I came to the front for the first time in 1943 I found amongst various units of the army and the Waffen S.S. in Italy – particularly among the paratroops, the Hermann Goering Division and the 16th S.S. Panzer Division; none of whom came in any way under my command – that it was a tacit and accepted custom in cases of reprisal action for a retribution of about 1 to 10 to be exacted, in order that such action might act as a deterrent.

The statement goes on, again in part,

... The continually recurring excesses on the part of the above mentioned divisions caused Field Marshal Kesselring the greatest difficulties, not only in respect of the maintenance of morale and discipline within his army groups but beyond that also with Il Duce who intervened with the Field Marshal for the protection of the Italian population.

The significance of General Wolff's statement lies in its acknowledgement that the Partisans severely endangered the German lines of communication, and specifically names the paratroops and the Hermann Goering Division as indulging in recurring excesses when carrying out reprisals against Partisans. Moreover, the statement conflicts in part with those of General Heidrich, the latter albeit made one and two years respectively after General Wolff's statement.

The second set of statements is by General Lemelsen, who commanded the German 14th Army between June and October 1944. During this period the formations under his command experienced great difficulties in keeping open their lines of communication and supply, particularly between Siena and Grosseto, due to Partisan activities. Because of these difficulties General Lemelsen, on the 13th June, sought from and was granted authority by Field Marshal Kesselring's headquarters to shoot up to ten Italians of military age for every German soldier killed by Partisans, or for proven acts of military sabotage.

General Lemelsen was not named as a suspect in the Reports by 78 Section of Special Investigation Branch which deal with the massacres by German forces in the Comune di Cavriglia. He was, however, apprehended for being suspected of involvement in anti- Partisan reprisals elsewhere in Italy, and detained in the London Cage. Here he made a number of statements, some as a witness in the trial of Field Marshal Kesselring.

In a statement dated the 26th February, 1946, General Lemelsen says, in part,

... With the fall of Rome and the beginning of the retreat a considerable increase in Partisan activity behind the Army set in with startling suddenness. Whereas until now only isolated raids had taken place, from now on not a night passed in which despatch riders, single lorries and soldiers were not ambushed, robbed and dragged away and their lorries burnt... Behind the Army was the broad belt of the Apennines which was bristling with organised Partisan bands, especially on the pass-roads. It was known that the guerrillas had received strong reinforcements from the large numbers of English prisoners-of-war who had been liberated by the defection of Italy, and who were good fighters in contrast to the Italians, who were, generally speaking, cowardly. The groups beyond the Apennines, who made themselves felt right behind the front, were not organised in units to the same extent.

... These mostly small communist bands at the same time terrorised the civilian population, who, according to their political opinions, either held back timidly or else supported them. For this reason it could not, in many cases, be established which of any prisoners taken were members of a Partisan group, which were collaborators with the Partisans and which were innocent civilians. Under these circumstances it was unavoidable that sometimes an innocent person lost his life.

... With the continuous retreats during this period of the fighting, the troops were often obliged first of all to clear their lines of retreat of Partisan groups. So, just at that time many actions had to be set in hand by the divisions against Partisan occupied places from which German soldiers had been fired upon. These were perhaps felt as being reprisals by the civil population. It is, therefore, quite possible that one or other of the incidents may have been an operation to clear the roads and not a reprisal.

As the guerrilla pest grew apace, Field Marshal Kesselring found it necessary, on the 17th June, 1944, to issue a stringent order about anti-Partisan measures. This order, which covered every officer who overstepped the prescribed measure in his choice of means to fight the Partisans contained, in my opinion, a great menace to discipline and order, considering the critical situation and the nature of the troops' moral tension.

Later in this same statement, and referring to the responsibility for the massacres in the Comune di Cavriglia on the 4th, 8th and 11th July, 1944, General Lemelsen comments,

Here it is obviously a question of operations in the eastern boundary of the 10th Army where strong Partisan groups were lurking immediately behind the front. The two flanking corps (76 Panzer Corps and 1st Parachute Corps, the former having at this time under its command both the 1st Parachute Division and the Hermann Goering Division) would have shared these operations between them.

In a further statement made on the 12th June, 1947 and declared to be supplementary to the statements he made as a witness in the trial of Field Marshal Kesselring, General Lemelsen, again in part, said,

... I remember that I was informed of Field Marshal Kesselring's order of the 17th June, 1944... and I ordered that verbatim copies of it with the Field Marshal's signature should be passed on to Corps... I cannot remember now whether I appended any additional instructions when I passed on this order.

... Partisan activities in the rear of my Army had increased so much at this time that thorough measures to eliminate this danger were urgently necessary. A few days previously I had discussed Partisan activities with the Field Marshal, whom I met almost daily on my tours of the front. On this occasion he said to me something like this: 'The restraint we have maintained towards the Partisans up to now, and the purely defensive attitude which we now take against Partisan attacks must be brought to an end. The Partisans must be attacked with all weapons and annihilated. I should not underestimate this serious threat to the rear of the Army.'

... Thus, the Field Marshal's order of the 17th June, 1944 regarding the conduct of the campaign against the Partisans was not unexpected by me. I was not at all upset by the stern content of the Field Marshal's order, which was well known to us all, and I did not hesitate to pass on the order to the Corps.

The statements both by General Wolff and General Lemelsen confirm the acute problems caused by the Partisans to the German lines of communication during the middle months of 1944. But in his statement of the 26th February, 1946 General Lemelsen showed distinct misgivings with regard to Field Marshal Kesselring's infamous order of the 17th June, 1944, believing that it protected and possibly had encouraged any German officer who acted or considered acting with excess either directly against the Partisans or when carrying out reprisals.

With regard to the massacres in the Comune di Cavriglia, General Lemelsen correctly identifies these as having taken place in the area occupied at the time partly by 76 Panzer Corps and partly by 1st Parachute Corps, with two of the formations suspected of being involved in the massacres, the Hermann Goering and 1st Parachute Divisions, being under the command of the former Corps.

Some fifteen months later, in mid June 1947, and while still in captivity, but subsequent to the trial of Field Marshal Kesselring (February to May 1947), General Lemelsen recalled having been informed of the Field Marshal's order of the 17th June, 1944, with himself ordering that it be passed on verbatim to the formations under his command, although he could not remember whether or not he had appended any qualifying instructions to the order. But he seems to have undergone something of a change of heart at this time from the opinion he expressed in his earlier statement, in which he criticised part of the Field Marshal's order as being 'a great menace to discipline and order'. Indeed, in his mid June 1947 statement General Lemelsen said that when Field Marshal Kesselring's order was issued he agreed to its contents without reserve, as he also did to the Field Marshal's verbal comments that any restraint heretofore shown towards the Partisans must end, with them being attacked by all weapons and annihilated.

There can be no doubt that with regard to the German reaction to the Partisans and reprisals against those sections of the Italian civilian population thought to be supporting Partisans, General Lemelsen's observations are amongst the most illuminating. Like General Heidrich, General Lemelsen was ultimately released without being arraigned for any war crime.

Field Marshal Kesselring was the senior German commander throughout the major part of the Italian Campaign. As such he bore the ultimate responsibility for all the massacres and reprisals carried out against the Italian civilian population by the German armed forces during this period.

He capitulated to the Allies and was detained at Berchtesgaden on the 7th May, 1945, being taken on the 15th May into the Ash Cage at Mondorf near Luxembourg. From Mondorf he was first taken to Oberusal and then to Nuremburg where he spent five months in solitary confinement starting just prior to Christmas 1945. Following his long stay at Nuremburg the Field Marshal was moved to Dachau before being returned again to Nuremberg. After a brief spell at Langwasser he was transferred to the camp of the American Historical Division at Allendorf. Then, during the autumn of 1946, Field Marshal Kesselring spent about a month in the London Cage, being interrogated there, before returning to Allendorf. It was mid January 1947 that he finally left Allendorf for Rimini in preparation for his trial at Mestre which opened on the 17th February, extending until the 6th May.

As indicated above, it was agreed that only the trials of senior German officers involved with the Ardeatine Caves massacre, and those responsible for planning and carrying out other German reprisals in Italy be dealt with under British Army Order. In keeping with this arrangement Field Marshal Kesselring was indicted to appear before a British Military Court Martial.

The charges against Field Marshal Kesselring were twofold: the first accused him of being a party to the murder of 335 Italians in the Ardeatine Caves near Rome on the 24th March, 1944; the second accused him of inciting by two orders the troops under his command to murder Italian civilians by way of reprisals in violation of the laws and usages of war.

With regard to the first charge, Field Marshal Kesselring argued that Hitler's arbitrary order fixing the reprisal ratio at one to ten and nominating the Sicherheitsdienst (the Security Service of the S.S.) to carry out the reprisal, removed all responsibility from the armed forces in this matter. The Field Marshal also advanced the parallel argument that, because of Hitler's order, both General von Mackensen and himself had not on their own responsibility permitted any reprisals. Indeed, they had on the contrary attempted to achieve a deterrent effect by the deaths of those who were so liable under international law. But the evidence showed that it was Field Marshal Kesselring who gave the order to the S.S. to kill ten Italians for every German who died as a result of the Via Rasella attack. Moreover, the Field Marshal stated in evidence that he was given to understand by Obersturmbannführer Kappler that only Italians already under sentence of death would be executed, and that no innocent persons would be killed. Under cross-examination, however, he conceded that he had taken no steps to ascertain whether the figure of 320 Italians said to already be under sentence of death, and to have been quoted to him by Kappler, but denied by the latter, had, in fact, received confirmation of their death sentences by him. This is astonishing, since some time earlier Field Marshal Kesselring had taken it upon himself to confirm all death sentences passed on Italians by German military courts. In fact, as of the 24th March, 1944, the number so confirmed totalled just three.

Generals von Mackensen and Mälzer had been jointly and similarly charged in respect of the Ardeatine Caves massacre. Their trial, also before a British Military Court Martial, which preceded that of Field Marshal Kesselring, and at which the Field Marshal gave evidence for the defence, was held in Rome between the 18th and 30th November, 1946. Both Generals were found guilty and sentenced to death by shooting. In the circumstances it would, therefore, have been somewhat surprising if Field Marshal Kesselring had not also been found guilty of the same charge and similarly sentenced, as indeed he was.

Germans involved in authorising and carrying out the massacres

In his memoirs Kesselring asserts that General von Mackensen, General Mälzer and himself were sentenced to death because of their failure to circumvent one of Hitler's orders, for which they were blameless. He concludes that the findings of the court were a travesty of justice.

Turning to the second charge with which we are principally concerned, since it covers the massacres in the Comune di Cavriglia, the Short Statement of Facts appearing on the charge sheet read as follows:

In June 1944 the Italian Partisans in Italy were having a considerable harassing effect on the German Army. On the 17th June the accused issued a written order to the effect that Partisans must be put down at all costs and that he would protect any officer who exceeded the usual restraint. On the 1st July he issued a further order to the effect that wherever Partisan activity was rife a proportion of the civil population should be taken as hostages and shot if the Partisan activities continued. As a result of these orders many hundreds of civilian men, women and children were shot all over Italy.

The two orders issued by Field Marshal Kesselring and referred to immediately above are set out in chapter 12 of this book.

To almost all observers the intention and meaning of these orders are quite clear, and from the German viewpoint in the current situation regarding the Partisans perhaps understandable, if not remotely justified. But at his trial much was made by the Field Marshal's defence team of the English translation and interpretation of some of the words and passages contained in the orders. In his summing up the Judge Advocate made reference to this, commenting,

...Now, gentlemen, dealing with it generally, ... assuming that we have really got a proper translation of the German text into the English one which we now have – you will ask yourselves: Is it really necessary to introduce into these sentences a suggestion that they are quasi-military, German military shorthand – that whenever you read a sentence which looks clear on the face of it you must assume it does not mean that at all, and you can only understand it if some eminent German Staff Officer translates it for you and explains its subtle and inner meanings?

It was also held that the order of the 1st July was simply a combat order and a reply by Field Marshal Kesselring to appeals broadcast by Marshal Badoglio in mid June and General Alexander on the 19th, 20th and 27th June to the Partisans to attack members of the German armed forces.

In a further attempt to show that no kind of terrorism was intended, Field Marshal Kesselring, in his memoirs, quotes from an order he issued on the 21st August, 1944, this order being submitted in evidence at his trial. The order, in part, states,

Field Marshal Kesselring.

> In the course of major operations against Partisans, incidents have occurred in recent weeks that seriously harm the good name and discipline of the German armed forces which had nothing to do with retaliatory measures.
>
> Because operations against Partisans must be conducted by the severest means, innocent elements will occasionally be affected.
>
> If, however, a major operation instead of pacifying a district only leads to greater unrest among the population ... this will be an indication that the operation was wrongly conducted and can only be regarded as pillage. Il Duce himself has bitterly complained to Dr Rahn, our ambassador to the Italian Government, of the manner in which various operations aganst the Partisans have been carried out, and of retaliatory measures which, in the last resort, have fallen on the local population rather than the Partisans.
>
> ... The responsible leader of the individual operation against Partisans must therefore issue before the commencement of the operation clear orders relating to the general situation, as to the treatment of the population in the Partisan infested district and specifically to the degree requisitioning is permissible and what punitive measures may be taken. Such punitive measures are not

General von Mackensen

General Malzer.

to be left to the discretion of subordinate commanders. The principle must be that measures are only to be taken against the actual Partisans and not the innocent civilian population... As heretofore the Partisans are to be attacked with all possible means; in the case of unjustified attacks on the civilian population I shall relentlessly bring those responsible to account.

Again, and in a similar vein, Field Marshal Kesselring issued an order on the 24th September, 1944 which stated, in part,

Il Duce has once again conveyed to me written statements about acts committed by members of units stationed in Italy against the population, which contravene my directive of 21st August, 1944; the manner of their commission is outrageous and such as to drive decent and spirited elements of the population into the enemy's camp or to the Partisans. I am no longer willing to condone such behaviour, being fully aware that such cowardly outrages result in hardship for the innocent.

Il Duce's complaints are being forwarded to the High Command authorities, and the competent general is being asked to have the worst cases investigated, to report the result of the investigation to me and to pass the matter to the responsible commander for a final decision. These officers will also report the result to me.

Despite the explanations and qualifications put forward by defence counsel regarding Field Marshal Kesselring's orders of the 17th June and 1st July, together with his subsequent orders issued on the 21st August and the 24th September respectively, the prosecuting counsel at the Field Marshal's trial showed that no instances had been brought to light by the German authorities of the improper killing of innocent Italian civilians at the hands of members of the German armed forces for so doing. Neither was there any evidence of disciplinary action against any member of the German armed forces in this context.

In the event, it was established that many innocent Italian civilians had been put to death as a direct result of the two principal orders issued by Field Marshal Kesselring and cited on the charge sheet. As a consequence on the 6th May, 1947 the Field Marshal was found guilty as charged by the British Military Court Martial, and sentenced to death by shooting.

Following the trial Field Marshal Kesselring wrote that not only his counsel, but many others, considered the verdict impossible. But he himself foresaw the outcome of the trial, not because he had acted illegally, but because his trial had been preceded by the trials in Rome of Generals von Mackenson and Mälzer, the activities by the Partisans could not be allowed to be judged by history as a criminal operation, and the German Officer Corps and German military profession had to be dealt a mortal blow.

Immediately after his trial Field Marshal Kesselring was taken to Wolfsberg in Carinthia. While he was there the confirming officer, General Harding, was advised by the Judge Advocate General that there was no reason to alter the death sentence passed on the Field Marshal or those passed on Generals von Mackensen and Mälzer. But General Harding did so modify them, commuting all three death sentences on the 4th July, 1947 to life imprisonment. Later, the sentences were again changed to twenty-one years imprisonment.

One of General Harding's reasons for commuting the sentence passed on Field Marshal Kesselring was not particularly convincing. It was that the Field Marshal's orders of the 17th June and 1st July, 1944 were operative for only a limited and comparatively short period. General Harding also advanced the somewhat stronger argument that it would be against his conscience to confirm the death sentence on Field Marshal Kesselring, as well as on Generals von Mackensen and Mälzer, since Obersturmbannführer Kappler, whose trial was due to open in Rome on the 3rd May, 1948, would certainly receive a lesser sentence. This was because Kappler would be tried by an Italian court, and the then new Italian Republic did not have a death penalty.

In October 1947, Kesselring, von Mackensen and Mälzer were transferred from Wolfsberg to the war crimes prison at Werl. While there, General Mälzer died. On the 24th October, 1952, as an act of clemency, both von Mackensen and Kesselring were released from the Werl prison. Kesselring retired to live near Munich where he died in July 1960, age seventy-four. Von Mackensen lived out the remaining years of his life in seclusion in the city of Kiel.

17

Castelnuovo dei Sabbioni and its
environs mid July 1944 to present day

Mid July 1944 to November 1955

It is said that as soon as the battle front had passed through Castelnuovo dei Sabbioni and the surrounding area, squads of men started immediately to work on restoring the industrial plants of the vicinity damaged or destroyed by the Germans, including the lignite mining complex. The writer saw no evidence of such activities during the period late July to mid August 1944 when British 13 C.T.W. was located near to the village of Santa Barbara. Indeed, at this time the lignite mining complex appeared to be deserted and the whole area was without a supply of electricity.

Be that as it may, quite fortuitously a German 'Tiger' tank having only a damaged track had been abandoned but a few kilometres distant from Castelnuovo dei Sabbioni. After all the live ammunition had been cleared from the tank and a mine removed from beneath one of its tracks, Engineer Ugo Mercante of the Società Mineraria del Valdarno (S.M.V.) was successful in getting the tank mobile and moving it under its own power to the workshops of the lignite mining complex. Here the engine was removed from the tank and coupled to an alternator which had been secreted in one of the remote galleries of the mine. In order to produce the components necessary for the tank engine/alternator coupling, two teams of men working continuously around the clock took turns to rotate by hand the lathe and other machine tools required in the components' manufacture. After several days of intense and difficult labour an electricity supply once more became available at the mining complex, albeit with a limited capacity. This essential utility allowed the pumps used to extract water from the galleries of the mine to be put back in service, thereby pumping out the then flooded galleries and permitting workers again to enter the mine.

The extraction plant, whose damage by the Germans is described elsewhere in this book, was raised and supported back into its original position using both 100 tonne jacks and railway sleepers, this vital operation again being carried out under the direction of Engineer Ugo Mercante, with British troops rendering valuable assistance.

Thus, during the latter part of August, the lignite mining complex at Castelnuovo dei Sabbioni was back in limited production. Such output of lignite that became available was immediately transported from the mine in Allied Army trucks for urgent use by the military, in industry, and for the heating of public buildings. Moreover, by means of temporary connections, electricity was supplied to nearby Santa Barbara, as well as being fed back through the damaged power station to Castelnuovo dei Sabbioni, these being the first villages in the area to be illuminated by electricity after the battle zone had passed northwards through them.

Fuel for the ex-German tank engine used to drive the alternator producing the electricity was provided by the Allied forces. The improvised generating set was required to operate continuously, the supply of fuel governing the availability in the evenings of a limited amount of electricity sufficient to light a local hall in which the British soldiers stationed in the vicinity could dance with the local ladies.

Over the following months and years life in and around Castelnuovo dei Sabbioni gradually returned to near normal. The conflict of war did not again blight the area, with peace arriving in Europe in May 1945. But Allied troops remained in the vicinity, although in diminishing numbers, until the late 1940s. During the latter part of 1944 all the inhabitants of the village of Santa Barbara were forced to leave their apartments and live elsewhere because the whole village was requisitioned by the Allies for use as a rest camp for front line soldiers. It was November 1945 before the inhabitants of Santa Barbara could return to their homes following the closure of the camp by the Allies and a total refurbishment of the properties by S.M.V.

But the memory of the brutal massacres by the Germans in early July 1944 lived on, overshadowing all the people of Castelnuovo dei Sabbioni, and particularly those who had lost relatives or friends.

On the first anniversary of the massacre, practically the whole population of the village assembled in the Piazza IV Novembre in commemoration of those who had died there. And a year later, on the 4th July, 1946, before an equally large gathering, the chapel in memory of those massacred at Castelnuovo dei Sabbioni and nearby Le Matole on the 4th and 11th July, 1944 respectively was inaugurated, having been built on the site of the massacre in the Piazza IV Novembre. This small chapel carries the poignant inscription 'I Massacrati Di Ieri Sono Gl'Immortali Di Oggi' (The Massacred of Yesterday Are The Immortal Of Today). Every year on the morning of the 4th July a commemoration service is held at the chapel. The numbers attending this service have diminished over the years, but many still remain in Castelnuovo dei Sabbioni, more than half a century after the event, who have good reason never to forget the barbarity of the Germans in early July 1944.

At the end of World War II the recovery of lignite at the Castelnuovo dei Sabbioni mining complex was still carried out predominantly underground. The reopening of worldwide coal and oil markets after the termination of the global conflict caused a crisis in the lignite mining industry. It became uneconomic to continue to recover lignite by the underground method and to transport it for use any distance away from the place where it was mined, since the heat value and cost of the lignite were acutely disadvantageous compared with those of the competing and ever cheapening coal and oil. This crisis, which was to span almost a decade, gave rise, in turn, to local unemployment and social unrest.

In the early 1950s Società Santa Barbara, the new licensee of the lignite mining complex at Castelnuovo dei Sabbioni, presented a project aptly named 'Santa Barbara'. It proposed the construction of a new 250MW thermal power station adjacent to the lignite mining complex which would consume the total output from the latter. Moreover, the mining operations themselves would be upgraded and changed from underground to opencast working. The proposals comprising the project were adopted in their entirety, and were to open a new era of economic prosperity and social stability for the area.

November 1955 to December 1986

Construction of the new power station commenced in January 1956, its two 125MW turbo-alternator sets entering operational service in December 1957 and March 1958 respectively. For the technically minded, the relatively modest steam conditions of 540°C and 105kg/cm^2 were adopted for use at the turbine inlets, steam condensing being effected by water itself cooled in two hyperbolic type towers, with their make-up water taken from the River Arno via an artificial lake formed at San Cipriano having an approximate capacity of 3,000,000m^3. Each of the two hydrogen cooled alternators have ratings of 156.25MVA., generating at 16.5kV.

Concurrent with the building of the power station, work commenced in the latter two months of 1955 to prepare for opencast mining of the lignite in sufficient quantity to meet the consumption requirements of the power station. Most of this preparatory work was carried out remote from Castelnuovo dei Sabbioni, and included the demolition of a number of isolated houses, most of which were the property of Società Santa Barbara. At this time few, if any, foresaw that in due course the almost total destruction of the old village of Castelnuovo dei Sabbioni would result from the opencast mining of the lignite. It was thought that the opencast operations would not extend much beyond the boundaries of the original lignite mining area, perhaps taking in the mining village of La Dispensa together with some further properties belonging to Società Santa Barbara. Thus, there was virtually no opposition to the advent of the opencast mining operations. On the contrary, since there had been many years of crisis in the local lignite mining industry, resulting in unemployment, poverty and a degree of discontent, the population as a whole was more than prepared to tolerate what they saw as only minor inconveniences in order to secure the stability brought about by long term employment either at the new power station or the opencast lignite mine. In the event, the power station engaged 175 operatives, the maximum number employed in opencast mining totalling 638. Many of those who could not obtain employment with the new enterprises moved to Florence which, at that time, had on offer much work, together with housing at an acceptable cost.

To the outsider it is ironic that much of the major equipment provided for the new power station and the opencast mining operation was of German origin, including the boiler plant and its auxiliaries for the former, together with the three massive excavators used to recover the lignite. Ironic, since it was the German military who, in July 1944, had destroyed the original power station at Castelnuovo dei Sabbioni, as well as damaging or destroying much of the equipment at the lignite mining complex.

It was in the July of 1959 that I first returned to Castelnuovo dei Sabbioni. Approaching from San Giovanni Valdarno and passing through San Cipriano and Santa Barbara, I saw first the blocks of apartments at the latter village just as they had been some fifteen years earlier, and then set eyes for the first time on the new Santa Barbara Centrale power station built, as best as I could recall, on or very near the location occupied by British 13 C.T.W. in July/August 1944. The road beyond Santa Barbara up to Castelnuovo dei Sabbioni remained much as I remembered it. Entering the old village, it too appeared not to have changed. Walking around the village I exchanged salutations with those local inhabitants who I encountered, including some ladies sitting in the shade outside their homes and engaged in needlework. As I entered the Piazza IV Novembre and walked up the steep slope to the church of San Donato a Castelnuovo I recalled the terrible happenings that had occurred there in July 1944 and what I had seen with my own eyes shortly afterwards. The local priest, who happened to be in the church, heard me enter, and came to greet me. We communicated as best we could, and I told him who I was and that I had been in Castelnuovo dei Sabbioni in July 1944 a short time after the massacres. After showing me around the church, the priest then escorted me to the chapel in Piazza IV Novembre and erected in commemoration of those who had died there and at Le Matole at the hands of the Germans.

By 1962–63 the opencast mine workings were approaching the then existing road between Santa Barbara and Castelnuovo dei Sabbioni. As a result this road, as well as the original road from Castelnuovo dei Sabbioni to Cavriglia, were both diverted. Around this time too, several small water courses were diverted, and the tiny villages of Basi, Bomba, Ronco, San Donato and San Martino were swallowed up by the opencast mining operations.

With the passing years the mining operations began to encroach on Castelnuovo dei Sabbioni itself. Properties in the lower reaches of the village became endangered as a result of the advancing lignite extraction works, and in order to rehouse the people living in these properties, work by a State Board commenced in 1962 on the construction of new dwellings in a zone of Castelnuovo dei Sabbioni known as Camonti. The first forty-nine houses were ready for occupation in mid April 1963, and over the next fifteen years or so the construction of further new housing continued until finally in ex-

Castelnuovo dei Sabbioni: Via Matteotti, barred and
closed to traffic, March, 1974.

cess of two hundred properties were built, all being available for letting. In addition, from about 1970, the building of privately owned houses commenced in the Camonti district, an enterprise still ongoing up to the present day.

Castelnuovo dei Sabbioni: demolition of the houses in Via Nuova, 25th May, 1974.

The people whose houses were threatened by the lignite mining operations became divided in their opinions as how best to proceed. Those who owned houses, either very old or new, were generally ready to sell them to Ente Nazionale per l'Energia Elettrica (E.N.E.L.), the state owned electricity company responsible since nationalisation for operating both the power station and the lignite mining complex. This willingness to sell was a result of E.N.E.L. being prepared to

Castelnuovo dei Sabbioni: 'Castello Alto' viewed from the 'Casale'. 25th March, 1975.

make generous payments for such properties, thus enabling those selling to acquire housing at the bottom of the valley between San Cipriano and San Giovanni Valdarno, and quite remote from the lignite mining area. There were also those property owners who were reluctant to sell, or for various reasons could not do so, and who as a consequence found themselves isolated and subjected to threats by E.N.E.L. of expropriation of their properties on the grounds of public service requirements. But towards the end of the 1970s those still unable to dispose of their properties banded together, and with the support of the Council of Cavriglia managed to obtain adequate rehousing grants, all with the proviso that the replacement dwellings had to be built in the Camonti district. A difference of opinion also arose between those who were not property owners.

There were those living in the areas affected by the opencast mining operations who wanted their new housing constructed in the style of their then existing housing, but at a nearby location. In contrast, there were others who wished for their replacement housing to be built in the Valdarno where it would be easier for those unable to obtain employment either at the power station or the lignite mining complex to seek for or travel to alternative work.

All the foregoing housing problems and solutions were, by their very nature, spaced out over several years.

Early in 1974 a substantial landslide occurred on the outskirts of Castelnuovo dei Sabbioni. Many of the houses at the edge of the movement were already abandoned, but others, a little higher up, were still occupied. At this time the Via Matteotti was already closed to traffic, with the doors and lower windows of the properties lining the street being bricked up in order to prevent entry therein. By May 1974 the demolition of houses in the Via Nuova had commenced, with those in Via Matteotti scheduled to follow.

On the 13th August, 1978 a major landslide occurred as a result of the opencast mining operations, engulfing what remained of Via Matteotti and Via Nuova. Such houses that survived on the edge of the landslip were demolished shortly afterwards. This large earth movement exposed the sandstone formation on which the highest and most ancient part of Castelnuovo dei Sabbioni is built, including the old church of San Donato a Castelnuovo. But for this different understratum the Piazza IV Novembre, the old church and parts of the Via Camonti and Via Vittorio Veneto would also have been

Castelnuovo dei Sabbioni: Via Matteotti and Via Nuova swallowed by a landslide on 15th August, 1978.

swallowed up by the opencast mining operations. In the event the mining operations left this central part of the old village undisturbed, although its inhabitants gradually moved away to live elsewhere, the last family departing in 1986. During this period the Castle of Pianfranzese was not so fortunate, since its understratum was of lignite rather than sandstone. This building, of immense historical importance and great aesthetic value, was destroyed in the latter half of 1983 as a result of the inexorable expansion of the lignite mining process.

January 1987 to Present Day

Although the area around the Piazza IV Novembre has been abandoned and is somewhat derelict in appearance, it has survived. Strong and local public opinion, supported by the Comune di Cavriglia, has opposed and so far prevented the demolition of the houses remaining in the centre of the old village of Castelnuovo dei Sabbioni, all of these having been acquired by E.N.E.L. Its historic significance apart, the piazza with the surrounding houses and the overlooking church is most attractive whether viewed from a distance or from within the piazza itself. Proposals have been put forward for the restoration and rehabilitation of the houses around the Piazza IV Novembre and the cultural use of the area, but these have yet to come to fruition. For what it is worth, the writer is very much in favour of these proposals, since they would preserve indefinitely the place where those innocent men of Castelnuovo dei Sabbioni were massacred in July 1944, together with the commemorating chapel.

By the end of the 1980s it was evident that the lignite deposits of the Castelnuovo dei Sabbioni area would soon be exhausted, the quantities of lignite recovered and the number of operatives employed in so doing both falling. On the 29th March, 1994 the excavation of lignite ceased, leaving a vast desolate and barren area of some 1,250 hectares. The power station continues to function, now using heavy oil rather than lignite as its fuel. Because of the high cost of the heavy oil, further elevated by its transportation to Santa Barbara, and the relatively low efficiency of the boilers arising out of their combustion chamber design, the power station normally operates at less than its rated output, the exception being when generating plant shortages occur elsewhere in the electricity supply network.

Currently there exist two major problems for the ex-mining area and its precincts. One is the replacement of the lignite mining industry as a provider of both direct and indirect employment, the other being the environmental restitution of what was once a quite beautiful area and which now, in large part, resembles a moonscape. Perhaps the first of these problems is the more easily resolved, since over a number of years there has been a steady decline in the numbers employed at the power station and the lignite mining complex. Many of those working in the mining industry have retired, with others leaving the area. Some younger people employed at the power station have taken transfers to other power stations operated by E.N.E.L. Moreover, in the area around Castelnuovo dei Sabbioni, in the Valdarno and at Florence there exist or have grown up numerous small industries and commercial businesses, as well as state organisations, which have together engaged increasing numbers of people, so that the area in the vicinity of Castelnuovo dei Sabbioni no longer depends, as it once did, almost exclusively on the power station and lignite mining to provide employment. But the problems associated with environmental restitution are profound. The responsibility of E.N.E.L. in the once mined area is limited to the movement of earth and spoil in order to achieve some degree of landscaping, and this is ongoing. Many grandiose and costly rehabilitation schemes have been proposed, some of which may eventually reach fruition. But the best and most extensive of these can only be a compromise, and none will ever return the area to its natural beauty which existed prior to 1956.

During discussions with members of the local authority and other interested parties in mid 1997, the opinion was formed that a firm view had yet to be reached as to what it was hoped to achieve overall for the area, taking cognisance of the industrial, commercial and environmental aspects.

It was learned that an architect had been engaged to advise on making the ex-mining area attractive both to tourists and light industry, paper plans being available of some of his proposals. In a somewhat cynical comment the writer said that architects were generally an expensive commodity and rarely produced what was required or expected of them. There was a knowing concurrence to this. It is anticipated that substantial European Union funds will be available to achieve the rehabilitation of the ex-mining area, while for their part the local authority is making only a very modest rental charge for land in order to attract industrial concerns to the area.

An example of the many and complex dilemmas facing the local authority embraces a proposal to convert the existing power station at Santa Barbara to combined cycle gas turbine (C.C.G.T.) operation, thereby increasing its capacity to circa 600MW. This, of course, is economically desirable, although the numbers employed subsequent to the conversion would be relatively small, with the C.C.G.T. design being environmentally acceptable. But the power station, no matter how modified, will remain a landmark, an eyesore and a disincentive for tourists to visit the immediate area. Indeed, the very attractive Villa Barberino with its magnificent dining hall and apartments is situated on the eastern outskirts of the village of Meleto, but its rear aspect looks out on to the power station.[1]

Thoughts have been given to camouflaging the cooling towers and chimneys of the power station so that they blend in with their surroundings. Asked to comment, the writer said that he thought this idea was a non-starter since the camouflage required varied with the seasons of the year, and in any event, the plumes from the cooling towers could not be disguised. Moreover, camouflaging techniques similar to those being considered had been used in the United Kingdom during World War II, but with only limited success.

In a summary session it was propounded that it would be difficult in a region as lovely as Tuscany to induce tourists to visit the ex-mining area no matter how well restored, although they could well be attracted to the more remote parts of the Comune di Cavriglia. For the ex-mining area and its immediate surrounds the aim should be to attract the types of light industry requiring a highly skilled and hence well paid workforce, since this would enrich the local economy together with the social and educational levels of the community. It was suggested that the initial approach should be to attract to this area one, but no more than two, principal and nationally or preferably internationally well known manufacturing companies. Once such a company or companies were established then others would soon follow. But to spread the net too widely at the outset would only dilute and make ineffective the resources available.

For the hotels and restaurants these, as a first priority, should concentrate on attracting industrial visitors by providing facilities for meetings, seminars, technical conferences and the like, whilst still being prepared to welcome tourists.

Time alone will decide as to whether or not the correct decisions have been made.

---

1 A new power station having C.C.G.T. operation and an output of 380–400MW is being built at Santa Barbara, comprising a single unit. Preparatory work commenced at the end of 2004/beginning 2005, the total project continuing until 2006. The north unit of the old Santa Barbara Centrale power station is scheduled to continue operating until September 2005, with the south unit remaining in operation until August 2006. Following the satisfactory functioning of the new facility, the old power station will be demolished.

18
Aftermath

W hen British 13 C.T.W. left Santa Barbara at first light on the morning of the 10th September the Italian Campaign still had almost eight months to run. The unit made its way back to San Giovanni Valdarno, then followed the valley of the River Arno north through Pontassieve and on to Sieci, a small village some 10km. due east of the centre of Florence, operating there for a little less than the next four weeks.

At this time British 13 Corps was under command of U.S. 5th Army which, on the same day as the above move by British 13 C.T.W. launched its offensive against the central Apennines as part of the Allied effort to breach the Gothic Line. Formations of British 13 Corps advanced north from the Florence area with British 1st Infantry Division on the left moving up Route 302 towards Borgo San Lorenzo, Marradi and Faenza, and British 6th Armoured Division on the right taking Route 67 from Pontassieve to Dicomano, the Muraglione Pass and Forlì .Between these two British divisions Indian 8th Infantry Division went forward from Sieci across the mountainous and trackless terrain in the direction of Vicchio, its objective being the seizure of Alpe di Vitigliano.

By the 11th/12th September U.S. 2 Corps, the corps additional to British 13 Corps comprising U.S. 5th Army and British 13 Corps, advancing side by side with the latter corps on the right, reached and crossed the River Sieve, taking San Piero a Sieve, Borgo San Lorenzo, Barberino di Mugello, Dicomano and Scarperia. But overlooking these small towns and villages the heights of the Apennines and the Gothic Line loomed and German resistance stiffened.

Then began six weeks of difficult, arduous and costly fighting in progressively worsening weather conditions in an attempt to breach the Gothic Line, to reach Route 9, the Via Emilia, to take Bologna, and to enter the valley of the River Po. British 1st Infantry Division advancing from Borgo San Lorenzo towards Marradi took Mt Prefetto by midnight on the 14th September, thus enabling U.S. 85th Division on their left to capture Mt Pratone, a key feature of the Gothic Line, on the 17th September. On the day following, Indian 8th Infantry Division, having passed through Villore, took Mt Femmina Morta which dominates the Casaglia Pass on the road to Marradi. Concurrently, British

6th Armoured Division took San Godenzo on the southern approach to the Muraglione Pass and went on to capture Mt Peschiena, which overlooks the pass from the north, on the 21st September. At the end of these operations the Gothic Line was effectively breached.

In late September the weather began to deteriorate with the fall of continuous heavy rain preventing significant air support to the ground forces, and making most difficult any further advances by the latter. Nonetheless, British 1st Infantry Division took Palazzuolo by the 25th September, going on to capture Mt Tocone on the 27th September and Mt Gamberaldi the day following. British 6th Armoured and Indian 8th Infantry Divisions also persevered, the former along Route 67, reaching Bocconi and taking Mt Fuso by the 26th September, while the latter division reached Mt Castelnuovo on the 29th September to find that it had been very recently abandoned by the Germans.

During a brief pause in activities some redeployment was carried out at the end of September/beginning of October by U.S. 5th Army. British 78th Infantry Division, which had recently returned to Italy after resting and refitting in the Middle East, joined British 13 Corps. This fresh division relieved U.S. 88th Division in the Santerno valley in order that the American unit could then operate northwards on the right flank of U.S. 85th Division in the direction of Castel San Pietro. In addition, British 1st Guards Armoured Brigade was detached from British 6th Armoured Division in order to relieve part of U.S. 88th Division holding Mt Battaglia.

At that time U.S. 2 Corps, on the left of British 13 Corps, changed its line of attack from the direction of Imola up Route 65 towards Bologna, moving forward on the 1st October and reaching Monghidoro, some 30km. short of Bologna on the following day. Meanwhile, British 13 Corps began its slow advance towards Route 9, the Via Emilia, along four river courses. On the immediate right of U.S. 2 Corps, British 78th Infantry Division aimed for Imola along the River Santerno. British 1st Infantry Division astride the River Senio moved towards Castel Bolognese, with Indian 8th Infantry Division advancing along the River Lamone in the direction of Faenza. Finally, British 6th Armoured Division moved along the River Montone towards Forlì .Although U.S. 2 Corps advanced with speed, British 13 Corps moved more slowly, much of its slow progress being attributed to the difficulties in repairing roads damaged by the Germans during their retreat, the incessant wet weather, and the relatively low powered British lorries which generally had only two-wheeled drives, making them incapable of moving and manoeuvring safely on the poorly surfaced and mud bound roads.

A problem arose too from the lengths of the lines of supply between the front line units and their essential services. In early October 1944, British 13 C.T.W. at Sieci was some 70km. behind the leading troops, thereby making it difficult to provide the latter with the engineering services they continually required. In order to minimise this distance British 13 C.T.W. moved forward on the 7th October from Sieci to San Piero a Sieve railway station situated some 22km. due north of Florence on Route 503 to Firenzuola via the Il Giogo Pass, travelling the distance of some 37km. via Pontassieve, Dicomano and Borgo San Lorenzo. This was as far forward as it was possible for the unit to go, since no sites were available in the mountainous region beyond to accommodate a workshop of this size. Indeed, only very small recovery units had room to operate in the higher levels, detachments from British 13 C.T.W. Recovery Section going forward to assist in the recovery of damaged and discarded vehicles littering the British 13 Corps area north-west of the River Sieve.

In his book The Gothic Line, Douglas Orgill makes particular reference to this situation. He says, The Royal Electrical and Mechanical Engineers (to which British 13 C.T.W. belonged), charged with the recovery of ditched, damaged and stranded vehicles, was now facing a situation in which the nearest major workshops were forty miles away, a distance which on crowded Arrow Route (Route 302) took between four and six hours to cover. The workshops could not be moved forward, for there was simply no site on Arrow Route where they could be re-established. Even a small recovery post of two or three vehicles was hard to accommodate in the sea of mud, where divisional artillery too was competing for the few possible pieces of open ground at the side of the road. The only consolation was that German shells, plunging deep into the semi-liquid ground, often failed to explode or had their blast effectively muffled, so that it took a direct hit to do real damage. Under these circumstances of near-impossible endeavour, the R.E.M.E. units, working prodigious hours in the driving rain, through slipping, crawling columns of men and lorries, carried out 339 vehicle recoveries in the first week of October.

A further phase of the attack was launched by U.S. 5th Army on the 5th October. As stated earlier, U.S. 2 Corps was aiming for Bologna, whilst the effort by British 13 Corps was directed at reaching the Via Emilia. British 1st Infantry Division, moving in difficult terrain along the valley of the River Senio, encountered determined German opposition at Mt Ceco which overlooks the villages of Castagno and Mercatale. The engagement stretched over five days, ending on the 9th October in victory for British 1st

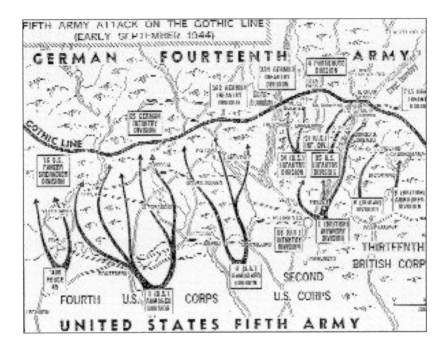

Infantry Division. Indian 8th Infantry Division following the River Lamone captured Mt Cavallera on the 7th October, but failed subsequently to wrest Mt Casalino from the Germans. As part of the same operation British 6th Armoured Division, still following Route 67 towards Forlì, entered Portico di Romagna on the 8th October, but failed to clear it of German forces. British 78th Infantry Division too made little progress. Its immediate objective was to secure Mt La Pieve which it reached and took on the 16th October, but failed to secure. Thus, by mid-October, British 13 Corps was at a standstill on the approximate line, left to right, Mt La Pieve, Mt Cappello, Mt Battaglia, Mt Ceco, Mt Casalino – Portico di Romagna.

There was to be one last attempt by U.S. 5th Army: by U.S. 2 Corps to take Bologna, and by British 13 Corps to reach the Via Emilia. This final effort commenced on the 16th October. Again, it was preceded by some redeployment of the British forces, with British 6th Armoured Division, excluding 26th Armoured Brigade, moving across from

Route 67 to enter the line between British 78th and 1st Infantry Divisions. The reconnaissance regiments of British 6th Armoured, Indian 8th and British 1st Infantry Divisions, together with an army field and medium regiment, joined British 26th Armoured Brigade in order to maintain pressure on the Germans along Route 67. Additionally, British 6th Armoured Division reassumed command of British 1st Guards Armoured Brigade on Mt Battaglia, whilst its 61st Infantry Brigade relieved the 38th Infantry Brigade of British 78th Infantry Division on Mt Cappello.

As part of this final effort British 78th Infantry Division renewed its attack on Mt La Pieve on the 18th/19th October. Mt Spaduro was captured on the 24th October, and the division reached Mt dell' Acqua Salata when outflanking Vena del Gasso. But these were the extent of the advance by British 78th Infantry Division. On the right of British 78th Infantry Division, British 6th Armoured Division made only limited gains in the area north-west of Mt Battaglia, British 1st Infantry Division faring likewise from Mt Ceco. Although Indian 8th Infantry Division was strongly opposed by German forces it did capture Mt Giro on the 23rd October and went on to take Rocca San Casciano. But by the 26th October efforts by U.S. 5th Army, including British 13 Corps, were suspended, all its formations going over on to the defensive. Units of U.S. 2 Corps were still some 15km. short of the centre of Bologna, with those of British 13 Corps, at their nearest point, 11km. from the Via Emilia. And so the situation generally remained until the spring offensive, the final major operation of the Italian Campaign, opened on the 9th April, 1945.

For a little in excess of six months, during the period of winter stalemate, British 13 C.T.W. remained at San Piero a Sieve railway station. Much work was done recovering, repairing and servicing guns, vehicles and equipment in preparation for the spring offensive. One significant accomplishment during early February was the fitting out of the first Universal 'Bren' Carrier as a 'Wasp' flame-thrower. This was followed by a series of satisfactory trials and demonstrations with an intensive work programme involving the similar equipping of a large number of carriers in time for use in the spring offensive.

In the period from mid-October up to Christmas 1944 there was almost continuous rainfall, the fields and roads being churned into a morass by the heavy military traffic. British 13 C.T.W. was fortunate in being at a railway station, and thus being able to utilise the rail tracks and sidings as hard standing for vehicles, generators and the like. But soon after Christmas the rain turned to snow, the temperature becoming increasingly

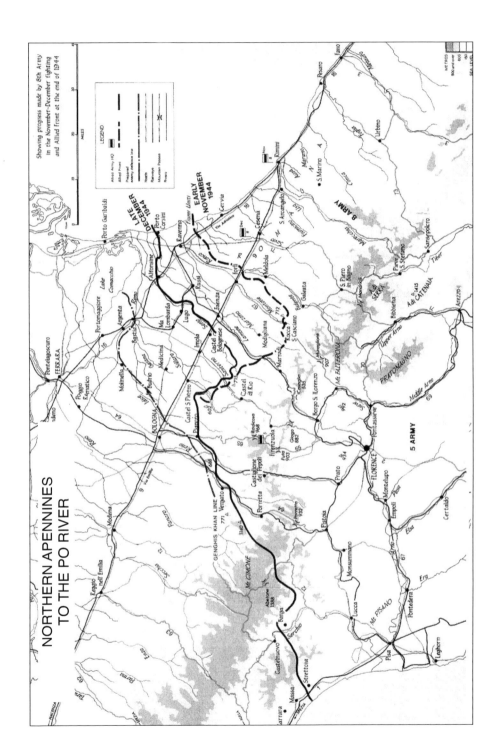

NORTHERN APENNINES
TO THE PO RIVER

cold and plunging to 17°F of frost on both the 11th and 22nd January. Because of the severe weather those soldiers living in tents were moved into houses in the village of San Piero a Sieve, the Italians generally opting to make room rather than to move out.

During the first three months of 1945 the opportunity was taken to grant leave to all members of British 13 C.T.W., most having been working continuously without any break for at least a year. I was fortunate to be given a week's leave in Rome in March, making the return journey partly in the back of a lorry and partly by train. In addition to visiting many of the notable locations in the Eternal City, I attended a performance of 'Madame Butterfly' at the Rome Opera House with the famous tenor Gigli singing the role of Lieut. Pinkerton. It was unforgettable.

Unusually, the initial reaction by several members of the unit when offered leave was to decline to take it, although in such cases those concerned were then ordered to accept. The refusals by those so doing appeared to stem from their wish to avoid being absent and other than fully involved in the coming spring offensive and its preparations. Having played a full part in the activities of the unit throughout the Italian Campaign so far, they wanted to be 'in at the kill'. In the event, all had taken and returned from leave well before the spring offensive opened.

The final phase of the Italian Campaign opened on the 9th April. British 13 Corps, which had reverted to British 8th Army command during the period of stalemate, advanced westwards with the Polish 2 Corps on their left, formations crossing the River Sillaro on the 15th April, and by the 19th April approaching the River Idice. Bologna itself was taken jointly by the U.S. 2 and Polish 2 Corps on the 21st April, with British 13 Corps then wheeling northwards to close up to and to cross the River Po on the 24th April.

Once across this great river barrier British 13 Corps, with British 5 Corps on its right and alongside, swept on in a northerly direction, crossing the River Adige on the 27th April, taking Venice on the 29th April and Trieste on the 2nd May. By 18.00 hrs. on the latter day the German forces in Italy had surrendered to the Allies, whilst on the 4th May the German General von Senger arrived at U.S. General Mark Clark's headquarters to formally capitulate. The twenty-month long Italian Campaign was indeed over.

During this last offensive British 13 C.T.W. finally left San Piero a Sieve on the 19th April, travelling the 130km. to Lugo via Dicomano, Forlì and Faenza. After a week at Lugo the unit joined the chase northwards moving through Medicina, Budrio, Lovoleto, San Pietro in Casale and Poggio Renatico to the small village of Chiesa Nuova. At the

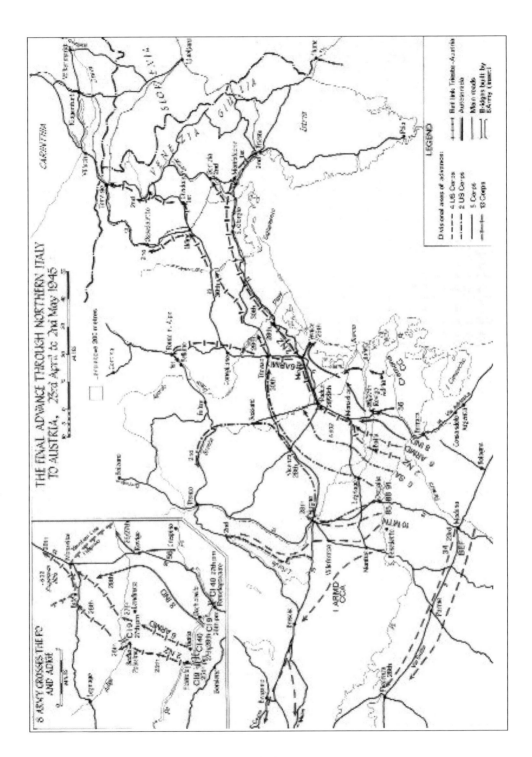

end of a further week at this location British 13 C.T.W. set forth at 03.40 hrs. on the 3rd May continuing northwards to cross the River Po by pontoon bridge and arriving at Mestre near Venice late that day. It was at Mestre that the soldiers of the unit learned that the Italian Campaign was over, and to a man were bewildered and apprehensive as to what now would become of them. It seemed as if the only way of life they had ever known was about to end. After five days at Mestre where little work was done, since the workshops were never properly established due to the pervading general uncertainty, the unit made its last move in Italy while I was a member of it to Cervignano del Friuli, some 45km. north-west of Trieste. It was there on the 13th May that British 13 C.T.W. paraded and went on to attend a service of thanksgiving to mark the end of the Italian Campaign and the war in Europe.

Four days later I left the unit to embark on the long journey to the R.E.M.E. Middle East School of Instruction at Tel el Kebir in Egypt.

19
Epilogue

There has always been controversy with regard to the importance of the contribution made by the Italian Partisans to the liberation of their country in World War II from both the Germans and the Fascists.

During the trial of Obersturmbannführer Kappler for his part in the massacre at the Ardeatine Caves on the 24th March, 1944, the Tribunale Militare di Roma were reluctant to support the attack by Partisans on German troops in the Via Rasella on the previous day as a legitimate act of war.

But in 1948, a small group of the relatives of some of those massacred by the Germans in the Ardeatine Caves took out a civil action against seven of the Partisans involved in the Via Rasella attack. This action was heard in the Italian courts, the court coming down firmly on the side of the Partisans, declaring the attack to be a legitimate act of war, and that those who organised and carried it out could not be made to answer for the Ardeatine Caves massacre committed by the Germans as a reprisal for the attack. Indeed, during the following year, three of the Partisans were decorated for their parts in the Via Rasella attack; Carla Capponi with the Medaglia d'Oro, together with Rosario Bentivegna and Franco Calamandrei each with the Medaglia d'Argento, all for military valour.

However, the small group of relatives of those massacred took their case to a higher court, the Roman Court of Appeals which, in mid 1954 confirmed the ruling of the lower court. Still dissatisfied, the relatives then moved their case to the Supreme Court of Cassation, advancing the new argument that Rome, at the time of the Via Rasella attack was an 'open city', and the action there by the Partisans could not, therefore, be an act of war. The Supreme Court gave its judgment on the 3rd August, 1957, declaring that, because of the occupying Germans, Rome could not have been an 'open city'. Moreover, Rome was never recognised as an 'open city' by the Allies. As a consequence, said the court, the Partisan attack in the Via Rasella was an act of war carried out when the city of Rome was but a short distance from the battle front. (In March 1944 the main front was, in fact, 120km. south-east of Rome through Cassino, with the Anzio beachhead 50km. south of Rome.)

Epilogue

But many factions of post World War II Italian society have continued to defame the activities of the Partisans during that conflict, and those involved in the Via Rasella attack in particular. Much anti-Partisan propaganda has been published over the years accusing those involved in that attack as being the murderers of innocent civilians who carried out a plot against the citizens of Rome which was designed by the Soviets. It has also been stated in many quarters, both verbally and by the written word, that the German authorities appealed to the Partisans who carried out the Via Rasella attack to give themselves up so as to allow the order to carry out the reprisal which involved the massacre of 335 innocent souls in the Ardeatine Caves to be countermanded. In fact, no such appeal was ever made.

From immediately subsequent to the 24th March, 1944, and since, the Vatican has taken the view that the Via Rasella attack by the Partisans was as much a massacre as were the killings by the Germans in the Ardeatine Caves. It is most unlikely that any protest by Pope Pius XII would have dissuaded Hitler and the Germans from proceeding with the Ardeatine Caves massacre. But protest or intervene he did not. The Holy Father never wished to appear anti-German to the many Roman Catholics of the German nation, and believed it was preferable to say nothing rather than to make any utterance showing a bias one way or the other in such matters. There was, as a result, no protest or condemnation by the Holy See of the Germans for the Ardeatine Caves massacre.

Another but non-religious view is that the Via Rasella attack was an error; a cowardly action carried out by youths having communist leanings, without due consideration as to its military use and possible German reprisals against the civilian population.

Much of the criticism of the Partisans stems from actions by them which resulted in reprisals by the occupying Germans. One such example is described in an article by Sebastiano Vassalli which appeared in the 27th June, 1997 issue of the *Corriere della Sera*. In it he tells how early on the morning of the 29th June, 1944, the 'Otello Gattoli' Partisan unit, about three hundred strong, was on the march from Guardistallo, some 15km. inland from Cecina on the west coast of Italy and 30km. south of Livorno, towards Casale Marittimo, approximately 21/2km. distant, when it encountered a German motorised column retreating northwards, being pursued by Allied forces. A fierce engagement took place in which the Partisans were overcome, two of them being killed, together with one German soldier. Subsequently, nine other Partisans who the Germans had taken prisoner were executed, as were forty-six civilians rounded up at random from the surrounding farming community. Thus, fifty-seven Italians were murdered as a result of one German death at the hands of the Partisans.

On the following day advance units of the U.S. 5th Army reached Guardistallo, while coincidentally there began a period of mourning for the Italian victims. The latter saw the majority of the local population apportion to the 'Otello Gattoli' Partisans a greater part of the blame for the killings than that attributed to the Germans. Amongst the accusers were the close relatives of those massacred and the local priest, Don Mazzetto Rafanelli who, a few days previous to the massacre had been mediating with the German command regarding the imminent arrival of Allied forces in the area. The priest pointed the finger of blame wholly against the Partisans, rather than against the authors of the slaughter. The reasoning of the accusers says Vassalli is simple and quite persuasive. They hold that the massacre was together foreseeable and useless. Provoking the Germans was not an act of war but a crime against the civilian population: a crime producing no heroes and only victims.

Thus, the events of the 29th June, 1944 at Guardistallo gave rise to two irreconcilable memories: the local one created by bereavement and from rancour, and the national one which is celebrated each year on the 25th April, and which, in turn, provokes reactions of intolerance. This situation continued for fifty years until a committee of the citizens of Guardistallo, with the Mayor as chairman, decided that it was time to put an end to the differences of memory with regard to the events of the 29th June, 1944, and to give an indisputable and definitive ruling as to responsibility and guilt. In order to make this pronouncement, Professor Pezzino of the University of Pisa was requested to give his opinion on the massacre at Guardistallo, and to rule as to who was the guilty party. The Professor was invited to hide nothing of the events of the 29th June, 1944, and to reconstruct honestly what took place on that day. Professor Pezzino's research extended over three years and resulted in his book Anatomy of a Massacre. In it he reconsiders the activities of the 'Otello Gattoli' Partisans outside the rhetoric of the activities of the Partisans in general, to which was attributed non-existent characteristics and daring exploits that were never carried out. Pezzino goes on to discuss some of the common platitudes about the Germans, including the distinction between the good and humane conscript German soldiers and those in the special corps and anti-Partisan units. The Professor also criticises the continuing and successive divisions between the inhabitants of Guardistallo in the context of the certainty of a section of the clergy of those years to exist and act over and above the differing lay factions.

Epilogue

In his *Corriere della Sera* article Vassalli does not divulge Professor Pezzino's conclusions directly, or the sentence as to who was the guilty party in respect of the Guardistallo massacre. Vassalli accedes that the reconstruction of the massacre by the Professor is reasonably accurate and definitive. He goes on to say that if more than half a century later the two opposing memories of the massacre do not, as a result of Professor Pezzino's book, begin to recompose themselves, then the research required to produce the book will have been in vain.

Vassalli foresees the possibility that those holding the two opposing memories of the Guardistallo massacre will continue to exist until death overtakes all those involved so long ago and time itself distorts, fades and finally obliterates all memory of the massacre. Whichever party Professor Pezzino's book declares 'not guilty' of the massacre will leave the other party in a state of discontent. Moreover, despite the honesty and clarity of Anatomy of a Massacre, the passions of the opposing factions remain unextinguished, and as a result of reading the book not one inhabitant of Guardistallo will have changed their opinion with regard to the circumstances of the events there on the 29th June, 1944.

A parallel analysis could well be written for the Via Rasella attack and the consequent Ardeatine Caves massacre, as well as for almost all other Partisan attacks and their resultant reprisal massacres by the Germans.

Arising out of correspondence with the authorities of the Comune di Cavriglia in Tuscany, I was provided with much valuable information for this book with regard both to the massacres carried out by the Germans in the area in early July 1944, and the lignite mining complex centred on Santa Barbara. Moreover, the Mayor of Cavriglia, Signor Enzo Brogi, and local historian, Signor Emilio Polverini, invited me, accompanied by my son John, to visit the Comune di Cavriglia from the 28th June to the 6th July, 1997, this period including the anniversary date for the massacres of the 4th July. The invitation was readily accepted.

Thus, on the first of these dates my son and I travelled by air and car to Tuscany, going from Milan by way of the Autostrada del Sole, the Passo della Raticosa and the Passo della Futa (part of the Gothic Line, where there is now a large German Military Cemetery), rejoining the Autostrada del Sole, and then taking Route 69 to San Giovanni Valdarno. From the latter we turned off towards the Monti del Chianti and Castelnuovo dei Sabbioni, soon reaching San Cipriano, which adjoins Santa Barbara, and locating the Hotel del Lago where we were to stay during our visit. The hotel is a converted farmhouse, and is so named as it is situated on the shore of an artificial lake containing reserve cooling water for the nearby Santa Barbara Centrale power station.

On the following morning, a Sunday, we were greeted in the hotel foyer by Emilio Polverini who was to accompany us to Civitella in Val di Chiana. The three of us were picked up by a police car from Civitella in which were its police chief and a driver. Travelling on occasion at speeds in excess of 200km./hour we believed the driver to be an experienced police driver in mufti; but subsequently discovered that he was, in fact, a general factotum in the employ of the Comune di Civitella whose varied duties included the odd spot of driving for the police.

At Civitella Town Hall our party collected a civic banner and numerous laurel wreaths, and were joined by the Mayor of Civitella, his councillors, and Dario, our interpreter for the day. The latter was a most pleasant young man, half Italian and half English, who had spent his childhood in London.

The purpose of the Civitella visit was to take part as guests in the ceremonies to commemorate the massacres there of two hundred and twelve men, women and children by the Germans on the 29th June, 1944, exactly fifty-three years earlier. It was through the association A.N.F.I.M., to which belong the various Comunes where massacres by the Germans took place, mainly during mid 1944, that we were invited, together with others from the Comune di Cavriglia and elsewhere, to visit Civitella. I was somewhat embarrassed to see my name, and that I had served with the British 8th Army during the Italian Campaign, prominently displayed on posters around Civitella.

Joining an assembly in the Piazza Lazzeri, the main square of Civitella, we listened to the town band perform two pieces, one of which was the Italian National Anthem. The Mayor of Civitella then made a short speech about the tragic events that had taken place at Civitella fifty-three years ago, during which he mentioned that my son John and I were present that day. This was followed by Mass in the lovely and beautifully restored Chiesa di S. Maria and a concert performed by the Hesperimenta Vocal Ensemble and the Polifonica San Lorenzo. It was interesting to note that the police officers present in the church did not remove either their head-dress or their small arms.

Leaving the church, we went with the Mayor of Civitella and his party to visit a number of isolated sites where citizens of Civitella had been put to death on the 29th June, 1944. Each location visited was marked by a memorial stone at which the Mayor placed a wreath of laurel leaves bearing the Italian national colours, this being followed by a brief period of reflection. Finally, we made our way to the cemetery where many of the victims of the massacres at Civitella are buried, outside which is a memorial bearing their names. By this memorial we met and spoke with the relatives of some of those massacred.

Following a protracted lunch in a local restaurant and a tour on foot of the very lovely Civitella, we were again taken by police car to the village of San Pancrazio, some 13km. distant. Here, also on the 29th June, 1944, in a cellar adjacent to the main square, the Germans massacred seventy-five local inhabitants.

In the late afternoon those of us from the Comune di Cavriglia and from Civitella joined a parade which formed up at the outskirts of San Pancrazio and made its way through the village to the main square, where a commemoration ceremony was held comprising several long political speeches and an open air Mass. During this ceremony we visited the cellar where the massacre had occurred. The cellar itself has recently been renovated and restored, much of it as it was in mid 1944, both as a museum and a monument to those put to death. Bullet marks can still be seen on the cellar walls, and a location is specifically identified where a local peasant was killed. In a small public garden adjacent to the cellar, its lower terrace contains a separate and different rose tree to commemorate each citizen of San Pancrazio murdered by the Germans.

After the Mass we accompanied those assembled in the short walk to the cemetery located on the slopes below the village where the communal grave of those massacred is situated, this being marked by a memorial stone bearing all the names and many of the photographs of those put to death. Another short ceremony was then held during which the names of all those massacred at San Pancrazio on the 29th June, 1944 were read out. This reading was made by Ugo Jona, the President of A.N.F.I.M., a diminutive figure, and a Jew, whose entire family was exterminated by the Germans.

Somewhat weary after a long and exhausting day, we were driven back to our hotel at San Cipriano via Bucine, Montevarchi and San Giovanni Valdarno.

Over the following days we visited most of the principal locations in the Comune di Cavriglia which were the site of or closely related to the massacres carried out in early July 1944.

On the Monday these included the Estate Santa Maria where the house of the Agricultural Agent was occupied as an H.Q. by troops of 76 Panzer Corps on the 29th June, 1944, the Villa Renacci at which Leut.-General Richard Heidrich, commander of German 1st Parachute Division and his staff took up residence on the 1st July, 1944, and the Scuola di Musica in the Via Verdi of Terranuova, where the main body of the anti-Partisan Unit commanded by Leut. Wolf was billeted.

In San Cipriano itself it was not possible to identify any of the properties used by the Germans in late June/early July 1944, since many had been demolished and much renumbering had taken place. Historian Emilio Polverini explains that prior to World War II the Societè Anonima Miniera Le Carpinete constructed some blocks of flats in San Cipriano. These were known locally as 'case della Carpinete' (Carpinete Houses), but no Via Carpinese or Via Carpinete existed as such. The blocks of flats still exist, but have been sold privately, with some being reconstructed, whilst others have been newly built nearby in the same style. As a consequence it is, in fact, difficult, if not impossible, to identify such properties as were used by the Germans in 1944. Some 1 1/2 km. distant from the above properties the original offices of the mine 'La Carpinete' have been replaced by the offices of the lignite mining complex. However, close to San Cipriano we did find the near derelict Villa Cetinale, once the home of Giuseppe Corsi. The villa was occupied by a German General and his staff as an H.Q. on the 2nd July, 1944. In Santa Barbara too, the flats constructed by the lignite mining company for its workers during the early years of World War II, and which were the assembly point for the German troops who carried out the massacres in the nearby villages on the 4th July, 1944 remained and were occupied by local citizens.

During the following day, Tuesday, our first call was to Montegonzi where the Castello was taken over on the 1st July, 1944 by troops of a German Hermann Goering 'Flak' Unit commanded by Major Seiler, the balance of this unit being billeted in the local school (now a library).

We then went on to the cemetery at Montaio where Ugo Bandinelli was buried on the 23rd July, 1944 after being shot by a German raiding party at his farm some fifteen days earlier. The grave of Ugo Bandinelli could not be located, although we did discover the grave of Teresa Bandinelli; most likely a relative of Ugo, but not his wife or daughter.

Next we visited the town of Cavriglia and found the Villa Bonarotti. This building is imposing, standing on high ground with its own gardens, and in 1944 would have been on the outskirts of Cavriglia. It was occupied from the 29th June, 1944 by a Colonel commanding German 11 Hermann Goering Panzer Grenadier Regiment.

From Cavriglia we made our way back to Castelnuovo dei Sabbioni; there in the Piazza IV Novembre, in the centre of the old village, which was the site of the massacre on the 4th July, 1944, we met up with the Mayor of Cavriglia, our interpreter Emma Pyke, and representatives of the local press, radio and television. Photographs and moving film were taken of me indicating the shrine commemorating those massacred, and in an interview I related the circumstances and details of my first entry into Castelnuovo dei Sabbioni in July 1944. A photograph and a verbatim report of the interview appeared in the supplement of La Nazione Arezzo dated the 4th July, 1997, the 53rd anniversary of the massacre.

Following an excellent lunch in the restaurant of the Parco di Cavriglia, situated at an elevation of some six hundred and fifty metres above sea level in the Monti del Chianti, we drove to Massa dei Sabbioni. There we saw and photographed the house that in July 1944 was the barber shop in which three men, one the local priest, were detained by German soldiers. On the opposite side of the road, some twenty-five metres further from the village centre, we visited the shrine where the barn Scala was once located, and in which the priest, Don Morini and Dante Pagliazzi were bayoneted to death and their bodies incinerated at the hands of the Germans on the 4th July, 1944. From the village we went to the local cemetery where the two men were initially interred in a common grave. Their remains are now in a small compartment in a wall of the cemetery, this compartment bearing the names and dates of birth and death of Don Morini and Dante Pagliazzi.

From the cemetery at Massa dei Sabbioni we went on to San Pancrazio, some 1 1/2 km. south of Castelnuovo dei Sabbioni, first visiting the lovely old church in which historian Emilio Polverini had been married. In the nearby cemetery we sought and found the common grave of Faustino Perini and Ivan Gelli (uncle and nephew) who were shot and killed by Germans while hiding in the woods near San Pancrazio. In the same cemetery we discovered the burial compartment of Antinesca Perini, the wife of Faustino, who found the bodies of her husband and nephew on the morning of the 9th July, 1944.

Leaving San Pancrazio we then motored through Il Neri and Castelnuovo dei Sabbioni to Meleto. Here we went to the locations of the Pasquini and Rossini farms at the south-west end of the village where seventeen and twenty-three men respectively were shot dead by the Germans and their bodies incinerated on the 4th July, 1944. Moving to the north-east end of Meleto, we visited the locations of the Benini and Melani farms where twenty-seven and twenty-two men respectively were similarly put to death. The barn of the Melani farm, although derelict, still exists. It is located at the rear of the

Villa Barberino, now, in part, an upmarket restaurant and apartments complex. In a conversation with the padrone of the Villa Barberino he explained that the twenty-two men killed there by the Germans had subsequently been incinerated by igniting hay then stored in the barn, and that no petrol was used. It was thought that this perhaps explains why the Melani barn was not totally destroyed by fire, as were the other barns at Meleto.

Finally, after a long and tiring day we went to the cemetery at Meleto, seeing there the common grave of thirty-one of the victims of the Meleto massacres, and discovering many but not all of the graves, some individual and some common, of the other sixty-two men put to death by the Germans.

While touring the lignite mining area on the Wednesday we visited the location where the village of San Martino had once been. The village itself no longer exists, having been engulfed by the opencast lignite mining operations. However, we saw and photographed the memorial to the four men killed in the village by the Germans on the 4th July, 1944. This memorial was first erected at the site of the massacre, but has been relocated on several occasions because of land slips and the encroachment of the opencast mining.

After touring the mining area and visiting the location where San Martino had once been, we were taken to Santa Barbara Centrale power station and given a short conducted tour of the facility. Lunch was taken in the canteen of the power station, and this was followed by a visit to Siena with a view to seeing the Palio. Unfortunately, rain had ruined the sand base laid in the Piazza del Campo on which the horses were intended to run, the event as a consequence being postponed for twenty-four hours.

Thursday morning was spent in discussion with Emilio Polverini at his house, in the company of his younger brother Leandro, a Professor of Ancient History at the University of Rome, who also acted as interpreter. Our talks ranged over the history of the lignite mining operations in the area, and the details of the massacres carried out locally by the Germans in early July, 1944. We went on to discuss the inquiry then currently being carried out by a Special Court in Rome to examine the activities of the Italian Partisans during the years 1943–45, and to determine if these were justified in the light of the resultant massacres meted out by the Germans on the civilian population, especially in June, July and August of 1944. This was followed by an analysis of War in Italy: 1943–45 by Richard Lamb and Mussolini by Denis Mack Smith.

We then turned to the subject of the Via Rasella bombing in Rome in March 1944, the resultant Ardeatine Caves massacre, and the trial of Herbert Kappler. In the context of tracing and bringing to trial those who carried out the massacres in the Comune di Cavriglia, I pointed out to Professor Polverini that a decision had been taken in October 1945 that only the most senior German officers responsible for planning and carrying out reprisals against the civilian population in Italy would be dealt with by a British Military Court, all lesser ranks being dealt with by the Italian Government. Thus, Generals von Mackensen and Mälzer were jointly tried by a British Military Court for their parts in the Ardeatine Caves massacre, while Field Marshal Kesselring was similarly arraigned for his part in both the Ardeatine Caves and other massacres. But Kappler and Caruso, the Fascist Police Chief of Rome, were tried by the Italians. In the event, all five men were found guilty, but only Caruso was executed. Continuing, I said that as far as I was able to ascertain no other German General such as Heidrich or Lemelsen had been put on trial by the British, neither did the Italians trace and put on trial any of the lesser German ranks who actually carried out the massacres in the Comune di Cavriglia and elsewhere. The recent trial of Priebke, one of Kappler's junior officers, is the exception.

Winding up our discussions, the Polverini brothers expressed their delight at receiving through me copies of the British Army S.I.B. Reports dealing with the massacres in the Comune di Cavriglia. I emphasised that these Reports were for the archives of the Comune di Cavriglia and Emilio Polverini's private collection only, making it clear that the part of this book which covered the massacres would be based on the S.I.B. Reports. Professor Polverini urged me to complete and publish my book without delay, since I must be regarded as a prime source of information, with first-hand knowledge of the happenings in the Comune di Cavriglia of July 1944. I promised to do my best, but said that completion was at least a year hence. Professor Polverini took the view that all my time should be dedicated to completing this book, and was surprised when I told him that some of my time was necessarily consumed with shopping, cleaning, laundering, correspondence, and the like. He indicated that I ought to employ someone to deal with such mundane matters.

We then visited the new local church of San Donato a Castelnuovo, which is much more attractive internally than it is externally, although "Il libro del ricordo" located in front of the church is most impressive. The nearby murals produced by Venturino Venturi appeared hoarding like, futuristic, and to me somewhat out of keeping. The bell of the church was cast to mark the fortieth anniversary of the Castelnuovo dei Sabbioni massacres, and rings out each day around sunset. Returning to Emilio Polverini's residence, we partook of an excellent lunch dispensed by Signora Polverini.

After lunch we spent time at the house of Emilio Polverini's recently deceased mother, where many of the historian's documents are kept. The meticulously maintained catalogue and the scale of the collection were most impressive.

Leaving the house of Emilio Polverini's mother, we commenced a tour of locations in and near to Castelnuovo dei Sabbioni that were the sites of significant incidents closely concerned with the massacres. First we went to a road bridge under which two German servicemen intended to spend the night, having lost their way to a German military hospital recently located in the vicinity. The presence of the two Germans was made known to the local Partisans who killed them both during the night of the 4th/5th June, 1944, and took the vehicle in which they were travelling. Moving on to the district of Castelnuovo dei Sabbioni known as Le Matole, we visited the site of the massacre there of ten Italian men in the early evening of the 11th July, 1944. The site is marked with a monument embracing ten truncated columns, each bearing the name of one of the men killed by the Germans. Nearby is a road drainage hole and channel in which one of the ten men shot hid overnight, being found dead on the morning of the 12th July, 1944. This spot is marked by a separate small monument. Ascending the steep slope up which the bodies were carried after the Germans had departed, we reached the two houses in which the bodies were cleaned up and kept prior to being taken for burial to the cemetery at Castelnuovo dei Sabbioni on the 12th July, 1944. Looking over a wall adjacent to the above mentioned two houses we observed and photographed a general view of Le Matole and the nucleus of the old village of Castelnuovo dei Sabbioni, including the old church and the Piazza IV Novembre. Following the route taken by those carrying the ten bodies from the houses where they had lain prior to burial, we made our way to the cemetery with its large communal grave containing the eighty-four bodies of those massacred at Castelnuovo dei Sabbioni and Le Matole.

Emilio Polverini explained that those massacred on the 4th July, 1944, including his father, were buried one week later in the communal grave. Since the bodies had been incinerated and partly destroyed, they were tipped into the grave in no particular order. However, the bodies of those shot on the 11th July, 1944 and buried on the following day, had not been burned, and were placed side by side in the north-east end of the same communal grave and adjacent to those buried the previous day. As a consequence, the length of the grave for the ten men killed on the 11th July, 1944 is considerably greater than that for the seventy-four killed one week earlier.

Epilogue

Friday the 4th July, 1997, being the fifty-third anniversary of most of the massacres in the Comune di Cavriglia, was the pinnacle of our visit, and proved to be particularly arduous. Punctually at 08.00 hrs., John and I were collected from the Hotel del Lago and taken by an official car to the nucleus of the old village of Castelnuovo dei Sabbioni. There, at the shrine in the Piazza IV Novembre was held the first commemoration ceremony of the day. This comprised a Mass with a dissertation by the local priest, the placing of laurel leaf wreaths in the shrine to honour those massacred in the piazza fifty-three years earlier and at nearby Le Matole on the 11th July, 1944, and the sounding of the Italian equivalent of 'The Last Post'. John and I, soberly dressed in dark suits, went forward to place a wreath in the shrine, similar wreaths being placed by representatives of the Comune di Cavriglia, the French town of La Chapelle Saint Mesmin (the French twin town of Cavriglia) and the Carabinieri.

After the ceremony we were introduced to Aldo Dini, looking much younger than his seventy-three years who, immediately prior to the massacre in the Piazza IV Novembre, managed to escape from the Germans, and thus avoided being put to death. We were also greeted with a smart salute by the Carabinieri Capitano of the district, a fine looking man, exquisitely turned out, and with a parachutist's wings on his uniform.

From Castelnuovo dei Sabbioni we went on to Massa dei Sabbioni. Here the Mayor of Cavriglia and others placed laurel leaf wreaths in the shrine on the site of the barn Scala where Don Morini and Dante Pagliazzi had been killed. Interestingly, the Mayor was not aware that the house on the other side of the road and some twenty-five metres nearer to the village centre had been the barber shop in which the two men who were subsequently killed, and another man who managed to escape, had initially been detained by German soldiers.

Making our way to Meleto we attended a further commemoration ceremony. This was quite protracted and embraced a Mass, a short address by Ugo Jona, the President of A.N.F.I.M., followed by his reading of the names of the ninety-three men massacred at Meleto on the 4th July, 1944. A further two speeches were then given, the first by Francesco Lelmi, an ex-Partisan and a member of Associazione Nazionale Partigiani Italiani (A.N.P.I.), and the second by the Mayor of Cavriglia. Lelmi read his speech from prepared notes, and I suspect that it was a version of his 'party piece', with a fair pro-communist content. By contrast, the Mayor of Cavriglia spoke but briefly and without the aid of notes. The ceremony took place in the War Memorial Square of Meleto where the men who were subsequently massacred were first assembled by the Germans.

Following the ceremony at Meleto we went again to the lovely Parco di Cavriglia for another splendid lunch. During the meal a policewoman from Terranuova, and a member of the local force of the Comune di Cavriglia, who sat opposite to John and me, remarked that he and I had been seen together in the area, many of the local inhabitants enquiring who we were. Having been identified as the ex-British 8th Army soldier whose name currently appeared on posters displayed locally, the policewoman went on to say that the people had taken John and me as brothers rather than father and son. John, in jest, stood up and acted as though he was offended by the inference that he appeared older than his forty-nine years, and I looked much younger than my seventy-four. The Italians present thought this to be highly amusing.

After lunch we returned to the Hotel del Lago to rest and prepare for the activities of the evening. Promptly at 17.30 hrs. we were collected and taken by official car to the Town Hall at Cavriglia. We were conducted into the Council Chamber where I sat on the platform with the Mayors of Cavriglia and La Chapelle Saint Mesmin and Emma Pyke, my translator. In the body of the Council Chamber were seated four small groups representing the four main political parties in the Comune, together with son John, and Emilio and Leandro Polverini. The Mayor of Cavriglia opened the proceedings by making a short speech welcoming the Mayor of La Chapelle Saint Mesmin and myself, then going on to introduce the representatives of the various political parties whose leaders responded by saying a few words. It was emphasised that, despite their political differences, the parties pulled together in their efforts to deal with the economic, social and environmental problems facing the Comune di Cavriglia.

I was then invited to say a few words through Emma Pyke. John and I were greatly honoured, I said, to be present in the Comune on this special day. I recalled that it was nearly fifty-three years since I had first entered Castelnuovo dei Sabbioni to learn of the massacres there and in other villages nearby. I was sickened by what had occurred and grieved for the people of the area then. More than half a century later I returned to grieve for them and with them again today.

Concluding, I said that the present gathering seemed ideally opportune for me to thank the Mayor of Cavriglia, Signor Brogi, and local historian Emilio Polverini for all their help and kindness, and to give them each a token gift from myself. The driver of our official car, who understood exactly what was afoot, had quietly brought in the two gifts from the car and placed them by the platform table. I then said that it gave me much pleasure to present the Mayor with a clock, emphasising that it was a fine English piece with Westminster chimes and suitably inscribed, and Signor Polverini with a Parker three piece 'Falcon' pen and pencil set in rolled gold, which was a collector's item. The gifts were unwrapped there and then, the recipients showing genuine delight.

Leaving Cavriglia Town Hall we were taken to a lovingly restored house and church high up in the Monti del Chianti. The church itself had once been a staging post for pilgrims en route to Rome. The location was quite beautiful, the charming and elderly owners being only too pleased to show us around and refresh us with a glass of their excellent home produced champagne. We then departed for Castelnuovo dei Sabbioni where we were given a simple meal in the working mens' social club which was served by its members. Coffee was subsequently provided in the adjacent bar where I was introduced to many of the local townsfolk.

Sometime between 22.00 and 23.00 hrs., almost sixty minutes later than scheduled, we made our way into the Conference Hall in the basement of the social club building. On the platform were the Mayor of Cavriglia, Emilio Polverini, my interpreter Emma Pyke and myself. Amongst the audience, which I estimated at between two hundred and two hundred and fifty, were Professor Polverini, Aldo Dini, Francesco Lelmi and Enzo Droandi, historian of Arezzo, together with my son John. The Mayor opened the meeting and introduced me to the audience. This was followed by some more than complimentary remarks regarding myself by Emilio Polverini. In part, he said that he knew of no one who possessed a broader and more profound knowledge than myself of the tragic events of July 1944, and the economic, social and environmental problems and developments of the area.

I was then invited to say a few words. Although I cannot remember exactly what I said, I recall that my initial remarks were an apology for speaking in English, since my knowledge of the Italian language was quite inadequate for what I wished to convey. I went on to say that I was greatly honoured to be allowed to be present with the people of Castelnuovo dei Sabbioni on this special day of commemoration, and I shared their sorrow and grief.

On a less sad note, I told of the immense pleasure it gave my son John and myself to be in the Comune di Cavriglia. I expressed our sincere thanks for all the kindness, courtesy and consideration extended to us wherever we had gone. We would, I said, be sad soon to have to depart for England, but I hoped that I would be permitted to return on occasion for as long as I was able to do so.

I then explained briefly what brought me to the Comune di Cavriglia, saying that I was in course of writing an account of my wartime journey through Italy, and my convergence at Castelnuovo dei Sabbioni with the terrible atrocities committed there by the Germans exactly fifty-three years earlier.

Aldo Dini then reiterated his experience of escaping death in the Piazza IV Novembre on the 4th July, 1944.

This was followed by Francesco Lelmi, the ex-Partisan, who delivered an illuminating speech in which he exhibited a view typical of that taken by the Partisans of the part played by the Allies in the liberation of Italy from both the Germans and the Fascists in World War II.

Lelmi told how the Partisans operating in the hills between the Valdarno and the Monti del Chianti found themselves faced with very difficult situations at the beginning of July 1944. The battle zone was approaching, and the women, children, older men and youths, who had escaped from the villages of Meleto, Castelnuovo dei Sabbioni, Massa dei Sabbioni and San Pancrazio, where massacres by the Germans had occurred, had now taken refuge in the Partisan controlled zone. The Partisans, as well as being engaged in guerrilla warfare, had to feed both themselves and those taking refuge, in addition to supplying arms for new recruits joining the Partisan movement. In these circumstances the command of the 4th Company 'Castellani' of the Sinigaglia Brigade of Partisans decided to send a courier to the British 8th Army in order to arrange for a supply of weapons, ammunition and medicines. Because of their knowledge of the Chianti region, two volunteers, 'Cecco'[1] and 'Gaiole'[2] were selected to act as the couriers.

The journey by the two Partisans was a hazardous one. They encountered a number of armed German patrols and saw from a mountain ridge the exact position of the battle front in movement in the valley below. Eventually 'Cecco' and 'Gaiole' reached a house inhabited by two old farmers who gave them food and lodging. The farmers told the two Partisans that the news was not good. The Germans had been to the farm several times threatening them with death and killing all the farm animals for food. A real danger existed that the Germans would return.

The route from the farm to the Allied lines presented many risks, and particularly so

---

1 Francesco Lelmi was known among the Partisans as 'Cecco', this being the local nickname for Francesco.
2 'Gaiole' was the name by which Lelmi's companion was known, Lelmi hailing from Gaoile in Chianti. Gaiole's real name was Girolamo Vannini.

.

for the two young Partisans who were armed only with a single pistol. At this point 'Gaiole' felt unable to continue with the mission, so 'Cecco' sent him back to his comrades. Then, after a further day of waiting and hiding, 'Cecco' finally encountered a patrol from the South African 6th Armoured Division.

A sergeant from the South African formation greeted 'Cecco', who amid the noise of warfare tried to explain the reasons for his mission. The pair went to the nearby Castagnoli farm where the farmer's wife, who spoke some English, acted as interpreter between 'Cecco' and a liaison officer. Having interrogated 'Cecco' at length, the liaison officer, while promising nothing in the way of supplies for the Partisans, arranged for 'Cecco' to be taken to British 8th Army headquarters near Panicarola sul Trasimeno where he could make the case for the urgently needed supplies.

Captain Gregor, an intelligence officer at British 8th Army headquarters, who spoke good Italian, listened intently to the requests made by 'Cecco' on behalf of the Partisans. He then began to ask many questions regarding German dispositions in the Valdarno, including the locations of their fuel and ammunition dumps, and the conduct of the Germans towards the civilian population. Continuing, Captain Gregor then asked 'Cecco' about the activities of the Partisans in the area, and whether or not the territory which they occupied lent itself to a drop by parachutes of the required supplies.

Since 'Cecco' answered fully and satisfactorily all of the questions put to him by Captain Gregor, he believed that he had fulfilled the purpose of his mission. Indeed, 'Cecco' could already visualise the precious supplies dropping from the skies into the waiting hands of the Partisans. But there was one last fundamental question to which the Captain required an answer: 'What was the political orientation of the Partisan groups to which "Cecco" belonged?' Without hesitation and with pride 'Cecco' replied 'We are Communists'.

As a result of 'Cecco's' answer, Captain Gregor began to put forward many difficulties in meeting the requirements of the Partisans. To surmount these difficulties 'Cecco' guaranteed with his own life the proper delivery of the supplies, volunteering to travel in the aircraft making the drop in order to indicate exactly the area in which the Partisans operated. 'Cecco' sought to convince Captain Gregor that if the supplies drop was not made, then the Captain would bear responsibility for the massacre of 'Cecco's' Partisan compatriots attempting to fight against the Germans without proper arms. But Captain Gregor was adamant: the anti-Communist ruling was paramount and ignored the possible loss of the lives of many Partisans and British soldiers, the latter having in the Partisans invaluable military support. The drop was never made.

'Cecco' met Captain Gregor again at Florence during August 1944. According to Lelmi the Partisans had already liberated that part of the city south of the River Arno prior to the advent of the Allied forces. In order to relieve the plight of the civilian population in the northern part of the city, who were desperately short of food and water, the Partisans wished to attack immediately the Fascists and German forces north of the River Arno. Lelmi, in his account, says that Captain Gregor, although being aware of the situation on the north side of the river, wished to delay the attack across it for two weeks or so.

In the light of this delay the Partisans attacked over the river the following morning, Lelmi thus claiming that Florence was liberated not by the Allies, but only as a result of the heroism and sacrifices of the Partisans. He relates that during the attack there was a moment when, near to the tobacco factory, the Partisans were likely to have been repulsed by the Germans because of a shortage of munitions. These were requested by the Partisans from the Allies, the latter turning a deaf ear.

Lelmi ended his account by saying that no one wished to throw doubt on the contribution by the Allies to the liberation of Italy from the Fascists and the Germans. He said, however, that his story gives the true facts as to how things happened, and this should serve to give due and just merit to the Partisan forces who participated in Italy's liberation. Indeed, he took the view that the Partisans could well have liberated Italy in World War II without Allied intervention, except by way of arms and supplies.

The ex-Partisan then produced a note issued to him by a South African Intelligence Officer on the 25th July, 1944, giving Lelmi safe passage to his then home in Siena, since for him the conflict was at an end. He went on to acknowledge that the time when I first entered Castelnuovo dei Sabbioni was commensurate with what he knew of the arrival of Allied forces in the area, and that I was certainly one of the first British soldiers, if not the first, to enter the village.

There was much I could have said in reply, but in order to avoid being contentious, I refrained from so doing. I might well have reminded Lelmi that the Italians were once closely allied to the Germans, and the former could not, therefore, expect the Germans to take over kindly to the Italians changing sides in the conflict and joining the Allies. I could also have remarked that many of the Partisan bands were simply a rabble and acted as terrorists. However, with enforced tact, I said that the contribution by the Partisans to the liberation of Italy was rightly and properly acknowledged by all who had any understanding of the Italian Campaign of World War II. I then drew attention to the fact that there are forty-two British Military Cemeteries in Italy, with one of the largest some twenty-five kilometres away and just west of Arezzo, while the British Military Cemetery at Cassino held four thousand known British dead and displayed the names of a further four thousand British soldiers who have no known graves. Moreover, a measure of the contribution made by the Allies was reflected in the official casualty figure for the Italian Campaign of three hundred and twelve thousand. Lelmi took my comments reasonably well and with equanimity.

After I had replied to Francesco Lelmi, Enzo Droandi, an elderly historian from Arezzo took the floor. From his opening remarks it was obvious that he was aware that I had unearthed the British Army S.I.B. Reports dealing with the atrocities carried out in the Comune di Cavriglia by the Germans, and prepared in the late autumn of 1944 under the supervision of W.O.II Crawley, W.P. It also appeared that Droandi knew I had made the Reports available for copying both by Emilio Polverini and the Comune di Cavriglia.

Droandi said that he considered W.O.II Crawley to be a fool, this opinion apparently being based on the brief affidavit prepared by W.O.II Crawley and submitted as evidence at the trial of Field Marshal Kesselring. This document simply states that he, W.O.II Crawley and his team investigated in depth the alleged atrocities in the Comune di Cavriglia, and these had been substantiated. Moreover, the atrocities had been committed under the orders and with the full knowledge of the senior German command in Italy. Enzo Droandi went on to complain that he had been refused permission at the British Public Record Office to see and examine the above British Army S.I.B. Reports.

In reply, I dealt with Droandi's last point first. I explained that it had taken me several days of searching to discover the Reports in question, which were an annexure to another and more broadly based Report. I remarked that indeed, I had happened upon the British Army S.I.B. Reports quite by chance, adding that up to 1994 they had been classified as 'Secret' for one hundred years, but in 1994 had been declassified after fifty years. In an attempt to clarify how things worked at the British Public Record Office, I said that documents such as the British Army S.I.B. Reports could only be found by continuous probing and searching. These documents were not, in general, readily identifiable for what they were, and the British Public Record Office staff, although most courteous and helpful, possessed no detailed knowledge of the British Army S.I.B. Reports on the atrocities in the Comune di Cavriglia and similar documents. I then refuted

Droandi's condemnation of W.O.II Crawley, and was tempted to add that he, Droandi, could hardly judge W.O.II Crawley as being a fool, based only on the affidavit put forward by the latter for the trial of Field Marshal Kesselring, when he had neither seen nor read W.O.II Crawley's full Reports, but withheld from so doing. Doubtless, the Comune di Cavriglia will now give Droandi access to the full Reports. At this juncture Enzo Droandi thanked me for my contribution and presented me with four pamphlets dealing with atrocities carried out by the Germans together with Partisan activities in the Arezzo area, prepared either by himself personally or under his guidance.

The Mayor of Cavriglia then invited those present to participate in the proceedings. Questioned by the current local priest as to how I felt when I first entered Castelnuovo dei Sabbioni nearly fifty-three years previously, I reiterated the events set out in detail in chapter 2 of this book.

An elderly lady present said that she had been interrogated almost continuously by the British Special Investigations Branch (S.I.B.) over a period of some thirteen days in late 1944, and asked what had resulted from these interrogations. I explained to her that the many statements taken by the S.I.B. team were contained in the Reports by W.O.II Crawley, which had been submitted to the British authorities. The lady persisted, saying that no action appeared to have been taken as a result of the S.I.B. Reports, despite the fact that the names and descriptions, together with several photographs and unit designations of many of the Germans involved in carrying out the massacres in the Comune di Cavriglia had been handed over to W.O.II Crawley and his team. In reply, I said that I understood and sympathised with her concern, but a decision had been taken at the highest level that only the most senior German officers would be arraigned before a British Military Court, all lesser ranks being dealt with by the Italian authorities. As a result only Generals von Mackensen and Mälzer, together with Field Marshal Kesselring were tried before a British Military Court, all three being found guilty of authorising the massacres of Italian civilians (all for the Ardeatine Caves massacre, Field Marshal Kesselring alone for all other massacres). Generals Heidrich and Lemelsen, who were both implicated in some of the massacres of Italian civilians were apprehended and interrogated, but avoided indictment. It would, I said, be recalled that Kappler, who was responsible for organising and carrying out the Ardeatine Caves massacre, was tried and sentenced by the Italian authorities. In conclusion, I said that as far as I could ascertain, not one of the Germans involved in carrying out the massacres in the Comune di Cavriglia had been apprehended, much less put on trial.

Epilogue

The Mayor then brought the meeting to a close, but there followed several informal conversations with various members of the public who were involved one way or another with the massacres of July 1944. I spoke with Giuliano Pagliazzi, a cousin of Dante Pagliazzi, the latter being one of those massacred at Massa dei Sabbioni. Giuliano had assisted in the recovery of the bodies of Don Morini and Dante Pagliazzi from the barn Scala and their transportation to the local cemetery for burial. And again I spoke with Aldo Dini. Somewhat embarrassingly, several people asked me to sign my name either on programme sheets or envelopes, whilst others came to shake my hand and say 'thank you'. I was quite touched emotionally.

Francesco Lelmi and I also talked. He is about my age and stature, and was, of course, 'Cecco'. I said I had noted that for him the war ended at the end of July 1944. But for me, when my unit left Santa Barbara there was yet another autumn, winter and early spring of war in the Gothic Line and northwards before peace came to both Italy and Europe. We spoke of how things were for each of us as the battle zone passed through the Comune di Cavriglia, and were saddened in our realisation of the dwindling numbers of those still alive who had experienced those days. He then addressed me as 'comrade' in, I think, the Communist and Partisan sense, presenting me with an A.N.P.I. scarf and banner. We embraced and parted as old comrades-in-arms and friends.

Finally, we all said our 'goodbyes', especially to our excellent and lovely interpreter, Emma Pyke, who thought that the proceedings at both Cavriglia Town Hall and the Castelnuovo dei Sabbioni Conference Hall had gone splendidly. Professor Polverini was quite fulsome regarding my performance that evening: he said I had spoken well, with clarity and proper authority. As on the previous Thursday, he urged me to complete and publish my book as a matter of urgency, as the time was now ripe for so doing. He also reiterated his earlier comment, saying that I must be regarded as a prime source regarding the material contained in my book, and the happenings of July 1944 in the Comune di Cavriglia in particular.

Our driver then conveyed John and me back to the Hotel del Lago at San Cipriano well after midnight. We were both pretty well exhausted after a long and arduous, but very satisfying day.

We were free of any commitments on the Saturday, deciding to visit Florence, and making the journey there by car and train. Subsequent to our return to San Cipriano we motored once again to Castelnuovo dei Sabbioni to photograph 'Il libro del ricordo', and the communal grave of those massacred in the village centre and at Le Matole on the 4th and 11th July, 1944 respectively. Leaving Castelnuovo dei Sabbioni and passing through the area laid waste by the open cast mining operations, Santa Barbara with its once lignite consuming power station and apartment blocks from which the Germans had set off to carry out the several massacres on the 4th July 1944 and San Cipriano where many of the German anti- Partisan units had been located, I wondered if I would ever pass this way again. Most likely not!

Around mid morning on Sunday, 6th July, John and I left the Hotel del Lago to motor to Milan, en route for Manchester and home. Both the Mayor of Cavriglia, Signor Brogi, and historian Emilio Polverini came to the hotel to say goodbye and see us off. The Mayor gave me a personal present of a small plaque made by an ancient wall painting technique. Both thanked us for making the journey to and our stay in the Comune di Cavriglia, wished us 'God's speed', and invited us to return whenever we wished to do so. I replied appropriately, saying what a wonderful experience our visit had been, and thanking them for their courtesy and kindness.

There were final handshakes, farewells and waves, and we all departed.

It was the 1st July 2004 when I travelled again to the Comune di Cavriglia. The purpose of the visit, on which I was accompanied by my dear friend Angela, was to attend the ceremony to mark the 60th anniversary of the massacre carried out by the Germans in the Piazza IV Novembre of Castelnuovo dei Sabbioni and nearby of 74 Italian men, all of whom were civilians and innocent of any subversive activities, which was to be held in the same piazza.

The ceremony itself, which embraced a mass, was held on the morning of the 4th July, and conducted by the Bishop of Fiesole. It was appropriately solemn, and many, both old and young, were present. Initially, Angela and I stood with Leandro Polverini and others on the sunny side of the piazza. Since Castelnuovo dei Sabbioni is a relatively small community where everyone is known to everyone, I suspect that it was being asked who Angela and I were. There were many friendly nods and smiles as it became known that I was the ex-British soldier who had entered Castelnuovo dei Sabbioni in July 1944, soon after the massacre had taken place. A most kind lady, who had been seated under the trees on the opposite side of the piazza, noticed that we were standing in the hot sun, crossed the piazza to us, and took Angela by the hand to sit with her in the shade. This gesture epitomizes the friendly, generous and courteous nature of the people of that remote Tuscan village.

Epilogue

The Hotel del Lago at San Cipriano where Angela and I stayed was as immaculately maintained and efficiently, but caringly run as ever, while the food at the nearby Taverna del Pescatore, where we ate, was an absolute delight.

On the morning of Friday 2nd July we were taken to Cavriglia, to be welcomed at the Town Hall by the new mayor, Signor Ivano Ferri, whom I had first met in 1997. While there I was greeted by a young lady who now works at the Town Hall, but who I had first met also in 1997 at lunch at the Parco Naturale di Cavriglia, when she was a police officer. Our conversation, in part, at that luncheon, which we both remembered, together with its amusing effect, is outlined in page 248 of the book. From the Town Hall we were taken to the beautiful Il Museo Della Pieve di Cavriglia, this being followed by a magnificent and protracted lunch at the Taverna del Pescatore.

At a meeting held during the evening of the same day, Friday, in the Conference Hall of the Castelnuovo dei Sabbioni social club, I was asked to say a few words about my book and the circumstances of my visit to the village. This I did. I was then questioned by a lady in the audience, Signorina Cosima Zanni-Dei, who asked me when, if ever, I could or would forgive the Germans for their barbarous acts, especially in the Comune di Cavriglia. Replying, I said that the question was a difficult one to answer, but my immediate response was that my forgiveness would come only with my death. In general, this was well-received by those present.

After the meeting I met again with ex-Partisan Francesco Lelmi. We greeted each other with warmth, and he gave me a copy of the authorisation dated the 25th July, 1944 he had received from the British 8th Army General Staff Intelligence providing him with military transport to Siena, where he had friends, and then permitting him to return to his home at Gaiole in Chianti.

During the morning of the following day, Saturday, we travelled by jeep through the Monti del Chianti to see some of the locations where the local Partisans operated from in mid 1944. The ride was very rough and hair-raising, being mostly over forest tracks, but was greatly enjoyed. Moreover, we were rewarded with the sight of some wild boar who were just a few days old, and a bottle of genuine Chianti vino presented to us by the jeep driver. Following the jeep trip we partook of a delicious lunch at the home of Emilio and Valeria Polverini. Signora Polverini herself prepared and served the meal, which culminated in a glass of the most excellent Vin Santo.

On the Sunday we lunched with Cosima Zanni-Dei at the Taverna del Pescatore. Then, in the late afternoon, we were joined at the Hotel del Lago by Leandro Polverini and his lovely wife Irene, who we were meeting for the first time, for drinks and the usual inspiring conversation led by Leandro. As a finale to our visit we had an evening meal alfresco at a local pizzeria with Enzo and Silvana Brogi and a group of their friends and neighbours. The Brogis then invited us to their home for coffee and ice cream, finally transporting us back to the Hotel del Lago.

Emilio Polverini picked us up from our hotel on the Monday morning, taking us to the railway station at San Giovanni Valdarno from where we commenced our journey to Merano in the South Tyrol. We bade Emilio a very fond farewell, and thanked him for all his help and kindness.

It is just conceivable that we may once again visit Castelnuovo dei Sabbioni after my book is finally completed. But much depends ...

*Rear of the Campo Imperatore Hotel. The Author is standing
at the approximate location where Skorzeny's glider landed.*

*Present-day view of the Campo Imperatore Hotel
and the surrounding terrain.*

The author at the River Rapido between Cassino and San Angelo where American 36th (Texas) Division attempted but failed to cross during 20th/23rd January, 1944.

Benedictine monastery at Monte Cassino from Point 593.

Polish Memorial on Point 593.

The author near Terelle (Elevation 2970 ft.).
The Monastery of Monte Cassino and Mt.
Trocchio are in the background.

Monastery at Monte Cassino from British Military Cemetery.

Polish Sherman Tank Memorial on track to Cavendish Road.

Terranuova: Via Vittorio Veneto 7. Lt. Wolf of
Anti-Partisan Unit was resident here
from 25th June, 1944.

*Terranuova: Scuola di Musica.
Anti-Partisan Unit was billeted here from
25th June, 1944.*

*San Cipriano: Villa Cetinale H.Q. 1st
Panzer Regt. 4 from 2nd July, 1944.*

Pasquini Farm, Meleto, where 17 men were massacred on 4th July, 1944.

Memorials at site of Rossini Farm, Meleto where
23 men were massacred on 4th July, 1944.

Remains of Melani Barn, Meleto, where 22 men were
massacred on 4th July, 1944.

*Headstone of communal tomb of unidentified
victims massacred at Meleto
on 4th July, 1944.*

*Castelnuovo dei Sabbioni: Chapel erected in Piazza IV Novembre
to commemorate the 74 men massacred there
on 4th July, 1944. (July 1997.)*

265

Mayoress Silvana Brogi, Historian Emilio Polverini and the author at the 'Madonnino' erected in memory of the four men massacred at San Martino In Pianfranzese on 4th July, 1944.

Castelnuovo dei Sabbioni: il Libro del Ricordo.

Memorial erected in memory of the ten Italian men put to death on the 11th July, 1944 at Le Matole. (15th July, 1984.)

Notes on Sources

Chapter 1
WO170 368. War Diary: British 13 Corps Troops Workshops.
Chapter 2
The Battle for Italy, W. G. F. Jackson, p. 85.
The Second World War, Volume V, Closing the Ring, Winston Churchill, p. 85.
Chapter 3
Benito Mussolini, Christopher Hibbert, pp. 192–216.
The Second World War, Volume V, Closing the Ring, Winston Churchill, pp. 45–48.
Chapter 4
War in Italy, 1943–45, Richard Lamb, p. 20.
The Second World War, Volume V, Closing the Ring, Winston Churchill, pp. 88–102.
Chapter 5
War in Italy, 1943–45, Richard Lamb, p. 23.
The Second World War, Volume V, Closing the Ring, Winston Churchill, p. 103.
My Commando Operations, Otto Skorzeny, Part 3, chapters 16, 17 and 18.
Benito Mussolini, Christopher Hibbert, pp. 223–235.
Chapter 6
Mussolini, Denis Mack Smith, p. 305.
War in Italy, 1943–45, Richard Lamb, pp. 24–33.
Benito Mussolini, Christopher Hibbert, p. 241.
Chapter 7
WO169 8631, WO169 12381. War Diary: British 13 Corps Troops Workshops.
Chapter 8
Private notes and diary of M. G. Nash.
Chapter 9
WO204 1454. Operations in Italy. January–17th March, 1944.
WO204 1455. Operations in Italy. 18th March–April, 1944.
CAB106 366. Operations of New Zealand Corps. 3rd February– 26th March, 1944.
Cassino: The Hollow Victory, John Ellis, pp. 41–221.
Cassino: Portrait of a Battle, Fred Majdalany, pp. 55–217.
The Battles for Cassino, E. D. Smith, pp. 31–118.
Chapter 10
WO204 1456. Operations in Italy. May–June, 1944.
WO204 8221. Operations II Polish Corps Against Monte Cassino.
Cassino: The Hollow Victory, John Ellis, pp. 267–383.
Cassino: Portrait of a Battle, Fred Majdalany, pp. 219–261.
The Battles for Cassino, E. D. Smith, pp. 145–172.
WO170 368. War Diary: British 13 Corps Troops Workshops.
Chapter 11
WO170 368. War Diary: British 13 Corps Troops Workshops.
Chapter 12
WO204 7283.
WO311 359.
War in Italy, 1943–45, Richard Lamb, chapters 11 and 12.

Death in Rome, R. Katz, pp. 1–114.

WO208 4591. Statement by General der Waffen SS, Karl Wolff, Hoechster SSund Polizei Führer und Bevolimächtigter, General der Deutschen Wehrmacht In Italien. (Highest SS and Police Officer and Military Plenipotentiary for the German Armed Forces in Italy), dated 5th August, 1945, re Activities by Italian Partisans and Reprisals by German Forces, including the Ardeatine Caves Massacre.

WO311 354, WO208 4672. Statements by General Joachim Lemelson, Commander German 14th Army, re Activities by Italian Partisans and Anti- Partisan Measures.

WO208 4672. Statement by Field Marshal Albert Kesselring, dated 18th October, 1946, re The Partisan War in Italy.

Chapter 13

E qui a parlar conviene: Quaderni di memorie, a cura di Carlo Fabbri e Dante Priore. *Quando c'era la miniera. La Storia Geologica e Mineraria*, Giovanni Billi, p. 19. *Il Comune di Cavriglia nell'* Ottocento, Rossella Valentini, p. 26.

Chapter 14

WO204 11477. Main and Supplementary Reports on Atrocities Committed by German troops in the Commune of Cavriglia, between 4th and 11th July, 1944.

WO204 11470. Atrocities: Summary of Cases Fully Investigated, including summary of atrocity in the Commune of Cavriglia.

Perché la memoria non si cancelli: Gli eccidi del Luglio 1944 nel territorio di Cavriglia, a cura di Emilio Polverini e Dante Priore.

Chapter 15

E qui a parlar conviene: Quaderni di memorie, a cura di Carlo Fabbri e Dante Priore. *Quando c'era la miniera, Il Commune di Cavriglia nell' Ottocento*, Rossella Valentini, pp. 41 and 42.

Photographs of one of two Ljungström turbo-alternators destroyed by a German mine and covered with machinery hall roofing, and boiler plant also destroyed
by German explosives.

Private correspondence from Emilio Polverini, historian for Castelnuovo dei Sabbioni and the Comune di Cavriglia to the author.

Chapter 16

WO311 354. Orders Issued By And On Behalf Of Field Marshal Kesselring re Operations Against Partisans:

> 1. New Measures in Connection with Operations against Partisans. Dated 10th May, 1944 and issued 17th June, 1944.
>
> 2. Anti-Partisan Measures. Dated 17th and 22nd June, 1944 and issued 1st July, 1944.
>
> 3. Operations Against Partisans – Order No. 2. Dated 20th July, 1944.

WO311 354, FO 647. Charges against Field Marshal Kesselring for Putting hostages to death, and Breaches of the laws and usages of war.

Trial held at Tribunali di Giustizia, Venice, between 10th February and 6th May, 1947. Verdict: guilty. Sentence: death by shooting.

WO204 11477. Main and Supplementary Reports on Atrocities Committed by German troops in the Commune of Cavriglia between 4th and 11th July, 1944. These reports identify the German units and many of the individuals who carried out the above atrocities, none of the latter being either detained, arraigned or punished.

Chapter 17

E qui a parlar conviene: Quaderni di memorie, a cura di Carlo Fabbri e Dante Priore.
Perché la memoria non si cancelli: Gli eccidi del Luglio 1944 nel territorio di Cavriglia, a cura di Emilio Polverini e Dante Priore.
Quando c'era la miniera. Un paesaggio minerario dal passato al futuro, Ivan Tognarini, pp. 9–17. Passato e futuro di un paesaggio minerario, l'area lignitifera del Valdarno di Sopra, Andrea Ensoli, pp. 52–68.
Dove c'era la miniera, Ing. Andrea Failli, Ing. Paolo Spinelli, Arch. Roberto Verdelli.

Chapter 18

WO170 368, WO170 4303. War Diary: British 13 Corps Troops Workshops. The Gothic Line, Douglas Orgill, pp. 163–216.
History of the Second World War, The Mediterranean and Middle East. Volume VI, Part II. The Campaign in Italy June to October 1944, W. G. F. Jackson and T. P. Gleave, pp. 51–105, 281–299, 369–371, 395–399, 411–421.
History of the Second World War, The Mediterranean and Middle East. Volume VI, Part III. The Campaign in Italy November 1944 to May 1945. W. G. F. Jackson and T. P. Gleave, pp. 34–36, 124–126, 198–199, 268–271, 294–295, 316–320, 324–328.

Chapter 19

Death in Rome, R. Katz, Foreword and Part Five – Epilogue.
Corriere della Sera, 27th June, 1997. Article by Sebastiano Vassalli.
'Missione fallita'. Annullato Il 'lancio di armi' per i Partigiani communisti. ('Failed Mission'. The 'Arms Drop' For The Communist Partisans Cancelled.), Francesco Lelmi, A.N.P.I.
Private notes and diary of M. G. Nash.

Appendices

Appendix A
WO169 8631, WO170 368, WO169 12381, WO170 4303. British 13 Corps Troop Workshops: Extracts from War Diary April 1943 to May 1945.

Appendices B and C
WO170 368. War Diary: British 13 Corps Troops Workshops: Movement Order and Route Card for Move from Presenzano to Cassino Area on 11th May, 1944.

Appendix D
WO311 0028. Letter Stating Levels of German Force Responsible for Carrying out Reprisals in Italy to be Dealt with Under British Army Order or by the Italian Government.
Report (in part) on German Reprisals for Partisan Activity In Italy.

Bibliography

Alexander of Tunis, Earl, *The Alexander Memoires 1940-1945* (Cassell & Co. Ltd, 1962).

Battaglia, R., *Story of the Italian Resistance* (Odhams Press Ltd, 1957).

Churchill, W. S., *The Second World War* (Cassell & Co. Ltd, 1948).

Contini, G., *La memoria divisa* (Rizzoli, 1997).

D'Este, C., *Bitter Victory* (E. P. Dutton & Co. 1988).

Ellis, J., *Cassino: The Hollow Victory* (André Deutsch Ltd, 1984).

Fabbri, C. and Priore, D., *E qui a parlar conviene* (Assessorato alla Cultura e Biblioteca Comunale di Terranuova Bracciolini, 1995).

Foley, D., *Commando Extraordinary* (Longmans, Green & Co. Ltd, 1954).

Hibbert, C., *Benito Mussolini* (Longmans, Green & Co. Ltd, 1962).

Jackson, Sir W. G. F., *The Battle for Italy* (B. T. Batsford, 1967).

Jackson, Sir W. G. F. with Gleave, Group Captain T. P., *History of the Second World War*. The Mediterranean and Middle East. Vol. VI, Part II. The Campaign in Italy June to October 1944 (H.M.S.O., 1987).

Jackson, Sir W. G. F. with Gleave, Group Captain T. P., *History of the Second World War*. The Mediterranean and Middle East. Vol. VI, Part III. The Campaign in Italy November 1944 to May 1945 (H.M.S.O., 1988).

Katz, R., *Death in Rome* (Jonathan Cape, 1967).

Kesselring, A., *The Memoires of Field Marshal Kesselring* (William Kimber, 1953).

Lamb, R., *The War in Italy: 1943–1945* (John Murray Ltd, 1993).

Liddell Hart, Sir B. H., *History of the Second World War* (Cassell & Co. Ltd, 1970).

Liddell Hart, Sir B. H., *The Other Side of the Hill* (Cassell & Co. Ltd, 1951).

Macksey, K., Kesselring: *German Master Strategist of the Second World War* (Greenhill Books, 1996).

Majdalany, F., *Cassino: Portrait of a Battle* (Longmans, Green & Co. Ltd, 1957).

Molony, C. J. C. with Flynn, Captain F. C., Davies, Major General H. L. and Gleave, Group Captain T. P., *History of the Second World War*. The Mediterranean and Middle East. Vol. V. The Campaign in Sicily. The Campaign in Italy September 1943 to 31st March, 1944 (H.M.S.O., 1973).

Molony, C. J. C. with Flynn, Captain F. C., Davies, Major General H. L. and Gleave, Group Captain T. P., revised by Jackson, Sir W. G. F., History of Second World War. The Mediterranean and Middle East. Vol. VI, Part I. The Campaign in Italy 1st April, 1944 to 4th June, 1944 (H.M.S.O., Second Impression, 1986).

Orgill, D., *The Gothic Line* (William Heinemann Ltd, 1967).

Pezzino, P., *Anatomia di un massacro* (Il Mulino, 1997).

Polverini, E. and Priore, D., *Perché la memoria non si cancelli* (Comune di Cavriglia, 1994).

Shepperd, G. A., *The Italian Campaign* (Arthur Barker Ltd, 1968).

Skorzeny, O., *My Commando Operations* (Edition Albin Michel, 1975).

Smith, E. D., *The Battles for Cassino* (Ian Allan Ltd, 1975).

Von Senger und Etterlin, F., *Neither Fear Nor Hope* (E. P. Dutton & Co., 1963).

Appendix A

British 13 Corps Troops Workshops: Extracts from War Diary:
April 1943 to May 1945

6/4/1943	Moved to Afuli, staging there for night of 6–7/4/1943.
7/4/1943	Moved from Afuli to Camp Kilo 89, Gaza, Palestine.
13/5/1943	Moved from Camp Kilo 89, Gaza to Kilo 76, staging there for night of 13–14/5/1943.
14/5/1943	Moved from Kilo 76 to Cowley Camp, Mena, Egypt.
11/6/1943	Bulk of Forward Party despatched to Haifa, Palestine, for loading on to M.T. ships.
12/6/1943	Further contingent of Forward Party despatched to Beirut, Lebanon, for loading on to M.T. ships.
14/6/1943	Balance of Forward Party (excluding Advance and Rear Parties) despatched to Haifa and Beirut for loading on to M.T. ships.
20/6/1943	Advance Party of Forward Party moved from Cowley Camp, Mena to 157 Transit Camp, Suez.
30/6/1943	Advance Party of Forward Party (4 Officers + 70 O.R.s) left 157 Transit Camp, Suez and embarked on H.M.T. K119 at Port Tewfik.
1/7/1943	Advance Party of Forward Party sailed from Port Tewfik to Port Said (via the Suez Canal) arriving 2/7/1943.
3/7/1943	Advance Party of Forward Party sailed from Port Said to Alexandria, arriving 4/7/1943.
4/7/1943	Advance Party of Forward Party disembarked at Alexandria and transported to Amiriya Transit Camp, Egypt.
9/7/1943	Advance Party of Forward Party transported from Amiriya Transit Camp to Alexandria and re-embarked on H.M.T. K119, sailing from Alexandria in D+3 Convoy.
9/7/1943	Rear Party moved from Mena to Giza, Egypt.
9/7/1943	Rear Party moved (by train) from Giza to Amiriya Transit Camp.
13/7/1943	Advance Party of Forward Party arrived at Syracuse, Sicily. Disembarked in afternoon and went to Assembly Area on Syracuse–Floridia road approximately 2 miles from Syracuse.
16/7/1943	Advance Party of Forward Party moved from Assembly Area to Priolo.
17/7/1943	Rear Party moved from Amiriya Transit Camp to Ikingi, Egypt.
18/7/1943	Rear Party moved from Ikingi to Alexandria, embarked on H.M.T. K119.
20/7/1943	Rear Party sailed from Alexandria in D+14 Convoy.
22/7/1943	Gun Shop, W/T and Instrument Sections moved from Priolo to north-east of Lentini so as to be in a suitable location to service the Medium Artillery Regiments (25 pounders).
24/7/1943	Rear Party arrived off Syracuse, Sicily, and then sailed on to Augusta, Sicily.

24/7/1943	Rear Party disembarked at Augusta and went on to Assembly Area approximately 3 miles north of Augusta.
25/7/1943	Balance of Advance Party of Forward Party moved from Priolo to Carlentini.
26/7/1943	Rear Party moved from Assembly Area to join up with balance of Forward Party at Carlentini.
Undated	Forward Party sailing from Haifa and Beirut in M.T. ships arrived in Sicily and joined up with Advance and Rear Parties (excluding Gun Shop, W/T and Instrument Sections) at Carlentini.
29/7/1943	Unit up to strength in men, vehicles and equipment.
9/8/1943	Gun Shop, W/T and Instrument Sections moved from north-east of Lentini to Misterbianco.
10/8/1943	Remainder of unit moved from Carlentini to join up with Gun Shop, W/T and Instrument Sections at Misterbianco.
5/9/1943	Moved from Misterbianco to Santa Teresa.
8/9/1943	Moved from Santa Teresa to Embarkation Assembly Area, Mili Marina.
9/9/1943	First Party of unit crossed to Italian mainland and went on to Palmi.
10/9/1943	Balance of unit (excluding 3 Scammell tractors) crossed to Italian mainland and went on to Palmi.
11/9/1943	Moved from Palmi to Mileto.
13/9/1943	Moved from Mileto to Nicastro.
29/9/1943	Moved from Nicastro to Cosenza.
30/9/1943	Moved from Cosenza to Scanzano.
1/10/1943	Moved from Scanzano to Castel del Monte.
4/10/1943	Moved from Castel del Monte to San Sevro.
7/10/1943	Major Hunter replaced Major Rundle as O.C.
22/10/1943	Fatal accident in 'B' Shops.
28/10/1943	Moved from San Sevro to Gambatesa.
7/11/1943	Moved from Gambatesa to Vinchiaturo.
16/11/1943	3 men killed instantly and 3 men injured by an explosion in a Blacksmiths' Shelter in Gun Shop. This was thought to be due to the explosion of an oxygen cylinder. (One theory was that the oxygen cylinder while being unloaded dropped on to a mine.) The 3 men killed were Sgt. Bamborough and Craftsmen Davies and Rushworth. A Court of Inquiry to investigate the incident was set up.
19–20/11/ 1943	Gun Shop, Armourers, W/T and Instrument Sections moved to a new location some 300 yds. distant so as to avoid mud and flooding caused by heavy rain.

23/11/1943   Because of bad weather, billets arranged in village of Vinchiaturo
             for all unit personnel.

27/11/1943   Gun Shop moved from Vinchiaturo to Archi station.

28/12/1943   Remainder of unit moved from Vinchiaturo, staging for night of
             28–29/12/1943 in a river bed near Gissi.

29/12/1943   Moved into Gissi, occupying whole of street area as workshops.

1/1/1944   Very heavy snowfall blocked all roads in and out of Gissi.
             Bad weather reduced work output.

20/1/1944   Moved from Gissi to Atessa (M.O. 09.00hrs. 181/2 miles.).
             Improvement in weather gave increase in work output.

9/2/1944   Heavy snowfall caused all work to cease except by those under cover.

9/2/1944   Visit by Major Palmer, W.T.S.F.F., re gun prematures.

19/2/1944   By working until 23.00 hrs. produced 10 sledges for Mountain
             Warfare School – based on skis and standard stretchers.

5/3/1944   Came under command of 5 Corps.

18/3/1944   Moved from Atessa to near Vinchiaturo (staging area)
             (M.O. 08.30hrs. 102 miles.).

18/3/1944   Came under command of 2 New Zealand Corps.

19/3/1944   Moved from near Vinchiaturo to Pietravairano
             (M.O. 08.30hrs. 45 miles.). 5 Corps Troops Workshops
             still in intended new location, so unit moved into adjoining field.

22/3/1944   5 Corps Troops Workshops moved. Unit relocated,
             reorganised and set up for work.

25/3/1944   Unit back under command of 13 Corps.

2/4/1944   Moved from Pietravairano to Presenzano (M.O. 08.00hrs. 101/2 miles.).

26/4/1944   Major Hunter and W.O.I. (A.S.M.) Wall Mentioned in Despatches
             for service in Sicily.

30/4/1944   W.O.I. (A.S.M.) Wall awarded an Immediate Emergency Commission
             to 1st Lieutenant for work on gun prematures.

11/5/1944   Moved from Presenzano to M.R.9516 (between San Pietro Infine and
             San Vittore del Lazio) (M.O. 01.25hrs. 111/2 miles.).

27/5/1944   Moved from M.R. 9516 to Piedimonte San Germano
             (M.O. 05.00hrs. 15 miles.).

7/6/1944   Commenced move from Piedimonte San Germano to Valmontone, but
             returned to Piedimonte San Germano (M.O. 23.15hrs.).

8/6/1944   Moved from Piedimonte San Germano to Valmontone
             (M.O. 23.15hrs. 55 miles.).

11/6/1944   Moved fromValmontone to Faleria (M.O. 23.40hrs. 55 miles.).

19/6/1944   Moved from Faleria to north of Orvieto (M.O. 04.00hrs. 50 miles.).

27/6/1944	Moved from north of Orvieto to south of Lake Trasimeno (via Città della Pieve) (M.O. 23.00hrs. 47 miles.).
16/7/1944	Major Hunter left unit to be promoted to Lt.-Col. and become C.R.E.M.E. at H.Q. 13 Corps. Captain Wallace took over as acting O.C.
22/7/1944	Moved from south of Lake Trasimeno to 6 miles south-west of Arezzo (near Mugliano) (Via Castiglione del Lago and Foiano della Chiana) (M.O. 05.07hrs. 55 miles.).
25/7/1944	Captain Wallace promoted to Major to become O.C. 13 Corps Troops Workshops w.e.f. 2/7/1944.
26/7/1944	Protection of King George VI during his visits to forward areas.
28/7/1944	Moved from 6 miles south-west of Arezzo (near Mugliano) to Santa Barbara (M.O. 05.30hrs. 32 miles.).
10/9/1944	Moved from Santa Barbara to M.R. Q9170 (near Sieci) (M.O. 06.45hrs. 20 miles.).
17/9/1944	R.C. church service held at Sieci.
22/9/1944	Lt. Wall awarded B.E.M.
7/10/1944	Moved from M.R. Q9170 (near Sieci) to San Piero a Sieve station (M.O. 05.45hrs. 23 miles.).
11 & 22/1/ 1945	Weather very cold: 17°F. of frost recorded.
6/2/1945	Lt. Page posted to 1st Guards Infantry Brigade Workshops.
12/2/1945	First Universal 'Bren' Carrier fitted out as a 'Wasp' flamethrower followed by satisfactory trials and demonstrations.
19/4/1945	Moved from San Piero a Sieve station to Lugo (via Dicomano, Forlì and Faenza) (M.O. 05.30hrs. 80 miles.).
26/4/1945	Moved from Lugo to Chiesa Nuova (via Massa Lombarda, Medicina, Budrio, Lovoleto, San Giorgio di Piano, San Pietro in Casale, Fiume Reno Bridge, Poggio Renatico) (M.O. 05.15hrs. 45 miles.).
3/5/1945	Moved from Chiesa Nuova to Mestre (M.O. 03.40hrs. 53 miles.).
8/5/1945	Moved from Mestre to Cervignano del Friuli (M.O. 07.00hrs. 100 miles.).
13/5/1945	Unit parade followed by Thanksgiving Service to mark the end of the war in Europe.
17–18 *or* 19/5/1945	M. G. Nash left 13 Corps Troops Workshops to attend a course at the R.E.M.E. Middle East School of Instruction, Tel el Kebir, Egypt. Travelled by road to Forlì (via Mestre), by train from Forlì to Taranto (via Rome and Naples), by ship from Taranto to Alexandria and by train from Alexandria to Tel el Kebir (via Cairo).

Appendix B

**Movement Order for British 13 Corps Troops Workshops
for move from Presenzano to Cassino area on 11th May, 1944. Secret.
Movement Order No. 12**

1. The unit will move to the Gun Shop site (MR.G9516) at 01.25hrs.
    11th May 44. The Gun Shop and a vehicle repair increment
    of 1 CDn. C. Tps. Wksps. will be under command.

2. The order of march will be as follows:

    H.Q.

    Veh Shop Store Section Tpt. & Rec.

3. *March Discipline*

    (a)   Speed 10 m.i.h.

          Density 40 V.T.M.

          Route as per route cards being issued.

    (b)   Halts – NIL

    (c)   Sidelights will be used by one veh in every four.
          Convoy lights will be used on all vehs as far as G9714
          (Horse Shoe Bend). ALL lights will be extinguished
          on passing G9714.

    (d)   Steel helmets will be worn.

4. *Administration*

    (a)   A hot cup of tea will be served from the cookhouse at 00.45hrs.

    (b)   On arrival at the new site bunching will not be allowed.
          As far as possible static vehicles will be moved into their
          correct positions and covered with camouflage nets.

    (c)   Each Shop will lift its own latrine and cause it to be properly
          filled in, the earth being thoroughly soaked in oil six inches
          below the surface.

    (d)   It is emphasised that all anti-malarial and blackout
          precautions must be strictly observed.

    (e)   The site is under enemy observation from the ground
          and is liable to occasional shellfire.

                              C.M. HUNTER Major E.M.E. C.M.F.

              May 44 O.C. 13 Corps Troops Workshops, R.E.M.E.

                        Distribution: O.C., R.O., O. i/c. Wksp.

                              O. i/c. 'A' Shop. O. i/c. 'B' Shop.

                                    O. i/c. Rec. & Tpt.

                                    O. i/c. Stores Section.

                                          A/C.S.M.

                                    War Diary (2) File

Appendix C

Route Card for movement of British 13 Corps Troops Workshops from Presenzano to Cassino area on 11th May, 1944

Route Card

Time	Place	Distance	Remarks
01.25hrs.	Present location	—	Through F.M.C. Area.
	Rd. Junction	31/2	Turn right, along Route 6.
	Rd. Junction	71/2	Back sharp right.
	Road and Track Junction	1/2	Keep left along hillside, in direction of Cassino – Very short steep hill, low gear required.
02.31hrs.	G.962163		NOTE: After passing the Horse Shoe Bend, you are under enemy observation and within shelling range. Do NOT show any lights, either while in convoy, or on arriving at the site as this only invites unwanted enemy attention. Speed: 10 m.i.h. Density 40 v.t.m. Halts – NIL

Route 6 and Naples–Rome railway line between Mignano and Cassino and location of British 13 Corps Troops Workshops during the Fourth and Final battle for Cassino in May 1944.

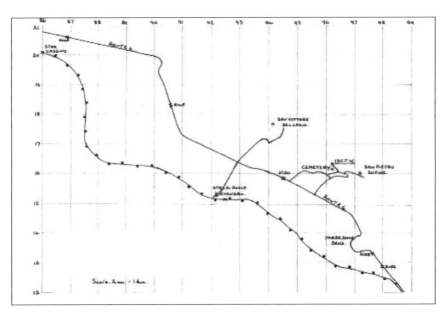

Appendix D

Letter & Report (in part) stating levels of German force reponsible for carrying out reprisals in Italy to be dealt with under British Army Order or by the Italian Government. Allied Forces Headquarters (British Section) Report on German reprisals for partisan activity in Italy

Register No.   Report dispatched
BM 115/1   5th October, 1945
A63(VW)

In (covering) letter to Under Secretary of State, The War Office dated 5th October, 1945 from F.N. Mitchell, Brigadier, G.H.Q., C.M.F., it was proposed (and accepted) that the Ardeatine Caves case and trial of Senior German Officers responsible for planning and carrying out German Reprisals in Italy be under Army Order. The remainder is to be handed over to the Italian Government.

Under the section of the above-mentioned Report headed CASES FULLY INVESTI-GATED items 46, 47 and 49 are as follows: 46. A study of the detailed reports of investigations in Annexures II to XXX reveals that there is a striking similarity in the facts of all cases which have been fully investigated. In each case the incident opened with the killing or wounding of a German soldier or soldiers by partisans; reprisal activity is then initiated either by the troops immediately on the spot, or in more serious cases, by the arrival of definite units and formations specially detailed for the purpose. There is no taking of hostages in the normal sense of the word; but a number of apparently innocent people are selected from the local population and are killed by shooting or hanging. Whole villages or a selection of farms or houses are then destroyed by fire; in a number of cases an announcement is then made to the population that the action taken was a reprisal for the death of a German soldier and will be repeated should further attacks on Germans take place.

47.   The worst of the cases of organised reprisal activity are those which took place on 6 July and 23 August 44 on the Fucecchio Marshes (Serial No. 2 in Appendix E. Detailed report at Annexure III), at Cavriglia from 4 to 11 July 44 (Serial No. 4 in Appendix E. Detailed report at Annexure V), at Civitella on 29 June 44 (Serial No. 6 in Appendix E. Detailed report at Annexure VII) and near Stia from 13 to 18 April 44 (Serial No. 15 in Appendix E. Detailed report at Annexure XVI). In each case the reprisal was carefully organised beforehand, and its direction from divisional or corps H.Q. is evidenced by the fact that troops from a considerable number of different units, specially brought to the spot for the purpose, took part in the operation.

49. The careful planning of the atrocities in the Comune di Cavriglia is evident on pages 1 to 3 of the opening summary in Annexure V. It will be observed that there is good reason to believe that General Heidrich, then GOC 1 Para Division and later GOC 1 Para Corps, himself directed the operation, and there is no doubt that it was carried out by troops under his command and also by Herman Goering Division. The dead in this case totalled 187 male civilians (see pages 43 to 48 of main report in Annexure V). It will be observed that a large number of them were over the age of 70 years, and there seems no doubt that almost all were innocent.

Index